_128_

THE COMPLETE
GRAND GRIMOIRE,
OR THE RED DRAGON

Interlinear Edition

THE COMPLETE ILLUSTRATED GRAND GRIMOIRE, OR THE RED DRAGON

Interlinear Edition

Aaman Lamba, Translator

Arundell Overman, Editor

The Complete Illustrated Grand Grimoire,

Interlinear Edition, French-to English

Translated by Aaman Lamba

Edited by Arundell Overman

Images from Public Domain sources and images created by Ville Vuorinen, Matti Sinkkonen, and Artem Grigoryev

Published by Aaman Lamba, United States of America

ISBN: 978-1-7345171-2-5

Dedication

The Spirits, The Teachers, The Students and The Way

CONTENTS

FIGURES

FOREWORD

In the mid-1980s, as I was starting my Occult journey, I was fascinated by the possibility that one could call upon Angels and Demons. One of the very first texts I encountered on my path that taught this most sacred art was *The Grand Grimoire*, a text that asserts to have knowledge passed down from King Solomon himself. This was very intriguing to me. I was raised with Hebrew and Aramaic and read so much about King Solomon's magical exploits in various Rabbinic texts. I felt *The Grand Grimoire* would fill in the gaps in my knowledge of this great King and his ability to control demons to conform to his will and frankly, to my own will.

However, as I read through the texts available to me, I found the content to be foreign and remote because of the inconsistent and partial translations that were available. This posed a challenge for me, which led me on a quest to learn more about this Grimoire and others like it. However, no matter where I looked for accurate information on it, I hit dead ends. Other books would reference it, but I questioned the integrity of the translations being used. Being multilingual myself, it was clear to me that the translations were not consistent, and in some cases, they were incorrect. In time, I resigned myself to the idea that I would never find a single comprehensive text that would cover the *Grand Grimoire* clearly and concisely.

Fast-word some three decades later.

When I heard that my friends, Aaman Lamba and Arundell Overman, announced that they would take on the enormous task of translating and interpreting the *Grand Grimoire* and that it would be the most complete one to-date, I was initially skeptical, but also intrigued. When I was presented with a review copy of the book, my skepticism vanished. This book is replete with images and in-depth explanations on all aspects of the text which I found incredibly useful. Being a scholar of the Occult myself, I immediately saw the value in the work presented in these pages.

The beauty of this translation is not only its accuracy, but also that it is in a clear interlinear format. This provides the reader with the opportunity to see the original text, side-by-side with the English translation, something that does not exist in any other edition of this text. This alone is an invaluable benefit to the reader. However, this is not a mere translation of the text. It is also groundbreaking in its scholarship. For centuries, certain items mentioned in the text were a mystery. Aaman and Arundell were able to decipher them, which is a historic achievement unto itself.

The book that you have in front of you is the result of painstaking and meticulous research, something I appreciate and value highly in a book. It is so well researched that I quoted it in my own work, *Beelzebub—A History*. Aaman's flawless translation of the original languages into English and Arundell's detailed contribution to the editorial and historical aspects of the text work seamlessly together.

Due to the nature of *The Grand Grimoire*, accuracy should be of the utmost importance to any Magician and Sorcerer who wishes to delve into the secrets and powers of this text. You, the reader, can rest assured that this is by far the most accurate rendition of this text to-date.

I am confident that this book will be referenced for many years to come. I know I will certainly refer to it time and time again as I further my own research on the subject of Solomonic Magic.

Congratulations, Aaman and Arundell on this monumental work, and thank you for asking me to write the foreword. I am truly honored.

So Mote it Be,

Baal Kadmon
New York City, New York – Winter 2020

PREFACE

Magical texts and practice evolve continuously but rely on a common substrate and community of practice, built over previous generations' efforts. We are fortunate to live in a period that is seeing an explosion of occult publishing, with significant advancements in research, practical innovation, a wide spectrum of multi-cultural texts, and a rediscovery of source materials that were lost in translation, as it were, by past generations of authors.

The Grand Grimoire is one such foundational work of magic that has had much bad press and ill repute. While it was considered the most famous "black grimoire", it has suffered from poor and incomplete translations and a lack of understanding of the context in which the book was written and published. It has been very influential in magic and occult studies, with its focus on making pacts with demons and infernal intelligences. It was often combined with collections of magic spells and sold under various titles, from the Red Dragon to the Black Pullet to the Grimoire of St. Cyprian. It borrows from older grimoires such as the Key of Solomon and the Ars Notoria. There is a close correlation with the Key of Solomon and the spirits of the Grimorium Verum. While it claims to be written in 1521, the publication history indicates an origin in the 19th century, during the explosion of the grimoire publication mania.

We identified the lack of a definitive translation of this important work as a critical gap in occult studies and we worked closely to parse through original manuscripts to arrive at the best possible version. We felt the best way to present this would be as an interlinear edition, or more precisely a parallel corpus, with the French, Latin, Greek and English texts side by side. We identified many interesting correlations to other grimoires, as well as the original items referenced. The introduction goes into these topics and the history of magic as an aid to interpreting the grimoire.

While many of the spirits have visual representations in the public domain, we felt there was an opportunity to synthesize these and develop

new original images for some, along with the seals as an aid to visualization & evocation of the spirits. Accomplished artists Ville Vuorinen, Matti Sinkkonen, and Artem Grigoryev, and Gregory Koon worked to develop these images and refine the seals for this book. The seals of 17 of the subordinate spirits are drawn from the 1904 Mathers/Crowley edition of the Lesser Key of Solomon. The seal of Pruslas was created by Gregory K. Koon and is in the public domain.

I found the original manuscript of a contemporaneous novel called *Le Dragon Rouge* in the archives of the *Bibliotheque Nationale*. I was enraptured by the characters & magical operations described, as well as folk beliefs on topics such as werewolves, mermaids & fairies. This novel was written in the spirit of the scientific temper of the time and serves as an interesting counterpoint to the grimoire. As so often with critical works, it helps illustrate the magical & divinatory practices it intends to critique. The complete translation has been included herein.

We are immensely grateful to the expert magicians & practitioners who have kept the flame of spiritual & occult studies burning through centuries of darkness, as well as the modern community that grows apace, and claims space to build a third perspective, synthesizing science, religion, folk beliefs and the role of spirits in this more-than-human world.

Baal Kadmon, thank you for the kind words in your foreword, as well as for your own rich scholarship and insights in your excellent books.

Arundell, it's been fun and exciting working on this with you. Looking forward to more productive collaborations and scholarship.

I would like to thank my amazing artist and fellow occultist wife, Deepti Lamba, for her creative and emotional support in this journey through the realms, besides her tolerance of my individuality. We are a sangha of two magical ronin, forging our own path to points unknown.

Aaman Lamba
Virginia, January 2020

INTRODUCTION

Hello and welcome to the Grand Grimoire! A book written in the nineteenth century, it teaches the reader how to invoke a demon, known as Lucifuge Rofocale and make a pact with him. Not by devoting yourself to him, but rather, by forcing him to obey you, through the power of God, and the mighty Blasting Rod.

In this chapter, we will discuss the origin of the magic arts, the laws against the practice of magic, the development of books used to conjure demons, witchcraft and the inquisition in Europe, the key themes of the Grand Grimoire itself, and finally, its method of Invocation.

ORIGIN OF THE WORD GRIMOIRE

The word Grimoire may come from the Italian name Rimario, meaning a collection of rhymes or verses from the Bible, or it may come from the Latin term Grammaria, meaning a book in Latin, and later, extending to all books on magic. A Frankish word, *grīma*, meaning mask or sorcerer may also contribute to the term grimoire. This root gives us the familiar 'grimace'. The Scottish word 'glamour' popularized by Sir Walter Scott in *The Lay of the Last Minstrel,* meant the usage of magical spells or 'grammar' for enchantment and attraction.

In the magical sense, a grimoire was a collection of prayers, invocations and spells, often personal to a practicing magician. The term has developed a reputation as being specifically for the dark arts and what is considered black magic, but occultists of varied persuasions have read and used grimoires. Many claimed an ancient heritage, dating back to King Solomon. They were influenced by a variety of sources, from East to West. Initially passed around in manuscripts in Latin, Italian, French, Greek and Hebrew, they gained popularity in the Middle Ages. The grimoires were widespread throughout Europe after the invention of the

printing press in 1450, and France was the country in which the most grimoires were produced.

MAGIC IN THE ANCIENT WORLD, AND THE GENERAL DEFINITION OF MAGIC

Let us begin with a definition of magic. In the Universal Dictionary of Antoine Furetière, dating from 1690, the term "magic" is defined as "a science through which one learns to do surprising and wonderful things." Magic is the understanding of the divine forces of nature, and the practical use of these for operations, such as divination, and the casting of deceptive illusions. It is also the art of conjuring demons, evoking the dead, using astrology, interpreting dreams, and fortune telling etc. It can be used to harm men and women, or to provide them with wealth, health or other benefits.

Witches, those who use magic, were thought to be able to control the laws of nature, prolong the night, stop time, create storms, etc. this is described by Lucan in the Pharsalia:

"They know the stones, the plants, and the powers within them. They can silence anyone. Their great knowledge gives them absolute power over all that surrounds them. They create potions that can make any man fall in love, even the most austere or the most reclusive. Finally, witches often have a connection with death and the deities of the underworld. The practice of necromancy is very common. It is a matter of bringing back to life a corpse, which has in particular the power to predict the future, but witches also have the power to kill. To achieve their ends, they sometimes use certain

objects, such as a cauldron to prepare the potions, a sickle to cut the herbs useful for the preparation of the potions and ointments, or nails, whose magic powers are said to immobilize anyone. The figurines are also used according to the principle of analogy. Any action done on the figurine is felt by the person it represents."

THE PERCEIVED DIFFERENCE BETWEEN MAGIC, SORCERY, WHITE AND BLACK MAGIC

Since ancient times, there has always been a distinction between white magic and black magic, depending on whether one wishes to do good or evil, or if the magic is harmful or not. White magic was thought to be an art that causes good effects, through the help of angels and positive spirits, and black magic an art of evil, causing ruin and destruction, through the aid of demons.

It has been said the devil gives himself to the magician and the sorcerer gives himself to the devil. The sorcerer is to the magician, what the superstitious and the fanatic are to the truly religious man. The magician has an art, a science he has learned to master, unlike the sorcerer who is only a vulgar copycat and cannot attain the sacred art. At least, this is what was believed. Yet, it should be kept in mind that these definitions are not always easy to apply, if for no other reason than the books of magic, including the one we are presently studying, are filled with a mix of white and black magic.

ORIGIN OF MAGIC - GREECE, EGYPT, PERSIA

Magic first began with shamanism. The medicine man of each tribe acted as an intermediary between the normal world and the spirit world, and was consulted on matters of healing, dream interpretation, and in all matters supernatural. Every known culture, tribe, or race on earth has had a shaman. As civilization developed into cities, the tribal shaman developed into the priestly class.

THE PERSIAN ORIGIN OF THE WORD

The word Magic comes from the Persian word Magush, which can be translated as "Power, or "to be able." The Magush were a tribe of the Persians, a priestly class. So, the term did not originally carry any negative meaning. They were one of the six tribes of Medes in Babylon, according to Herodotus. They are also used to refer to both the teaching of Zoroaster and the community that accepted his teaching. Their function as priests included the interpretation of dreams, making of sacrifices, the observation of astrological phenomena, and the making of predictions from that observation. The Gospel of Mathew refers to the μάγοι or magoi from the East, familiar as the Three Wise Men. The Greeks began to refer to the activity of the magos as *mageia* or *magike*, and Herodotus refers to the magi as interpreters of omens and dreams

Other early terms relating to magic are *defixio*, meaning to make immobile or freeze, and *amuletum*, the creation of amulets and talismans. This kind of magic was believed to make people get sick, fall in love, do actions contrary to their nature, go insane, or even die.

In truth, the distinction between white magic and black magic can become somewhat thin at times and depend on if the magician is within

the ordinary priestly class, or outside of it. Generally white magic is used for good, and black magic for evil, but the definition of good and evil differ from person to person, and it is not always easy to apply a universal definition here.

ZOROASTER

Zoroaster is considered the first practitioner of magic. Pliny the Elder, in his natural history, presents him as the inventor of magic in Persia. However, he goes on to describe the mystery surrounding this character: There might have been several Zoroaster. This is probably because no one seems to be able to agree on his date of birth, and many different stories are given for his origin. The Greek mathematician Eudoxus and the Greek philosopher Aristotle place his birth 6,000 years before Plato's death, while others like Hermippus of Smyrna place him 5,000 years before the Trojan War, much earlier in history.

He was considered the first and the oldest of the magicians. Sextus Sinensis recognized two enchanters of this name; the king from Persia and author of natural magic; the other, King of the Bactrians, and inventor of the black or diabolical magic. Justin said Zoroaster ruled in Bactria long before the Trojan War, was the first magician, and that he infected humans with the errors of magic.

According to legend, he began to train as a priest in his home country at about 7 years of age and became one at 15. He traveled for some time learning from other teachers, and at the age of 30 years old experienced a life changing vision. On the bank of a river, during the spring festival, he saw a shining being, who revealed itself as Vohu Manah (good purpose) and taught him about Ahura Mazda (wise spirit) who was said to be the highest god. Ahura Mazda is opposed to the Persian devil known as Angra Mainyu, also known as Ahriman. It is believed that these concepts of an ultimate good and evil were borrowed by and blended into Judaism, and eventually Christianity, and Islam.

MAGIC IN EGYPT

Egypt is one of the countries in which the earliest traces of magic have been found in the form of papyrus, wax figurines, and amulets. Here, magic, religion and science were all one thing. Heka is the divinity that represents magic power. It is symbolized by the Sceptre HÉQA, a bent cane, or crook, a short wand with a hook on the end, carried by the Pharaoh to show his divine magic power.

The Egyptian texts in the Greek language translate Heka as "sacred Magic" and "sacred energy". Besides this god, the goddess Isis, and the god Thoth were also related to magic. Isis was said to have used magic to resurrect her husband Osiris after he had been slain by the god Set, and Thoth was credited as the inventor of writing and a god of magic. Many of the characteristics of the god Thoth, shown with the head of an Ibis bird, and carrying a stylus, or instrument for writing, were transferred to the Greek god Hermes, and the Roman god Mercury. In 332 BC, Alexander the Great conquered Egypt. This began a fertile period of cultural and religious exchange, especially with magic.

GREEK WITCHCRAFT

Many gods and heroes of Greek mythology relate to magic. The goddess who was most associated with this art though, is Hecate, daughter of Astéria, the starry night. A goddess of the moon, along with Selene and Artemis, she represents the new moon, a symbol of death. She is both a beneficent goddess linked to fertility, wealth and wisdom, but also the goddess of shadows and the dead, and the mystery of the night. She is considered the goddess of magic and witchcraft. Hecate is often invoked in ancient texts as a protector of witches. She is an expert in changing shapes, metamorphosis, but also in the composition of poisons and the handling of herbs.

THE FIRST LAWS REGULATING MAGIC IN THE ANCIENT WORLD

With the increasing development of magical practices, it became necessary to create laws to limit them. This was particularly the case in Rome, where between 451 and 449 BC, the Decemviri, a group of Roman lawmakers, enacted the law of the Twelve Tables, the first written Roman law and the oldest document on Italian magic. Its purpose was to sanction the magic practices that affect the health, property and reputation of others. However, no documents concerning it have been preserved, so its contents are only accessible thanks to a reference made by the Latin author Seneca who says: "The law of the Twelve Tables punishes those who, by spells, destroy the crops of their neighbor."

Moving forward in time several hundred years, the Codex Theodosianus, by Theodosius II in Constantinople in 438, describes the laws issued since the reign of Constantine I. There we find a law dating from the year 321 that forbids evil magic that affects the health and the reputation of others. However, Constantine authorized magic used in medicine or to control meteorology, which he considered to be of public value. Constantine II, in 356, forbade magicians to seek the spirit of the dead or practice black magic.

MAGIC AND WITCHCRAFT IN THE BIBLE, THE BATTLE BETWEEN MOSES AND THE WIZARDS OF EGYPT

Witchcraft is mentioned in many different forms in the Christian Bible, the earliest example being the wizard's duel between Moses and the magicians in the court of the Pharaoh. As he demands for the release of the Israelites from their slavery in Egypt, he is instructed by the Lord to

use his magic rod to perform various miracles. For each miracle he performs, the Egyptian magicians find some way to duplicate it. Exodus chapter 8 tells us in verse 5

> *And the Lord said to Moses, "Tell Aaron, 'Stretch out your hand with your staff over the rivers and canals and ponds and cause the frogs to come up onto the land of Egypt." 6. So, Aaron stretched out his hand over the waters of Egypt, and the frogs came up, and covered the land of Egypt. 7. But the Egyptian magicians did the same by their magic arts, and they also brought frogs up onto the land of Egypt...*

As the battle rages on, the magicians of pharaoh throw down their magic wands, which become snakes. Moses then throws down his magic rod, which also becomes a snake. The snake that was the rod of Moses then swallows the snakes that were the magic wands of the Egyptian magicians. Eventually, the battle is won, only by the fact that the lord sends an angel of death, which slays the first-born son of the Egyptian leader, and thus, he gives in, and allows the Israelite group to leave Egypt.

THE WITCH OF ENDOR

Another famous story from the Bible concerning witchcraft is the story of the witch of Endor. The story goes like this. The first king of Israel, named Saul, was getting ready to go into a fierce battle with a neighboring tribe of Philistines.

He had normally been used to receiving advice on such matters from Samuel, the one-time prophet of Israel, who was now dead. So, he decided he wanted to consult with Samuel anyway, and the only way to do that was to get a witch to summon up the ghost of the dead prophet.

He went to the witch, in disguise, but she figures out who he is, after

all, she is a witch, and she is also worried he might have her put to death. She makes him promise that she won't be punished for doing such an illegal act as calling up the spirit of a dead man, and when he does, she proceeds to summon up the ghost of Samuel. The king asks the ghost about his fortunes in the upcoming battle, and unfortunately, the news is not good. The spirit predicts he will die in the coming battle and he does, losing his head, along with his son.

THOU SHALT NOT SUFFER A WITCH TO LIVE

Exodus 22 verse 18 states in the King James version of the Bible that *"thou shalt not suffer a witch to live,"* and this verse sent many witches to be burned at the stake or hanged, after all, the ultimate law in the Christian world was the bible, until the age of reason.

The exclusion from Church activities and leadership, combined with persecution, might have contributed to women adopting folk magic practices, and developing a deeper engagement with the forbidden arts, often enough through a greater familiarity with herbs, potions and magical workings.

SOLOMON AND THE TEMPLE OF ASTARTE, BELZEBUTH AS A PAGAN GOD, AND THE TRANSLATION OF ALL PAGAN GODS INTO DEVILS IN THE NEW TESTAMENT

The most famous of all magicians in the bible, by far, was the second king of Israel, Solomon. The legends of Solomon as a magician spread far and wide and exist within Jewish, Christian, and Islamic mythology. Solomon's reputation as a magician, like Moses, would even be lent to add credibility to magic books written 2500 years after his death such as the Lesser Key of Solomon, the Goetia.

The various Keys of Solomon popular in the Middle Ages were compendiums of spells and protective talismans dating back to Biblical times. A book of demon incantations was popular in the first century of the Common Era attributed to Solomon, according to the historian Flavius Josephus, who described a Jew named Eleazar's feats at exorcism by applying a ring within the presence of the Emperor Vespasian using this book.

"For I have seen a certain man of my own countrey, whose name was Eleazar, releasing people that were demoniacal in the presence of Vespasian, and his sons, and his Captains, and the whole multitude of his soldiers: the manner of the cure was this: he put a ring that had a root of one of those sorts mentioned by Solomon to the nostrils of the demoniack: after which he drew out the demon through his nostrils: and when the man fell down immediately, he abjured him to return into him no more: making still mention of Solomon, and reciting the incantations which he composed. And when Eleazar would persuade and demonstrate to the spectators that he had such a power, he set a little way off a cup or basin full of water, and commanded the demon, as he went out of the man, to overturn it; and thereby to let the spectators know that he had left the man. And when this was done, the skill and wisdom of Solomon was shewed very manifestly. For which reason it is, that all men may know the vastness of Solomon's abilities,

and how he was beloved of God, and that the
extraordinary virtues of every kind with which this
King was endowed, may not be unknown to any
people under the sun; for this reason, I say, it is, that
we have proceeded to speak so largely of these
matters."

The Bible says that Solomon's heart was led away from Yahweh in his later years by his foreign wives, and that they seduced him into the worship of their gods. Therefore, Solomon built temples to Astarte the "abomination" of the Sidonians, and to Chemosh. He offered prayers at the benediction of the Temple in the form used by the Canaanites, on bended knee with arms outstretched.

The Bible says he slept with his fathers, leaving his demise ambiguous. He is reputed to have asked God to keep his demise hidden from the demons so long as his works remained unfinished. He thus remained kneeling on his staff in prayer while the demons labored, until a reptile gnawed at the staff and he fell.

Solomon is even named as having been the author, way back in time, of course, of the Grand Grimoire, the Red Dragon, of which this present work is a study. The goddess Astarte becomes the demon Astaroth, one of the three principal spirits of the book. Belzebuth, as well, is often mentioned in the Bible, and in the old testament is called "the god of Ekron." By the New Testament, the image of Belzebuth has shifted into that of a devil rather than a god, as he is then called "the prince of demons." So, it is for all pagan gods, in the mythology of the new religion, they fell into hell and became the devils.

THE FIRST BOOKS OF MAGIC

There have always been books or scrolls of some kind concerning magic, since the dawn of time, and the invention of language. Written on papyrus, or goatskin, or whatever else was available, in whatever language

was known to the writer. With the invention of the printing press in 1450, however, the spread of magical books took a distinctly different turn, as they could be mass produced.

Some of the first books to be printed, hot off the presses, were instruction manuals of various types. Marcelin Berthelot, writes in his encyclopedia that there "existed in the Middle Ages a whole literature of recipes of chemistry, industry, medicine, magic, etc." Known as books of secrets, these "instruction manuals" became the first grimoires and, as time went on, the content of some of them shifted into darker and darker realms involving the devil, and his demons.

THE LITTLE ALBERT AND A BRIEF MENTION OF OTHER GRIMOIRES

Published for the first time in 1658 in Belgrade, "the wonderful Secrets of the natural and Kabbalistic magic of the *Petit Albert,* or the Little Albert, was said to be written by Albertus Magnus, just like the Grand Albert, a previous book of recipes and magic formulas. Combined editions of these books were also published from the nineteenth century onward. They were the subject of several police convictions, due to the "hand of glory," a magical object said to aid criminals, and were often banned. The content of the Little Albert deals with love and profit, but also astrology and medicine, and it also contains practical recipes for everyday life. About love, we find chapters such as "for the reciprocal love between the sexes", "or "to know whether a girl is chaste."

THE PICATRIX, OR THE GHAYAT AL-HAKIM

Astrology was very popular during this time period. It consisted in the

casting of horoscopes and texts devoted to the meaning of the stars in relation to human fate and destiny. One of the most well-known works on astrology was the Picatrix, a Latin translation of a compilation of Arabic magic titled the Ghâyat al-Hakîm.

This grimoire dates from the 11th century, but no manuscript prior to the 14th century exists today, except for a 13th-century fragment. It is made up of instructions for the use of astrological images, incenses, prayers to planets, and magical compounds created for various purposes such as love, or the destruction of one's enemies. Agrippa is said to have been exposed to the Picatrix in his travels to Spain, and took much of the ideas, particularly the concept of the Occult Philosophy.

GRIMOIRE OF HONORIUS

Some Grimoires, especially the earliest ones, deal with "natural magic" and were not considered diabolical for the most part. The further away from the invention of the printing press we get, the more diabolical the nature of the grimoires become.

Many of the later grimoires deal with the devil and his court. The devil is seen as a spirit to compel, to force to obey ones wishes, to provide treasure, wealth, and the things that the devil and his demons are thought to have control over. Since the grimoires were written by the more wealthy and literate class of people, they were usually developed in places of learning, whether that be the university, or often, the church. One important example of a grimoire that was believed to have been written by a Pope is the Grimoire of Honorius.

The Grimoire of Honorius is believed to be the work of Honorius the First, Pope from the years 625 to 638. It is said that he gathered in Rome, the greatest magicians of his time. He was also convicted as a heretic at the council of Constantinople in 680. Since this book was widely possessed by nobles and clergymen one thousand years later, it seems unlikely that it was written by Honorius the First, but rather that it was written in his name, in a similar manner as books claiming to be written

by Solomon or Saint Cyprian.

THE GRIMORIUM VERUM

Another important Grimoire from this time period is the Grimorium Verum, also called the True Grimoire. Its hierarchy of spirits is very similar to the Grand Grimoire with the same three superior spirits of Lucifer, Belzebuth, and Astarte, and six spirits directly under them.

It will be noted by the careful study of these two books that the spirit Tarchimachae is in the same place in the hierarchy of the Grimorium Verum as is occupied by Lucifuge Rofocale in the Grand Grimoire and Red Dragon. Various editions of the Grand Grimoire, and the Red Dragon have been published, and there are slight differences between the two, but they are so close as to be almost identical and are considered most of the time to be the same book.

THE READERS OF THE GRAND GRIMOIRE, LITERACY OF THE TIME PERIOD, SIMPLY OWNING THE BOOK WAS CONSIDERED A MARK OF POWER

At the beginning of the eighteenth century, about 95% of the French population was illiterate, and a majority of 63% remained illiterate up to the French Revolution. Therefore, it is complex to know how the grimoires were used. Faced with the mass of these works produced over the centuries, it seems impossible to think that they could have been possessed and used only by a literate elite. Thus, historians believe that, in the countryside, the physical book itself was believed to have conferred to its possessor, power, for good or evil. There was no need to read it,

just having it on you could protect you from your enemies. The book was in this way considered a protective talisman.

Magic, religion, and superstition are often blended together in strange ways. Superstition is perhaps more frequent in the countryside, among the common folk, although who can say is the difference between superstition and religion? At any rate, in 1854, Victor Joly stated that there were 400,000 volumes of magic circulating in rural populations. This number can't be verified, but many copies of the various grimoires have been found in attics or barns. The belief and practice of the common people was often different than the official church doctrine, and it seems likely that the grimoires and books of magic were, in a sense, underground religious texts.

PAPAL MAGIC

The sixteenth-century Scottish mathematician John Napier counted twenty-two popes practicing necromancy, among them Alexander VI, Gregory VII and Boniface VIII, who were believed to have conspired with Satan to satisfy their desire for power. On the outside though, the church tried to ban the practice of magic and decrees would be published, which marked the beginning of a great repression of it through the power of the Inquisition.

POPE INNOCENT VIII OUTLAWS MAGIC

The church was always against the practice of magic, from antiquity onward. At the synod of Laodicea, which took place between 343 and 381, clergymen were forbidden from practicing magic, as in the Canon 36 it is written *"that clerics of a higher or lesser degree were neither sorcerers, nor magicians, nor mathematicians, nor astrologers; That they do not produce so-called amulets that are chains for their souls. Those who wear these so-called amulets must be excommunicated."* Numerous other councils within the church pronounced the same ruling.

During the pontificate of Pope Innocent VIII, in the fifteenth century, witchcraft was officially compared to heresy, and declared to go against the values of the church. From that point on, Papal bulls and decrees continued to be written, to limit the expansion of the occult sciences, and even to eradicate those who dared to employ them. The Council of Orleans in 511, Auxerre in 578 and 583, Reims in 630, the Council of Toledo in 694, on and on they go. The Canon XIV, *Indiculus Superstitionum et Paginarum*, condemned superstitions such as divination and spells, which were considered pagan customs. In 743 the council of Leptines convened, which banned the practices of magic and astrology. By the year 1234 the first papal bull condemning witches came out. Penned by Gregory IX, it precisely describes the Sabbath of the witches, and the cult of the Devil.

In 1445, the provincial council of Rouen condemned superstitions and devil worship, stating:

If there are people who have invoked the Demons, & who are rightfully convinced that they did, we want them to do public penance with a mitre on their heads, for a mark of perpetual infamy. If they renounce their error, Bishop Diocesain may reconcile them with God, but in case they remain obstinately in their sin, if they are ecclesiastical, they will be degraded, & remain in a prison forever; If they are secular, they will be abandoned to the secular justice, so that it may punish them. As for the sorcerers & the other superstitious, The Holy Council orders that they will fast a month in prison for the first time, & that if they continue to use superstitions, they shall be more severely punished.

Around one hundred years later, the Council of Trent created the Index *Librorum Prohibitorum*, a catalogue of forbidden books, which

included most of the grimoires. On November 1, 1578, Pope Sixtus IV promulgated the papal bull *Exigit sincerae Devotionis*, which allowed the Catholic monarchs to establish the Inquisition. On January 5, 1586, Pope Sixtus V published the Bull *Coeli et Terræ* which condemned the practice of magic, connecting it with the devil, and forbidding all forms of astrology, geomancy, hydromancy, pyromancy, palmistry and necromancy.

THE INQUISITION AND THE HAMMER OF THE WITCHES

It was during this same period that demonology, a science that studies the nature of demons, developed. It was aimed at making a classification of the Demons, but also at knowing their history and their attributes. This demonology was at the heart of the fifteenth century debates on witches and sorcery, and many treaties were printed.

The inquisitors, the main editors of demonology treatises, attempted to represent the demonic society according to the Christian model. Perhaps the most famous book of its kind, The Malleus Maleficarum, meaning hammer of the witches, announced that demons were determined to destroy the Christian religion, and were aided by the witches. In the face of constantly growing grimoire production, the church and the state put in place a violent system of repression. The magic books were censored, and their owners arrested.

A true witch hunt, the Inquisition, was established in the 13th century during the pontificate of Gregory IX. Its goal was to fight all forms of heresy, including witchcraft. The accused had to go before an ecclesiastical court. The testimony of two individuals was enough to convict an accused person.

The Papal Bull *Ad Extirpanda* promulgated by Innocent IV in 1252

legalized the use of torture to extort confessions. There were few who openly praised the devil, the accused person usually admitted to being guilty because they accepted the views of judges and public opinion due to torture. The sentences were generally harsh: the accused might lose their property, be sent to jail, or even sentenced to death, often at the stake. Signs of shame were also used, such as a yellow cross placed on the chest or on the back of accused heretics. The Inquisition marked the beginning of a witch hunt that continued for centuries.

FLYING AND THE JOURNEY TO THE SABBATH

As the inquisition wore on, the tales of witches and their doings became more and more outrageous. Witches were said to have the ability to fly to the sabbath, a meeting of witches and sorcerers, on brooms, pitchforks, or sticks. They were said to have been able to do this by means of a magic salve, which, when rubbed upon their bodies, or on the broomstick, made them fly to the sabbath, where they would meet with the devil and his demons and perform acts such as dancing backwards, fornicating with demons, and cursing the crops, livestock, and health of their neighbors.

The recipes for these magic potions still exist, and a careful examination of their components reveal that they contained deadly poisons such as Belladonna, Hemlock, or Datura, drugs such as opium, or hallucinogens made from mushrooms, or the skin of poisonous toads. It is certain that at least some people were involved in the creation of and experimentation with such substances, which were known as witch ointment, sabbath ointment, fairy ointment, and even lycanthropic ointment. Smearing such an ointment on the skin, with the right expectation and ritual setting, might make a person believe they had traveled to the sabbath, or become a werewolf.

Witches and sorcerers were also reputed to have recourse to seven, or

twenty-league boots or garters, by means of which they could cross as many leagues in an hour. We see recipes for preparing such garters and plasters in the Grand Grimoire's collection of spells.

NICOLAS REMY

Nicolas Rémy (1530-1612) was provost of Nancy from 1575 to 1591 and the Attorney General of the Duchy of Lorraine. He wrote a treatise on demonology from his direct experience with witches. This book was called the *Daemonolatreiæ libri tres* and was published in 1595. He boasted of having burned 900 sorcerers and witches in the sixteen years he served at his post.

According to him, demons and sorcerers have a perfect knowledge of nature, and of men, which allows them to use illusion, but he did not believe they could turn into animals. It is hard for us today to imagine the seriousness with which people treated this subject at this time in history, almost 500 years ago. Imagine for a moment a man who had sent 900 people to their deaths for the crime of witchcraft. How many of them were completely innocent? How many of them really did believe they were witches, and were attempting to practice witchcraft?

It is logical to assume considering the magic books that did exist at the time, that at least some people did attempt to carry out the instructions contained in them, and caught in the act, lost their lives for it.

WIER'S REFUTATION, THE TIDE STARTS TO TURN SLOWLY TOWARD SCIENCE AND REASON

One of the first men to speak against the hysteria of the witch hunts was

Johann Wier. A Dutch physician, he was a student of Henry Cornelius Agrippa of Nettesheim, renowned magician and author of the Three Books of Occult philosophy. In 1563, Johann Wier published the book *Praestigiis Daemonum et Incantationibus ac Venificiius* (On the Illusions of Demons & On Spells and Poisons) which refutes, among other things, the ideas of the Malleus Maleficarum and fights against the trials of witchcraft.

Johann Wier was committed to distinguishing the difference between magicians, poisoners and witches. He criticizes the magicians, whose purpose he says is to subdue the demons and then control their nature, as well as the poisoners who use poisons to kill. In contrast, he describes witches as victims of the devil who do not deserve the death penalty but are rather to be cared for, as they are not aware of their actions, and, are what might be termed today, mentally ill.

SYMPATHY FOR THE WITCHES

Fredrich Spee von Langenfeld (1591-1635) also wrote against the witch hunts. He was a prison chaplain where people accused of witchcraft were held. Convinced of the innocence of the witches, in 1631 he wrote the Treatise *Cautio Criminalis*. Before writing, he attended torture sessions and accompanied convicts to the gallows or the pyre, to better understand the mechanics of the trials. Concerning torture, he writes:

> *The tortures usually used are very violent and cause terrible pain. The pain is so terrible that, in order to escape it, one does not fear to save themselves even from death. There is therefore great danger that those who are put to torture do not confess to a crime they did not commit and confess all that the inquisitors suggest to them, even what they have premeditated to declare as true, to deliver themselves*

from such torment.

He even goes so far as to advise the innocent to confess a crime they did not commit to escape the inhumanity of torture. After the publication of Spee's work, the persecutions died down somewhat, and many other works denouncing the cruelty of the witch hunts were published.

WHY DID THE WITCH TRIALS HAPPEN?

The witch hunt has been attributed to the Reformation, the Counter-Reformation, the Inquisition, the wars of religion, the religious zeal of the clergy, the birth of modern states, the development of capitalism, the use of narcotics, hallucinogens present in mold on rye bread, mutations of medical knowledge, social and cultural conflicts, attempts to eradicate the last remnants of paganism, hatred of women, etc.

The witch trials were in full force by 1480, this was only 30 years after the invention of the printing press. The fires died down a bit, and then flared up again ever larger between 1580 and 1639. The witch trials spread through England, Germany, France, Switzerland, Scotland, and even, for a short time, in the American colonies, such as the famous witch trials of Salem, Mass. It has been estimated that at least 100,000 people lost their lives as a result of the trials. 50,000 in Germany alone.

If we put these events in context with the history of the grimoires, it is easy to see why many of them were destroyed during this tormented time period. However, compared to the large number of accused, few books of magic were discovered. This can be explained partially by the fact that many of the accused were innocent. Also, women were not usually the main owners of grimoires, as they were not allowed to learn to read as often as men, and more often women were accused of being witches than men.

CENSORSHIP OF BOOKS AND GRIMOIRES

In the year 1515 Pope Leo X wrote the Papal bull, *Inter Solicitudines,* which began the censorship of books. Before being printed, each book had to be examined by the bishop of one's area, and if noncompliance was found, a person could be excommunicated. By 1549, under Pope Paul III, this list of banned books had grown to over 1000. All works without indication of author, printer, date of publication etc., were immediately banned by the church. The purpose of such a ban was to prevent the public from reading books considered to be dangerous to faith or morals.

This repression also provoked the opposite effect, the censored books were avidly searched for, and many people wanted to read them. This created contraband literature. The church and the state, having set up this censorship, caused the printers to create false addresses, to not to be arrested and condemned to death. This explains the difficulties in dating many of the grimoires and it is why some editions of the Red Dragon are simply undated, and some have false dates of printing in the frontispiece such as 1411, which would have been even before the invention of the printing press.

THE BLUE LIBRARY AND THE BOOK PEDDLERS

One important part of the development of the Grand Grimoire and the Red Dragon, was the Blue Library. Historians are of two minds about where the term Blue Library came from. One idea is that the term described the color of the paper, a blue gray, lower cost paper used to pack sugar. Others say that the name comes from the content of the books, and that the term blue was a slang term for tale, or "fairy tale." These books were hastily printed, and poorly inked, and sometimes filled with illustrations that came from other books, as the woodcuts used to

make the illustrations were reused to save costs. They were sold by peddlers, to the public, and spread into the countryside.

Most of the books of the Blue Library had a pleasant character, with the grimoires being the darker part of the collection. Among these books are works detailing the lives of saints, reflections on death, religious education, romance, chivalry, fairy tales, and even practical almanacs and cooking guides. Historians have discovered and cataloged over 1,200 different titles so far, and it is probable that many were lost, or destroyed. These books were despised by the elite class of society, and looked at as vulgar literature, for the common folk,

Among the books of the blue library, we find the *Grand Albert*, the *Grimoire of Honorius*, the *Echiridion of Pope Leo*, the *Veritable Key of Solomon*, and the Grand Grimoire, from which the Red Dragon was derived. The clergy condemned the books of the Blue Library for having demonic content. It was blasphemy to read them, or even to own one. In fact, we do find in these works some rather dark secrets, such as the Hand of Glory. Thanks to this collection, the contents of the grimoires, both of black magic and of white magic, became accessible to all.

THE PRINTING PRESS AND THE EXPLOSION OF BOOKS

In 1450, the printing press was invented by Johann Gutenberg, In the fifty years that followed this invention, 40,000 different books were printed. With these books, producers saw a demand among the populace for classic knowledge, such as the *Corpus Hermeticum* and the *Grand Albert*. Works which were believed to be heresy by the Church. The Pope quickly stated that the printing press was a satanic invention, used by the devil to spread heresy.

Indeed, if it were not for the printing press, there would have been no

Protestant Reformation, and we would probably never have heard of Martin Luther, as it was the printing press that allowed the Bible to be spread to the common people. As this was going on, so were the witch trials, and the grimoires themselves were feared, banned, and yet in demand. They were printed in many different forms and editions, sometimes without a date of printing, or the name of the printer, and in secret, and spread through all of Europe.

ON THE IMAGES IN THE GERMAN EDITION

Soon after its printing, the Red Dragon was translated into Italian and German. Numerous editions were published, up to thirty-three have been documented, twelve are in languages other than French, or one third, which represents a strong proportion for a book rather poorly edited. Most of these foreign editions are in German, which can be explained by the importance given to magic in this country. Germany was the place where the witch hunts were the most violent. Many people accused of witchcraft were burned at the stake. It was also the land of demonologists, such as Henrich Kramer (Heinricus Institoris) and Jacob Sprenger, the authors of the *Malleus Malleficarum*. Superstitions and belief in the existence of the devil were well established. The additional images of the spirits of Lucifer, Belzebuth, and Astaroth, can be found in the German edition of the Grand Grimoire. These are the same three major spirits of the Grimorium Verum.

ON SIZE AND FEEL OF THE ORIGINAL

BOOKS

Originally, the Red Dragon was printed in a very small format. This was for several reasons. During this time period, larger books were more for scholarly use, and smaller books were more for personal use. Among the copies we have that still exist today, the largest of the original works had

an 8-inch spine on the book. For a book whose purpose it was to summon demons, it would be logical that it should be made somewhat small, so that it could be held in one hand as the ritual was taking place and the book was being used to invoke the spirits. A small size would also be useful when it came to hide the book from suspicious family members, or even the witch hunters.

The cover of the Red Dragon had Lucifuge on it, in all his Satanic glory. The letters of the title, the Red Dragon, a name for Satan, and the letters being written in red, reinforced the lurid, exciting nature of the work. This was probably aimed at both terrifying and intriguing the reader. It is most likely that the image of Lucifuge had some roots in the common depiction of the devil as half-man, half-goat, which in turn developed from the classical image of the Greek god Pan. As the early church grew, the god of forests, nature, lust and revelry, became a ready symbol of the devil to the early Christians. Easy to discredit and place blame on for his lust, in comparison to their sterile depiction of Jesus. Yet Pan was not unknown among the common people, and perhaps, despite his devilishness, perhaps there was some association between the image of Lucifuge, and the old god.

DIFFERENCES BETWEEN THE RED DRAGON AND GRAND GRIMOIRE

A word could be said here concerning the different editions of the Red Dragon, and the Grand Grimoire. The earliest edition of the Grand Grimoire can be dated back to 1750. Over the next hundred years, the book was printed in dozens of cities across Europe, and in many different forms. There is even a "Grand Grimoire of Saint Cyprian." Other editions combined the Red Dragon with another grimoire, the Black Hen.

The present edition is composed of texts from multiple public domain manuscripts of the Grand Grimoire and the Red Dragon. The oldest

extant versions can be dated to 1821. The main portion of the book stayed the same, with the invocation of Lucifuge and the hierarchy of spirits being the central core of the book, but, the frontispiece, and other details often changed. Sometimes the title of the work was written backwards to show the sinister nature of the work, and a little devilish looking mask image was placed at the start of the book as well.

In some editions there was a false date, such as 1411. Some editions had no illustrations, and some editions have borrowed illustrations of the spirits that don't seem to go with the book at all. Some show Lucifuge with two horns, some with three, and some with four. A few have the devil pictured as a large, wicked looking bull with the face of a man. The core of the books always stays the same, with the French versions of the book bring the oldest, and the German, Italian, and later Spanish versions of the book coming after it and based on it. From what we see in the study of the books that have survived, it is possible to theorize that, the Grand Grimoire came first, and some editions of it were named the Red Dragon later.

THE LINK WITH THE BLACK HEN, AND THE DESCRIPTION OF THE DEVIL'S COAT OF ARMS

The Red Dragon is often combined with another grimoire, the Black Hen. Let's take a moment here to study more precisely this book of magic as well as the joint editions that have been produced.

The Black Hen, sometimes called the hen with the golden eggs, is a grimoire whose first known edition dates from 1820. Its main subject is how to make a pact with the devil, through the sacrifice of a black hen. This is described in the Black Hen:

Take a black hen that has never laid eggs and no rooster has approached; Go on a great road, in the place where two roads intersect; There, at midnight, make a circle on the ground with a magic wand made of cypress, put yourself in the middle and split the body of the hen in two while pronouncing these words three times: Eloïm, Essaïm, Frugativi and Appelavi. Then turn your face towards the east, kneel and say a prayer; That done, you will make the great conjuration; Then the spirit will appear to you. He will ask you for your orders; You will give them as you deem fit, for he will not refuse to obey you, and you will be able to make yourself the richest, and therefore, the happiest of all men.

Some variations of this ritual require digging a hole, spreading the blood of the hen and burying it there. The words spoke are also sometimes different. If the devil does not appear immediately, he may appear nine days later. He is said to provide money in exchange for the sacrifice, or another black hen who lays golden eggs.

Sometimes joint editions of the two grimoires were produced. The frontispiece of these editions was something that we might call the devil's coat of arms. On it was shown a red dragon, the symbol of the devil from the Biblical book of Revelations, with two demon horns on his head. His tail is curled like a pig, which might be intended to show greed, and thus by extension, wealth. Upon the shield held by the dragon, is the black hen. This might also be a sly reference to the French jester or fool, a popular figure in the French court, and in the Tarot as the Fool.

A BOOK BY THE SAME NAME THAT DENOUNCES THE ORIGINAL

There is also a book which denounces the Red Dragon. It appears in 1866 and has 108 pages just like the original Red Dragon but is critical of everything within it. The author mentioned on the title page is Mr. Robville, but nothing else is known about him. The frontispiece shows a magician, recognizable by his silly hat and long dress. He carries in his right hand a magic wand. This was a popular representation of the sorcerer at the time.

The book tells the story of Claude Michu, the son of a weak-minded and gullible farmer, who thinks that he is the victim of a bad fate because the whole village mocks him. At an evening soiree, the Shepherd Simounen, a shady character and seller of talismans at odd hours, tells the young boy about the legend of the black hole. Claude decides to prove his courage, and find the black hole, which was said to be guarded by demons. The shepherd Simounen, who was described as someone "living on the credulity of the peasants, who were filling his purse with handsome coins and making an income through their foolishness," decides to trick the young boy. He tells him about, a "Little book printed in Red," which he describes as "a treasure of science, it's the sorcerer's bible, and inside are the great conjurations that make the spirits obedient."

There are many quotes from the Red Dragon, showing that the author knew this grimoire perfectly, such as the fact that in the Red Dragon, the treasure is said to be guarded by a demon. As the story continues, Bernard Morand, the pharmacist of the village, discovers what is going on, and steps in to educate young Claude. According to Bernard, everything in the world is explained by natural laws and magic does not exist. Bernard says to Claude:

> "All the power of the sorcerer lies in the knowledge of
> certain practices that will no longer seem wonderful
> when the instruction of the thing is known. In the eyes
> of the vulgar, they seem to operate wonders; They
> make the spirits speak, they change the places of
> objects by only the speaking of a magic word; It is

after all, only skillful conjurers or cunning knaves who misuse their science by lending it a supernatural character."

Concerning the Red Dragon, the book used by the shepherd Simounen, Bernard explains that:

"It is a sample of human silliness, a bunch of absurdities, written a long time ago by a man named Antonio Venitiana, who was not lacking in pride and presumption."

This shows once again that the author, knew the real Red Dragon well. He describes Lucifuge Rofocale as *a "red demon adorned with three horns and mounted on goat's feet"*. Bernard Morand then attempts to pass on some scientific knowledge, on electricity, to the youths of the village, so that they are no longer victims of superstition. The book closes with Simounen being sent to prison for having killed a peasant with his potions.

The full text of the novel titled the Red Dragon by M. Robville has been included at the end of the grimoire for reference. It illustrates the social and scientific context in which the grimoires were being published and received and is a good counterpoint to the ideas of the Red Dragon. This book has never been translated before into English. It is interesting to note that it contains excerpts from the grimoire which are nearly identical to the original manuscript. It also includes illustrations of other divinatory practices that were popular in the day.

There are sections discussing local folk traditions such as mermaids or water dragons, werewolves, and will-o-the-wisps. There is also a medieval tale about a half fairy Queen, Melusine, who reputedly built the French fortress of Lusignan. There are disquisitions on the rise of the scientific temper that moved magical work to the sidelines, and warnings about Spiritualism and false magic practitioners.

THE MAGICAL REVIVAL, DEMONOLATRY, SATANISM, AND THE SOLOMONIC MAGICIANS OF TODAY

Finally, we come to the modern day. In 1888 the Hermetic Order of the Golden Dawn was founded, and many of the magicians that were members of that order, such as Aleister Crowley, Macgregor Mathers, and A. E. Waite were influential in the publication of many grimoires such as the Lesser Key of Solomon, the Book of the Sacred Magic of Abramelin the Mage and the Grimoire of Armadel.

The Golden Dawn was an important influence on all the magic and occultism that would come after it, and interest in and seeking out the grimoires was a part of that magical revival. A. E. Waite was perhaps the first to publish portions of the Grand Grimoire into English, but he did not publish the full translation, as he strongly felt that all such books were diabolical, and his interest was in holy magic.

Nevertheless, knowledge of the Grand Grimoire and Lucifuge Rofocale spread in English-speaking magic circles, and many different mangled translations of it have spread around the internet. It has even been featured in popular culture in movies like The Warlock with the actor Julian Sands.

In modern times magicians tend to take one of two different approaches for the work. In the first approach, they attempt to follow the book exactly as it was written, step by step, even if that involves finding hard to acquire items, such as a Hazel wand with a forked tip, or a blood stone. There are many grimoires, including the Grand Grimoire and the Red Dragon, that are said to be written by Solomon, and the traditionalist magicians who practice the art as closely as they can to the way it was written in the book are often called "Solomonic" magicians.

The other school of magic that practices out of the grimoires is generally termed Satanism, or Demonolatry, and their method is basically to simply take the names, descriptions, images and sigils from the grimoires and use them in rituals that praise the demons, and approach them as friends and allies. This group of magicians do not use the Hebrew names of God to threaten and bind the spirits, but instead reveres and worships them as ancient gods, and cosmic forces. Both groups use magic to affect change in the world using demons, but the approach to the religious component in the grimoires is different.

THE AUTHORSHIP AND KEY THEMES OF THE RED DRAGON AND GRAND GRIMOIRE

Who wrote the Red Dragon? There is no way for us to be sure, but in the title page, it is signed Antonio del Rabbia. Antonia being an Italian name would seem to indicate that the author, if he existed, was Italian. del Rabbia meaning the Rabbi, a spiritual leader in the Jewish religion. Venitiana might mean, from Venice, or it might be a surname. It is possible that there was a real Antonio, who did compile the book, or it is also possible that this was simply used to give authority to the work, as the common people might be more inclined to trust a rabbi.

Some editions of the book are signed "Doctor J Karter" instead. Once again it seems that the title of doctor might have been added to give a kind of authority to the text. It is easier for a reader to trust a doctor, or a rabbi. In either case, we know nothing more about the author of the work, and it is likely that he compiled it from earlier writings. As this book was written during the time when people were tried, convicted, and killed for being witches, it is unlikely the real author would be willing to place his name on the work. Perhaps Antonio the Rabbi, or Doctor Karter, was a code name, or had some meaning to the original creator that is now lost.

There are also indications that this grimoire is part of, or perhaps blends the Faustian tradition with the Solomonic grimoires. Multiple themes such as the large dog guarding the treasure and the daemonic pact are found in the Faustian grimoires, and the devil in Doktor Faustus, Mephistopheles can be translated, in one way, as Lucifuge, the arch-demon in the Grand Grimoire.

LANGUAGES IN THE GRAND GRIMOIRE

Although the Red Dragon is written mainly in French, Hebrew and Greek terms are found in the text, as well as long passages in Latin and Italian, such as the "promise of the Spirit" in the chapter of the Sanctum Regnum. This added a mysterious and coded dimension to the Grimoire, which had to be deciphered by the reader who wished to make a pact with the devil. In fact, understanding of Latin and Italian would be necessary to assimilate and follow the instructions in the ritual of invocation.

In this interlinear edition, we have taken the time to translate every word into English, and to produce the most complete version ever printed.

STRUCTURE OF THE GRIMOIRE

The work is divided into two parts. In the first part, the precise instructions for the creation of the Blasting Rod, and the evocation of Lucifuge Rofocale are described. The would-be magician, referred to as the Karcist is told to sacrifice a goat, and make its skin into a magic circle, in which to stand during the conjuration of the demon. In the second book, the author outlines a method whereby one may go about the process, even if they don't have the means to sacrifice a goat, make the magic circle or prepare the blasting rod.

Although the ritual structure is geared to invoke Lucifuge Rofocale, the book mentions that any one of the spirits listed can be invoked for

the purpose of making a pact with it. No information is given on the 18 spirits who are under the 9 superior spirits, perhaps it was felt that these were well known demons and they would already be known about by anyone who practiced the book, or perhaps there was once more information on these 18 spirits within the book, and at some time it was edited for reasons of size.

A NOTE ON PURITY AND PREPARATION FOR EVOCATION

Éliphas Levi writes in his book *The Dogma and Ritual of High Magic*:

> *The purification of the mage must consist in abstinence, in a vegetable and gentle diet, in the deprivation of strong liqueurs, and in the settlement of the hours of sleeping. This preparation was indicated and represented in all the cults by a time of penance and hardship.*

Before beginning the ritual of summoning a demon, it is written in the Red Dragon that the magician must be "armed with fearlessness, prudence, wisdom and virtue." It is then added: "you will spend a whole quarter of a moon without attending any company of women or girls so as not to fall into impurity." To put this plainly, before calling up demons, you must not have sex for a week.

Many grimoires mention this purity requirement. This may have been influenced to some degree by the monks and priests, the first creators of medieval grimoires, who took a vow of chastity. This condition also demonstrates that the grimoires were intended for a male audience, since the sorcerer should not be associated with women. A notable exception to this occurs in the Grimorium Verum however, as that book gives a note on slightly different practices for men and women. Perhaps in this instance if a woman were to perform the ritual, she would have to avoid

the company of men during this preparation period.

The aspiring wizard also passes through a fast, or at least a meal regulation. Indeed, it is noted in the Red Dragon: "You will begin your quarter-moon, in the moment that the quarter begins, promising to the great Adonay, who is the head of all spirits, to have only two meals a day, or every twenty-four hours, which you will take at noon or at midnight, or, if you like better, at seven o'clock in the morning and at seven o'clock in the evening." In the Christian religion, fasting is equated with a penance in which the believer atones for his sins and approaches God. From a magical perspective, this along with all the other preparations can be seen from another perspective, that of purification, and through it, the generation of additional personal energy in preparation for the ritual.

ON THE BLOODSTONE

To get in touch with the devil, or Lucifuge Rofocale, or any other spirit, it is necessary to make a sacrifice. Before that though, you must protect yourself. The Grimoire thus advises the magician to buy "a blood stone called ematille" that he must always carry with him to prevent being tormented by the spirits.

It is probably a stone called a blood jasper or heliotrope. A green-colored stone, it is veined with red and when put in water and turned towards the sun, it gives the impression of being stained with blood, hence its nickname of Blood Stone. Claude Lim, in his Dictionary of Magic and Medicinal Stones, describes it in this manner: it *"gives the gift of prophecy, health, a long life, provides praise and fame, draws out poisons, stops blood flowing, prevents being deceived etc."*

Note the last line here, *"it prevents being deceived."* This is interesting considering it being used to conjure demons, and especially in the fact that the magician is told to always carry the stone with him . Claude Lim adds that "that the heliotrope gives its possessor power over the demons

THE COMPLETE ILLUSTRATED GRAND GRIMOIRE, INTERLINEAR EDITION

provided a bat is engraved on it." This can be compared with the Grimorium Verum, where the sigils of the demons are sometimes engraved onto an emerald.

ON THE CLAVICULE

The Grand Grimoire refers to a Clavicule often as the means to access the power and majesty of Solomon's powers, and by means of which to command the spirits. This has often been literally translated as 'Collarbone' or left untranslated.

While one could consider the collarbone as akin to the tantric aghoris brandishing a human collarbone in their dark rites, this is a minor blind, if one were to consider it thus. The Clavicule, from Latin, gets its name from the Latin *clavicula* or little key, and this clearly reveals that this is nothing but the grand conjuration of the Key of Solomon. This is further confirmed by usage such as *"C'est par le moyen de la clavicule du grand roi Salomon"* which means, "This is by means of the Key of the Great King Solomon" and the actual usage of the text of the grand conjuration in the Sanctum Regnum chapter of the Grand Grimoire.

ON VERVAIN

The idea of purity is found in abstinence, the fasting, the Virgin Kid goat, and with the use of vervain. This plant has purifying virtues and was used to purify places and people before magic rituals. In antiquity, it is said that some priests washed their altars with an infusion of Vervain. The herb was said to have the power to cure all diseases and destroy hexes. It is also a symbol of peace and good luck. Tying a garland of this herb around the neck of the goat might have been intended to show that the sorcerer comes in peace to bargain with the evil spirits.

Vervain is a variety of the woody plant *Verbena Officinalis*, which bears

five-petalled flowers in a variety of colors and has been used in herbal medicine and folk magic as a tonic. It is one of the 38 plants referenced in Bach flower remedies and in a popular essential oil sold as Spanish vervain as well as the popular perfume oil of lemon verbena, which is a different plant.

In ancient Egypt, it was referred to as the 'tears of Isis' the goddess, and in Greece, 'Hera's tears'. Pliny the Elder cited it as being offered on Jupiterian altars. It was considered a sacred herb that was used to sweep the altars of Jupiter. Christian lore said it was used to staunch Jesus' wounds, giving it the name 'herb of the cross'. Cimaruta, the Italian folk charms used against stregeria or witches, were imprinted with vervain flower images. Victorian floriography gave it the attribution of love and sensibility, while European folk healers considered it an 'iron plant', with names referencing iron, such as the German Eisenkraut. To drive evil spirits out of houses, holy water was sprinkled with sprigs of verbena in the ritual of aspersion. Druids used it with a high degree of superstition, picking the herb during the hot summer, but at the break of day, before the sun rose. Some demonographers believed one must wear a crown of verbena if one is to evoke evil spirits.

ON THE HAZEL WAND

Before being able to encounter these dark forces, it is necessary to make the tools needed for the ritual. The mysterious wand, also called a blasting rod, is essential. It can be described as a sort of ultimate magic wand of the wizard, without which he could not summon the spirits. Its length must be nineteen and a half inches and have a forked tip.

The wood of the Hazel tree, also called Coudrier, is associated with fertility because of the abundance of hazelnuts produced by the tree. Divination wands, used by alchemists to find metals such as gold, or treasures, were made from hazel wood. When the wand approaches what you want to discover, it turns and bows. It is an instrument that gives the one who uses it power. A wand of this type is described in the spells and recipe section at the end of the book.

In the Red Dragon, the forked tip Hazel wand is described as the greatest treasure of the light and said to make the spirits tremble. It is said to be infused with the power of Samson, and other biblical figures such as the angel that drove Adam and Eve from the garden of Eden, as well as Jacob, Moses, and Emanuel.

The branch used for the future wand must be identified the day before the invocation, however, it must not be touched. On the great day of the operation, the sorcerer must go and cut it. It is written: "you will strip it of its leaves and small branches, if it has any, with the same blade of steel which was used to slit the victim, which is still dyed with its blood, whereas you must be careful not to wipe the said blade, starting to cut the wand when the sun begins to appear on the horizon."

The fact that it happens at dawn is symbolic and may also be magical in the sense that its aim is to capture the energetic power of the rising sun. Dawn marks the beginning and the birth of the day. It is also associated with promise and hope. The dawn, "Aube" in French, from the Latin "Alba." meaning white, is also a symbol of purity, an essential theme throughout the whole book. It was believed that one must be pure to encounter demons, or else they risk becoming their slave, rather than commanding them.

Finally, the sorcerer must apply a magnetic lodestone to the two tips of the wand, to magnetize them. The lodestone has long been considered to have magical properties in popular folk beliefs. Being magnetic, it is a symbol of invisible forces.

ON THE MAGIC CIRCLE

The summoning of Lucifuge Rofocale was considered very dangerous, so the sorcerer must be careful and protect himself, not knowing how the spirit will react to him. This protection includes the drawing of a magic

circle on the ground, called in the Red Dragon the "great Kabbalistic Circle".

The person performing the ritual is called the Karcist or the Operator. The number of people must always be odd, with either one, or three persons present, never two. The Karcist is the only one who has the right to hold the blasting wand and speak to the spirits, even if the spirit addresses the other people present or threatens them. The place chosen for the ritual is important: it must be solitary, and hidden away from the world, to avoid being disturbed during the evocation of the demon. Then,

"You start by forming a circle with the skin of the Kid, that you will nail to the ground with four nails; You will then take your Ématille stone and draw a triangle within the circle, as it is depicted, starting from the side of the rising Sun; You will also draw with the bloodstone the great A, the little E, the little A, and the J around the edge of the circle, as well as the Holy Name of Jesus in the midst of two crosses, so that the spirits cannot attack you from behind."

A.E.A.J refers to the Holy Names "by Adonai, by Elohim, by Ariel, by Jehovah", used often throughout the Grand Grimoire. The Grimoire performs its operations under these and other holy names and is replete with Catholic prayers and benedictions to invoke the spirits.

The four nails referred to were supposed to be drawn from the coffin of a dead child. Nails are often used in magic, especially nails taken from a coffin or the wood from the gallows, the structure from which criminals were hanged. Having been in contact with the dead, these were believed to contain a certain power, and were also often used in necromancy.

The Sorcerer then traces a triangle using his Bloodstone. The geometric shape of the triangle might have referred to the Holy Trinity, the number of people advised to participate in the ritual, or it may also refer to the three Chief spirits, Lucifer, Belzebuth, and Astaroth. The JHS at the base of the triangle is an abbreviation of the name of Jesus in Greek.

Thus, the sorcerer is placed under the protection of Christ, which might seem odd for a book supposedly compiled from the writings of King Solomon and is another indication of the context and usage of these rituals in the educated, church-oriented circles. The Karcist must then place two candlesticks with two verbena wreaths wrapped around them, on the right and left of the triangle, then light the candles. The candles must be virgin wax, blessed and made by a virgin girl.

The ritual is like a religious ceremony, where God and the devil are both invoked. The Karcist stands in the first small circle inside the Triangle of Pacts and his two assistants in the other circles. Once the Karcist and the other sorcerers are inside the circle, the Karcist lights a fire in a new vase, filled with willow charcoal. In the fire, he throws brandy, which would have to have been highly distilled and thus flammable, incense, and camphor. Camphor is a waxy, flammable, transparent solid with a strong aroma. It is found in the wood of the camphor laurel. These last two elements are often used in magical rituals. They are believed to purify the premises, while creating a mysterious atmosphere for invocation. It is also noted that the magician must not wear on his person metals such as iron, but only gold or silver, and they must have ready a piece of this, to throw to the demon that will appear.

In the course of the conjurations, we encounter Latin terms, such as "Venite" (come) or "in Suddeno." (suddenly, immediately, or, in an instant) This use of Latin gives religious authority to the ritual, but also makes it more mysterious. If no spirit appears, the Karcist must then plunge the metal coated tips of the blasting rod into the fire. This would show that the wand should be held by the base, and not the forked end, which would be the opposite of how the treasure finding wands or divining rods were used. This opposite use of the wand, like the reverse title, the words Grand Grimoire written backwards, may have been to show that the work was sinister, or in opposition to how these wands were normally used. In any case, after the two points of the wand are thrust within the fire, obviously not too deeply, or the wand would catch fire, the spirits will immediately utter "appalling howls" and soon show themselves.

ON LUCIFUGE ROFOCALE - NAME, MEANING AND FORM

Lucifuge Rofocale is, according to the grimoire, the Prime Minister of the underworld. The very name is symbolic, since in Latin Lucifuge comes the name "Lux", the light, and the verb "fugio", fleeing, thus designating the one who flees the light, the opposite of the name Lucifer, which means light bearer. The name Rofocale is the reverse of the name Lucifer, Reficul, "Rofocale", symbolizing that he is the opposite of Lucifer by his name and surname. The name Lucifuge is first found in the eleventh-century, within Michael Psellus' *De Operatione Daemonum*, adding to the hierarchy of demons first found in Iamblichus and the Neoplatonists.

> he counted off six species of dæmons, and first he mentioned Leliurium,23 speaking in his barbarous vernacular tongue, a name which signifies Igneous. This order of dæmons haunts the air above us, for the entire genus has been expelled from the regions adjacent to the moon, as a profane thing with us would be expelled from a temple, but the second occupies the air contiguous to us, and is called by the proper name Aërial; the third is the Earthly, the fourth the Aqueous and Marine, the fifth the Subterranean, and the last the Lucifugus, which can scarcely be considered sentient beings. All these species of dæmons are haters of God, and enemies of man, and they say, that the Aqueous and Subterranean are worse than the merely bad, but that the Lucifugus are eminently malicious and mischievous, for these, said he, not merely impair men's intellects, by phantasies and illusions, but destroy them with the same alacrity as we would the most savage wild beast. The Aqueous

suffocate in the water all that approach them; the
Subterranean and Lucifugus, if they can only insinuate
themselves into the lungs of those they meet, seize
and choke them, rendering them epileptic and insane;

The Grand Grimoire takes pains to indicate that the operator must not agree to the initial demands of Lucifuge Rofocale to surrender himself to the spirit.

I cannot agree to your demands unless you agree to
surrender yourself to me in twenty years, to do with
your body and soul as I please.

He must instead insist on keeping his soul inviolate and that the spirit must accede to his demands in the names of the Most Holy. Lucifuge Rofocale ends up obeying the Karcist so that he will no longer be beaten by the blasting rod. The Karcist then states his demands: The Spirit must appear to him, or to the one who will be in possession of the Grimoire. In addition, the Karcist asks for the location of the nearest treasure, in exchange for returning a gold coin to Lucifuge, on the first day of every month. The demon, not wishing to become a slave, accepts on one condition:

I cannot grant you what you ask of me under these
conditions or under any other, if you do not give
yourself to me in fifty years, to do with your body and
your soul what I like.

In an almost story-like fashion, the book explains that the will of the devil is only to possess the sorcerer and to make him a slave. To punish him for his rebellion, the Karcist then plunges the wand into the fire to make the demon suffer, until he submits, which he does finally end up doing. He then approves the pact and signs his true signature to it. He also promises to deliver the treasure's location under three conditions:

keep this secret always, that you are charitable
towards the poor, and that you grant me one piece of

gold or silver on the first day of every month, if you
miss this, you will be mine forever.

So, the pact with the devil is realized. He has approved it and is subject to the sorcerer, to whom he must now obey without being rebellious. However, should the wizard make the slightest error, the demon will be there to take his body and soul.

Such pacts were commonplace in occult writings, from the first century tale of Theophilus of Adana, who sold his soul to the devil to retrieve his church offices and the more contemporary priest of Loudon, Urbain Grandier, who neglected to hide his pacts with the devil while ministering to the Ursuline nuns, leading him to be burned at the stake. The pact of Urbain Grandier, autographed by him in his own blood can be found in the *Bibliotheque Nationale,* and appears to be drawn from the Grand Grimoire.

At the end of the ritual, the Karcist has everything he had desired. Through God's help, the devil is under his command and delivers access to a treasure, or whatever else the spirit might have been called to deliver. The spirit is then returned to his kingdom.

Once the promise of the spirit is made, the Karcist follows him to the treasure. The magician's assistants must remain within the triangle, within the magic circle. He is first blocked by a large dog, a gnome, the elemental Earth spirit reputed to protect treasures. The magician brandishes the blasting Rod and the gnome leads him to the treasure.

When the magician arrives at the treasure, he must throw a sheet of parchment over the treasure, on which is written the conjuration of the Key, while taking a piece as a token of recognition and throwing a coin of his own money, which he will have bitten before, to the demon. The sorcerer must go back and forth to the treasure without looking back, even if it seems as if "all the mountains of the world will topple over on him."

Once the Karcist is back in the cabbalistic circle that protects him, it is time for him to return the spirit to its normal abode, in hell or wherever that may be, the latter having fulfilled his duty for the moment. The spirit is also reminded to,

> *think about your commitment, because if you miss it for a moment, you can be sure that I will strike you forever with the lightning rod of the Great Adonay, Eloïm, Ariel and Jehovam. Amen.*

The sorcerer then thanks the devil for what he did and allows him to return home in peace. He warns the demon that he must withdraw in silence, without doing any bad deeds or trying to rebel. In the end, he reminds him of his commitment and threatens him with the power of the blasting rod. Finally, he thanks God for helping him to survive the ritual and bestowing his grace and blessings upon him.

THE HIERARCHY OF DEMONS IN THE BOOK

The 18 subordinate spirits are all well-known and can be found in the Lesser Key of Solomon and many other works. The Spirit Pruslas is the one spirit among the 18 that is not listed in the Lesser Key, and from what historians can tell, that is because he was missing from the list given by Wierus, and the Lesser Key was developed from that list of demons.

Pruslas is described as appearing with a flaming body, and the head of an owl. It is said that his abode is outside the mythical Tower of Babel, wherever that may be, and that he is the promoter of strife, war, and conflict. He may not be admitted into some places.

ZARIATNATMIK

In one of the prayers of the Red Dragon, besides invoking various powerful names of God and Emmanuel, the Sorcerer also calls on Zariatnatmik, who can be found in the 1863 Dictionnaire Infernale with the note "unknown person, but very powerful".

This mysterious figure appears in H P Lovecraft's horror novel *The Case of Charles Dexter Ward,* wherein the title character attempts to invoke demons using cabbalistic rituals inherited from his ancestor, but, taken from Eliphas Levi's *Transcendental Magic,* which in turn, borrowed this character from the references in the Grand Grimoire.

THE SANCTUM REGNUM AND ITS IMPORTANCE

The second part of the grimoire of the Red Dragon contains the SANCTUM REGNUM, which can be translated as "Holy Kingdom" or "Kingdom of God." There we find a hierarchy of spirits, as well as how to make them appear and force them to obey.

These steps are useful for those who do not know how or fail to make the blasting rod and the cabbalistic circle. The invocations of this part are claimed to have been taken from the Great Key of King Solomon. It is the second book that would probably have been used more often, since it does not contain the goat sacrifice, yet, the name is curious, since, the spirits within it are more what one would call the unholy kingdom, the kingdom of the devil.

WHAT N.N. MEANS, BECOMING SOLOMON

In addition, the requests in mind are signed "NN" within the Red Dragon. It may be the author's initials, but it is more likely to be the initials of the terms "*nomen nominandum*", meaning that the person reading the grimoire should be named, or write their own signature there. The idea here was that the magician had taken the place of Solomon, and could deal directly with the spirits, as Solomon did, thus receiving the same benefits as Solomon, of wealth, wisdom, power, the love of women, the destruction of enemies, etc.

A NOTE ON HOW THE DEVILS ARE BOTH PRAISED AND REVILED

Once all the tools are prepared, with the Blasting Rod in hand, the sorcerer can finally invoke the name of the spirit with which he wants to make a pact. The example here is given with Lucifuge Rofocale, but any of the 27 demons in the book could be invoked for the purpose of making a pact with them.

We must first ask for the agreement of Lucifer since he is Emperor of the underworld and directs all the demons. It is interesting to note that the Three greatest spirits of Lucifer, Belzebuth, and Astaroth are both praised and even asked for their protection and blessing at this point in the book, and this seems to contrast with the idea that these spirits are out to destroy the magician. In any case, the idea of hierarchy is strong, with the idea being that the higher spirits control the lower spirits as if they were workmen or slaves.

ON THE PRAYER FROM THE FALSE HIERARCHY OF DEMONS AND ITS USEFULNESS

The Latin prayer at the end of the Red Dragon is an entire ritual within itself. We can trace it back to a document on demonology by Wierus called the false hierarchy of demons, and it is also in the book the discovery of Witchcraft by Reginald Scot. This fragment, left in Latin in the original Red Dragon, dates to the 1500s and the time of the King James Bible.

It mentions going three days without sex before invoking the spirit, and is a one size fits all form of ritual for the use of invoking any demon or spirit, and was probably even, at one time extended to use for invoking ghosts or even fairies, as is evidenced in the book, the Discovery of Witchcraft, where the fairy Sybilia and other spirits are described. Since it was written in Latin, these instructions would have been more cryptic to the ordinary person, but a priest might have been able to read them, or employ that part of the book, as many of the religious texts were in Latin, and that Language would have been familiar to a priest.

ON NECROMANCY AND THE GREAT SECRET OF TALKING WITH THE DEAD

Some editions of the Grand Grimoire came with an additional section on Necromancy and conversing with the dead. While this is an age-old practice with examples as far back as the episode in the Odyssey, the Nekyia (νέκυια ἡ νέκυα), where Odysseus is advised to *'make a journey of a very different kind, and find your way to the Halls of Hades ... across the River of Ocean'*. He makes a trench and pours a libation to the dead, with milk, honey, wine and water, followed with barley meal and the sacrifice of a black ram.

> *Then there gathered from out of Erebus the spirits of those that are dead, brides, and unwedded youths, and toil-worn old men, and tender maidens with hearts yet new to sorrow, and many, too, that had been wounded with bronze-tipped spears, men slain in fight, wearing their blood-stained armour. These came thronging in crowds about the pit from every*

side, with a wondrous cry; and pale fear seized me. Then I called to my comrades and bade them flay and burn the sheep that lay there slain with the pitiless bronze, and to make prayer to the gods, to mighty Hades and dread Persephone. And I myself drew my sharp sword from beside my thigh and sat there and would not suffer the powerless heads of the dead to draw near to the blood until I had enquired of Teiresias.

The necromantic rite in the Grand Grimoire is far simpler. It involves attending the Midnight Christmas Mass at a Catholic church, and when the Priest raises the Holy Host, the Sorcerer intones under his breath the words *"Arise ye dead and come to me."*

He then quickly leaves the church and goes to the nearby cemetery, where he asks the Infernal Powers to release the dead from their dark kingdoms so he might converse with them.

Infernal Powers, you who bring trouble into all the universe, abandon your dark dwellings and go beyond your abode by the River Styx

Then he scatters some graveyard dirt, 'like one might cast grain in a field before intoning

He who is only dust, rise from thy tomb, from thy ashes, and answer the questions I will make of him in the name of the Father of all men

He then casts a cross of bones towards the nearby Church before a period of contemplation. Finally, he lies on the ground, facing the sky and begins to feel the shade's presence. He can also invoke the spirit to visible appearance for conversation before dismissing it.

Finally, the sorcerer leaves the graveyard after returning to the first tomb and making the sign of the cross with his knife. He is cautioned that

> one must not omit a single point or slightest circumstance of what is described herein, without which we run the risk of becoming ourselves the prey of all the denizens of Hell.

ON LUCKY AND UNLUCKY DAYS

At the end of the Red Dragon, between the text of the book, and the section on spells and recipes, there is a table of lucky and unlucky days.

It seems surprising to find such a table, in a book on how to summon demons, but it was probably placed there to give the book an extra selling value, among the common people, who were fond of such almanac-style instructions. It even comes with a note, delivered in all sincerity, about how these days were given by angels to Adam, the first man.

THE SPELLS AT THE END OF THE BOOK

The recipes presented in this last section of the Grimoire are very diverse, and have some similarities with the earlier grimoire, the Little Albert. There are recipes related to black magic, such as the "composition of death, or the Philosopher's Stone." It is hard to tell what the "composition of death" even is, but it is definitely NOT the Philosopher's Stone. The Philosopher's Stone was said to be an alchemical creation, capable of giving eternal life, and for its part, whatever the "composition of death" is, it is certainly a deadly poison.

One love spell refers to Solomon's true love, the Queen of Sheba, here referred to as Sheva, and an unusual herb, literally translated as 'the herb of nine shirts' that can be identified as the Alpine Leek or Victory Onion (*allium victorialis*), and is a perennial of the Amaryllis family. In German,

this plant is called Siegwurz, or the Root of Victory, and was worn as an amulet, 'to be as a safeguard against the attacks of certain impure spirits.'

Curtis' Botanical Magazine notes about this herb,

> *Bulb within the loose outer netted coverings of a deep purple colour, growing out into long thick fleshy fistular stem-sheathing petioles, which terminate in broad flattish elliptically-lanceolate green blades, from four to fix inches long, from half an inch to near two in breadth ; corolla of dirty sub diaphanous white colour, sometimes suffused with red; the whole plant, when bruised, has a very rank scent of Garlic. Native of Spain, Italy, France, Switzerland, and Germany. The root was considered by the Bohemian miners, when worn as an amulet, to be a safeguard against the attacks of certain impure spirits, to which they deemed themselves exposed; among them it was surnamed Siegwurz (Root of Victory); hence Victorialis. By the shepherds of other districts, it has been used internally as a preservative against the effects of fogs, and noxious exhalations; a purpose to which every species of Garlic is more or less adapted.*

Many recipes include the sacrifice of an animal. "To make the garter of seven leagues per hour," a young wolf should be slaughtered, and then his skin cut into one-inch wide garters. But this tool can lose its magic if a woman sees it or if its user crosses a river without removing it.

A black cat, an animal associated with the devil and witches, is employed to become invisible. According to the directions in the spell, it is necessary to boil the cat for twenty-four hours and throw its meat over the left shoulder, perhaps as if to feed the infernal spirits often associated with this side. Finally, you must place the cat's bones under your teeth, looking in a mirror, until you find the right bone and no longer see yourself in the mirror. The sorcerer must then say "*Pater, in Manus Tuas*

Commendo spiritum meum." (Father into your hands, I give my spirit.)

Other unusual ingredients within the spells include human fat and natural mummy. Ground up Egyptian mummies were a popular medicine in Europe, including the bitumen in which they were embalmed. This may come from Pliny the Elder who wrote that this ingredient had healing powers. The spell here uses these ingredients along with deer oil, laurel oil, wine and verbena leaves to prepare a plaster that would make one 'go like the wind', requiring a dilution of three drops of blood in white wine when stopping so as to not be sick.

The last recipe, including only plants, concerns the "composition of ink to write the pacts". Indeed, this ink is special and must be changed in every contact with the devil or an infernal spirit. It is composed of gallnuts, copper sulfate, rock alum and gum Arabic in boiling river water in a fresh glazed clay pot.

The book closes with a heartfelt warning to the reader to be wise and prudent like the Great Solomon, to be able to enjoy the wealth one might generate through these methods. A salutary caution is provided to, 'be humane to your fellow-men, comfort the unfortunate, live content.'

As a final note concerning the spells at the end of the book, we would add that, as in the case of the second book of the Red Dragon, which allows for an alternate method of calling the spirits, without the sacrifice of a goat, it may be that some of these final spells could be done without the use of a cat, or a wolf, etc.. Macgregor Mathers, head of the Golden Dawn, in his edition of the Key of Solomon, discouraged the use of animal blood or body parts in magic, feeling that the same effects could be achieved with the use of substitutes such as consecrated ink. Many magicians in modern times as well, have echoed these sentiments.

The Red Dragon also states that the spells in the final part of the book can only be performed by one who has had success in calling the spirits, and this should also be taken into consideration concerning them. With these words, we wish you well.

IMAGES, SEALS AND RELATED ART

The following images, seals and related art are drawn from various sources, including original art to represent some of the demons mentioned in the Grand Grimoire.

The seals of the 9 superior spirits were drawn from original editions of the Grand Grimoire and placed within the circles with their names for the purpose of this book.

The seals of 17 of the subordinate spirits are drawn from the 1904 Mathers/Crowley edition of the Lesser Key of Solomon.

The seal of Pruslas was created by Gregory K. Koon and is in the public domain.

The images of many of the spirits come from the 1863 edition of the Dictionnaire Infernale, and the remaining pictures have been created by the artists Ville Vuorinen, Matti Sinkkonen, and Artem Grigoryev, except for Fleurety, which is from the private collection of one of the authors.

The Seal of LUCIFUGE ROFOCALE

Figure 1: The Seal of LUCIFUGE

LUCIFUGE ROFOCALE is the primary spirit in the Grand Grimoire. He is the one with whom the pact is made and governs the Superior and Subordinate spirits. He is the Infernal Prime Minister. He has the power that LUCIFER grants him over all the wealth and all the treasures of the world. He has under him BAEL, AGARES and MARBAS, and thousands of demons or spirits who are his subordinates.

Figure 2: Lucifuge Rofocale, Grand Grimoire, Public Domain

The Seal of LUCIFER

Figure 3: The Seal of LUCIFER

The first conjuration in the Grand Grimoire is addressed to LUCIFER, 'prince and master of the rebel angels.' The second and third conjurations are also addressed to LUCIFER, and he is praised as 'One hundred kingdoms call unto Lucifer'. He makes the promise cited in the Grand Grimoire and can thus be interchangeable with LUCIFUGE ROFOCALE, although he is distinguished by citing LUCIFUGE ROFOCALE as his Prime Minister. He describes himself thus: "the powerful and supreme independent Emperor, free and absolute master of all the subterranean kingdom, despotic Lord in all my jurisdiction, formidable, terrible, very noble, who governs all fortune, all sages, wise, sagacious, fortuitous and sublime bright character. I am the dominator of Europe and all misfortunes of Asia in particular."

Figure 4: Lucifer, Dictionnaire Infernale, Public Domain

The Seal of BELZEBUTH

Figure 5: The Seal of BELZEBUTH

BELZEBUTH, Beelzebub or Belzebub or Beelzebuth. Prince of Demons, according to the scriptures; The first in power and in crime after Satan. According to Milton, Supreme Leader of the Infernal Empire, according to most demonographers, his name means Lord of the Flies. He was the Demon most revered of the peoples of Canaan, who sometimes represented him under the figure of a fly, most often with the attributes of the sovereign power.

We see in the Keys of Solomon, that Beelzebub sometimes appears under monstrous forms like those of a huge calf or a goat followed by a

long tail; often, however, he shows under the figure of a fly of an extreme size. When he is angry, one adds, he vomits flames and howls like a wolf. Sometimes Astaroth appears at his sides, in the guise of a donkey.

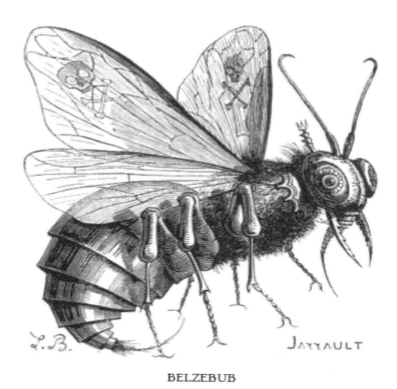

BELZEBUB

Figure 6: Belzebub, Dictionnaire Infernale, Public Domain

The Seal of ASTAROTH

Figure 7: The Seal of ASTAROT

ASTAROT is one of the three 'principal infernal spirits' in the Grand Grimoire. He is appealed to during the Conjurations, similar to the Conjuration of the Greater Key of Solomon.

In the Dictionnaire Infernale, he has the figure of a very ugly angel and shows himself straddling an infernal dragon; He holds in his left hand a viper. Some magicians say that he presides over the West, that he provides the friendship of the Great Lords, and that he must be evoked on Wednesday. The Sidonians and the Philistines adored him. He is said to be the great treasurer in Hell.

He knows the past and the future, and he would be happy to answer questions on the most secret things. It is easy to cause him to talk about the creation and the faults and fall of the Angels, about which he knows the whole story. But in his conversations, he argues that he was punished unjustly.

He teaches liberal arts in depth, and commands forty legions. He who invokes this spirit must be careful to let himself be approached, because of his unbearable stench. That is why it is prudent for the magician to hold under his nostrils a magic ring, made of silver, which is a protection against the evil odors of demons.

Astaroth has been referenced in several traditions. He is quoted as one of the seven princes of hell who visited Faust, according to the English tradition; He appears as a snake with a colorful tail like changing bricks, two short feet, all yellow, white and yellowish belly, reddish brown neck, and arrow points, like those of the hedgehog, as long as the length of a finger.

ASTAROTH

Figure 8: Astaroth, Dictionnaire Infernale, Public Domain

The Seal of SATANACHIA

Figure 9: The seal of SATANACHIA

SATANACHIA has the power to submit to himself all women and make them do what he wishes. He commands a great spirit legion; he has under him Pruslas, Aamon and Barbatos.

He also appears in the Grimorium Verum, directly under Lucifer, as well as in the Grimoire of Pope Honorius.

Figure 10: Image of Satanachia

The Seal of AGLIAREPT

Figure 11: The Seal of AGLIAREPT

AGLIAREPT has the power to discover the most hidden secrets, in all the Courts and Governments of the world, he reveals the greatest mysteries. He commands the second legion of spirits, he has under him Guer, Gusoan and Botis.

In the Grimorium Verum, he reports directly to Lucifer, and in an edition of the Veritable Key of Solomon, he approves 'the great Kabbalah of the Green Butterfly' (*le grande cabale dite du papillon vert*)

Figure 12: Original Image of Agliarept

The Seal of FLEURETY

Figure 13: The Seal of FLEURETY

FLEURETY has the power to perform any task he wishes during the night; he can also cause hail or raise a storm where he wishes. He commands a very considerable corps of spirits, he has under him Bathim, Pursan and Abigar.

Fleurety also appears in the Grimorium Verum as a subordinate of Beelzebuth.

Figure 14: Fleurety, inspired by Boreas from Atalanta Fugiens

The Seal of SARGATANAS

Figure 15: The Seal of SARGATANAS

SARGATANAS has the power to make one invisible, to transport one anywhere, to open all locks, to grant one the power to see whatever is happening inside homes, to teach all the tricks and subtleties of the Shepherds. He controls several brigades of spirits. He has under him Loray, Valefar and Farau

He is mentioned in the Grimorium Verum as subordinate to Astaroth.

Interestingly, in a newspaper article in September 1922, the author compares a Senator who voted for peace accords with the German Reich

to the demon Sargatanas, showing the longevity and popularity of this demonic figure in popular culture.

Figure 16: La Lanterne, Sep 8, 1922, citing Sargatanas

The highlighted text reads:

*But it is still the famous agreement, which, from him, will surprise the most. The friends, the allied candidates, the senator's newspapers from Aisne have always considered as 'defeatists of peace' those who, for the purposes of the treaty, spoke of an agreement with our debtor, and the members of the League of Human Rights, in Aisne, were still designated by a sharp and venomous index for having applauded the manifestation of Buisson in the Reichstag. **Now the Senator Marquis has just signed a pact with the demon Sargatanas!***

Figure 17: Original image of Sargatanas

The Seal of NEBIROS

Figure 18: The Seal of NEBIROS

NEBIROS in the Grand Grimoire is a Superior Spirit. He has the power to harm whoever he pleases, he can reveal the Hand of Glory, he educates on all the qualities of Metals, Minerals, Plants and all pure & impure Animals.

He also grants the art of predicting the future, being one of the greatest necromancers of all the infernal spirits. He can go anywhere and inspect all the infernal militias. He has under him Ayperos, Nuberus and Glasyabolas.

Figure 19: Original Image of Nebiros

The Seal of BAEL

Figure 20: The Seal of BAEL

BAEL is directly under LUCIFUGE in the Grand Grimoire.

In Weir's Dictionnaire Infernale, followed by the Lesser Key of Solomon, he is cited from the Grand Grimoire as leading sixty-six legions and being the head of the infernal powers. Ruling the East, he is said to appear with three heads – of a toad, a man, and a cat. His voice is hoarse, but he fights very well. He makes those who invoke him purposeful and cunning and teaches them the way to be invisible if needed.

He may be the same as the Canaanite god Baal.

BAËL

Figure 21: Bael, Dictionnaire Infernale, Public Domain

The Seal of AGARES

Figure 22: The Seal of AGARES

AGARES is subordinate to LUCIFUGE in the Grand Grimoire.

The Dictionnaire Infernale terms him the Grand Duke of the East in hell. He shows himself under the features of a Lord, riding a crocodile, the hawk in hand. He brings back fugitives from the party he protects and routs the enemy. He gives the dignities, teaches all languages, and makes dance spirits of the earth. He is of the order of virtues and has thirty-one legions.

Figure 23: Agares, Dictionnaire Infernale, Public Domain

The Seal of MARBAS

MARBAS is the third Chief under LUCIFUGE in the Grand Grimoire.

In Weir's Dictionnaire Infernale, he is termed the great president of the underworld; he shows himself in the form of a furious lion. When he is in the presence of an exorcist, he takes the human figure and responds on hidden things. He sends diseases; he gives the origins of the mechanical arts; he can change men into different forms; he commands thirty-six legions.

Figure 24: Original Image of Marbas

The Seal of PRUSLAS

Figure 25: The Seal of PRUSLAS

PRUFLAS or BUSAS, reports to SATANACHIA in the Grand Grimoire.

In the Dictionnaire Infernale, he is listed as a great prince and Grand Duke of the Infernal Empire. He reigned in Babylon, though he had the head of an owl. He excites discords, ignites wars & quarrels, and reduces men to begging; he answers profusely all that is asked of him, he has twenty-six legions under his orders.

Figure 26: Original Image of Pruslas

The Seal of AAMON

Figure 27: The Seal of AAMON

AMON, or AAMON, reports to SATANACHIA in the Grand Grimoire.

He is a big and powerful Marquis of the Infernal Empire. He has the figure of a wolf, with a serpent's tail; He vomits flame when he takes the human form, he has of man only the body; its head looks like an owl and its beak shows very sharp teeth. He is the more solid of the demon princes: He knows the past and the future, and reconciles, whom he wants, friends or enemies. He commands forty legions.

AMON or AAMON

Figure 28: Aamon, Dictionnaire Infernale, Public Domain

The Seal of BARBATOS

Figure 29: The Seal of Barbatos

BARBATOS is subordinate to SATANACHIA in the Grand Grimoire.

He is a great and powerful demon, Count-Duke in hell. He is similar to Robin in the Woods (Robin Hood?). He shows himself as an archer or a hunter. We meet him in the woods. Four kings sound the horn in front of him. He teaches divination by the singing of birds, the roar of the bulls, the barking dogs and shouting of various animals.

He knows the treasures buried by the magicians. He reconciles scrambled friends. This demon, which was once in the order of virtues of

the heavens or that of the dominions, is reduced today to command thirty Infernal legions. He knows the past and the future.

Figure 30: Barbatos, Dictionnaire Infernale, Public Domain

The Seal of BUER

Figure 31: The Seal of BUER

BUER reports to AGLIAREPT in the Grand Grimoire.

He is a second-class demon, president in the underworld; He has the shape of a star or a wheel with five branches and moves forward rolling on himself. He teaches philosophy, logic and the virtues of medicinal herbs. He boasts of giving good servants and giving health to the sick. He commands fifty legions.

Figure 32: Buer, Dictionnaire Infernale, Public Domain

The Seal of GUSOYN

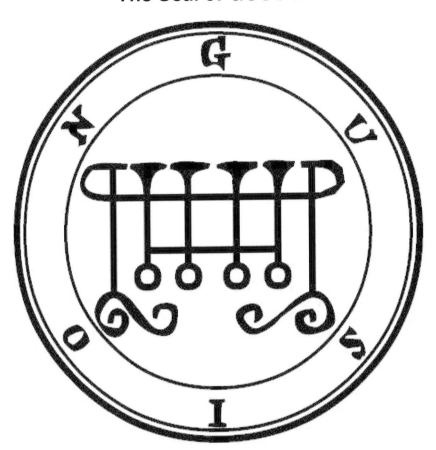

Figure 33: The Seal of GUSOYN

GUSOYN is under AGLIAREPT in the Grand Grimoire

Gusoyn is a Grand Duke in hell. He appears in the form of a camel. He answers questions about you, the past, the future, and discovers hidden things. He increases dignities and confirms the honors., He commands forty-five legions.

Figure 34: Image of Gusoyn (Public Domain)

The Seal of BOTIS

Figure 35: The Seal of BOTIS

BOTIS reports to AGLIAREPT in the Grand Grimoire.

The Seventeenth Spirit (of the Lesser Key of Solomon) is Botis, a Great President, and an Earl. He appears first in the form of an ugly Viper, then at the command of the Magician he puts on a Human shape with Great Teeth, and two Horns, carrying a bright and sharp Sword in his hand. He tells all things Past, and to Come, and reconciles Friends and Foes. He rules over 60 Legions of Spirits.

Figure 36: Original Image of Botis

The Seal of BATHIM

Figure 37: The Seal of BATHIM

BATHIM or MARTHYM is subordinate to FLEURETY in the Grand Grimoire

Bathim is a Duke of hell, tall and strong he has the appearance of a man robust, and behind a snake tail. He rides a horse of a whiteness livid and knows the virtues of herbs and precious stones. He transports men from one country to another with an unbelievable speed. Thirty legions obey him.

Figure 38: Original Image of Bathim

The Seal of PURSON

Figure 39: The Seal of PURSAN

PURSON, PURSAN or CURSON reports to FLEURETY in the Grand Grimoire.

He is a great king of hell. He appears in human form with a lion's head; he is wearing a snake, always furious; he is mounted on a bear and proceeded continually by the sound of the trumpet. He knows the present, the past, the future, discovers buried things, like treasures. If he takes the form of a man, he is aerial. He is the giver of good familiar spirits. Twenty-two legions receive his orders

Figure 40: Pursan, Dictionnaire Infernale, Public Domain

The Seal of ABIGOR

Figure 41: The Seal of ABIGOR

ABIGOR, or ELIGOS is subordinate to FLEURETY in the Grand Grimoire.

In the Dictionnaire Infernale, he is described as a demon of a superior order, grand duke in the infernal monarchy. Sixty legions march under his orders. He appears as the figure of a handsome horseman carrying the lance, the standard, or the scepter; he responds skillfully on everything related to the secrets of war, knows the future, and teaches to the chiefs the means to have themselves loved by the soldiers

Figure 42: Abigor, Dictionnaire Infernale, Public Domain

The Seal of LORAY

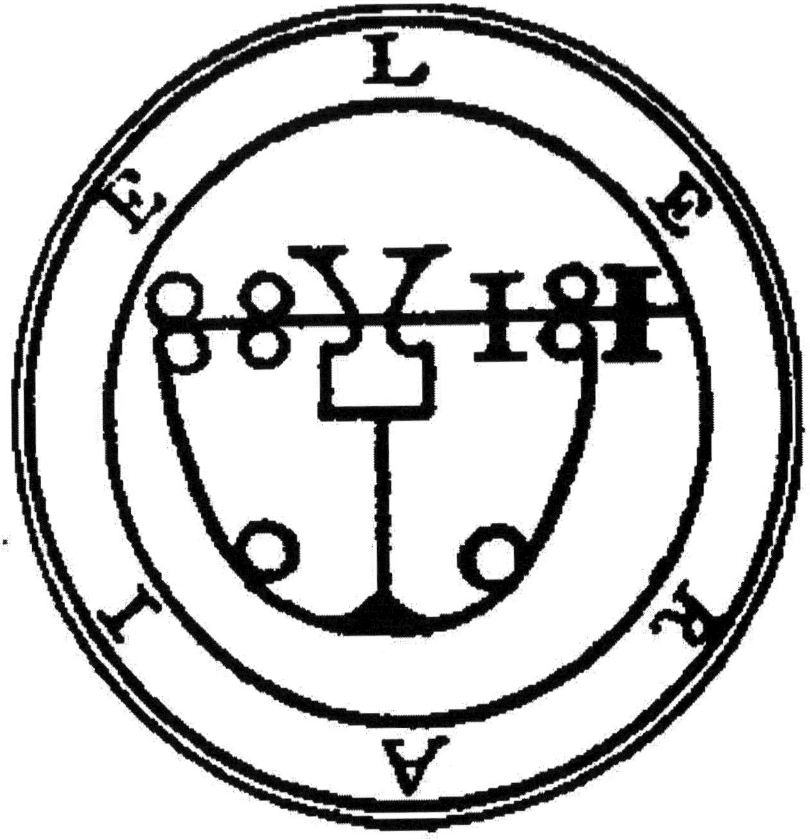

Figure 43: The Seal of LORAY

LORAY, ORAY or LERAIE is subordinate to SARGATANAS.

In the Dictionnaire Infernale, he is described as a great Marquis of Hell, who appears in the form of a superb archer carrying "a bow and arrows; he leads the fighting, causes major wounds by the archers, throws deadly javelins. Thirty legions recognize him as the dominating sovereign.

Figure 44: Original Image of Loray

The Seal of VALEFAR

Figure 45: The Seal of VALEFAR

VALEFAR, VALAFAK, or MALAFAR is subordinate to SARGATANAS in the Grand Grimoire.

In the Dictionnaire Infernale, he is described as a big and powerful Duke of the Imperial Empire. He appears in the shape of an angel, sometimes in that of a lion with the head and legs of a goose and a hare's tail. He knows the past and the future, gives genius and daring to men, and commands thirty-six legions.

Figure 46: Original Image of Valefar

The Seal of MARAX

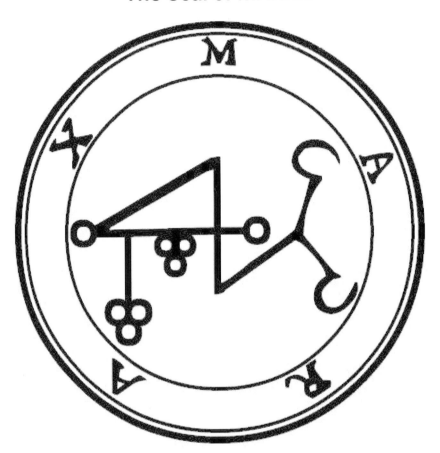

Figure 47: The Seal of MARAX

FARAU, FORAI or MARAX is subordinate to SARGATANAS in the Grand Grimoire.

In the Dictionnaire Infernale, he is described as Captain, count and president of several infernal bands; he is seen in the form of a bull. When he takes the human figure, he instructs man in astronomy and in all liberal arts, He is the prince of familiar spirits who are gentle and wise. He has under his orders thirty-six legions.

Figure 48: Original Image of Marax

The Seal of IPOS

Figure 49: The Seal of IPOS

IPOS, IPES, or AYPEROS is subordinate to SARGATANAS in the Grand Grimoire.

In the Dictionnaire Infernale, he is described as Prince and count of hell, he appears in the form of an angel, sometimes under that of a lion, with the head and the legs of a goose and the tail of an hare, which is a bit short; he knows the past and future, gives genius and daring to men, and commands thirty-six legions.

IPÈS

Figure 50: Ipos, Dictionnaire Infernale, Public Domain

The Seal of NABERUS

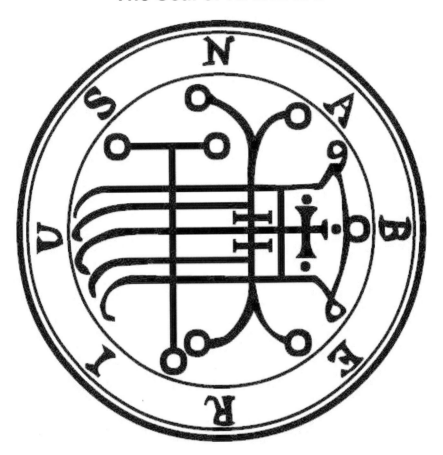

Figure 51: The Seal of NABERUS

NABERUS, perhaps representing Cerberus is subordinate to NEBIROS in the Grand Grimoire. While the names are similar, these are very different spirits.

In the Dictionnaire Infernale, he is described as Marshal-de-camp and Inspector General of the Armies.

He shows himself as a raven. his voice is hoarse, he gives eloquence, kindness, and teaches the liberal arts. He helps find the hand of glory; it indicates the qualities of metals, plants and all pure and impure animals. One of the leaders of the necromancers, he predicts the future. He

commands nineteen legions.

In the Grimorium Verum, he rules over Hael and Surgulath.

CERBERUS

Figure 52: Cereberus, Dictionnaire Infernale, Public Domain

The Seal of GLASYALABOLAS

Figure 53: The Seal of Glasyalabolas

GLASYALABOLAS, CAACIUNOLAAS, also named Caasstmolar. and Glassialabolas is subordinate to NEBIROS in the Grand Grimoire. The Grimoire calls him Classyalabolas, and makes him just a sort of sergeant, sometimes the mount of Nebiros or Naberus.

In the Dictionnaire Infernale, he is described as the grand president of hell. He is in the form of a dog, and he has the gait, with wings of a griffin. He gives the knowledge of the liberal arts and, by a strange contrast, inspires homicides. It is said that he predicts well the future. This demon makes the man invisible and commands thirty-six legions.

Figure 54: Glasyalabolas, Dictionnaire Infernale, Public Domain

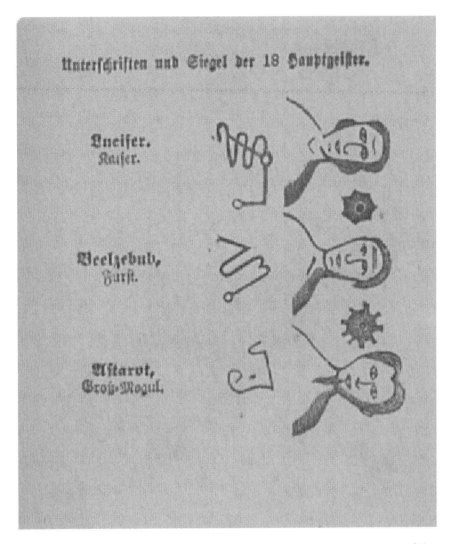

Figure 55: Images and seals of Lucifer, Beelzebub, and Astaroth, From a German edition of the Grand Grimoire, the Public Domain

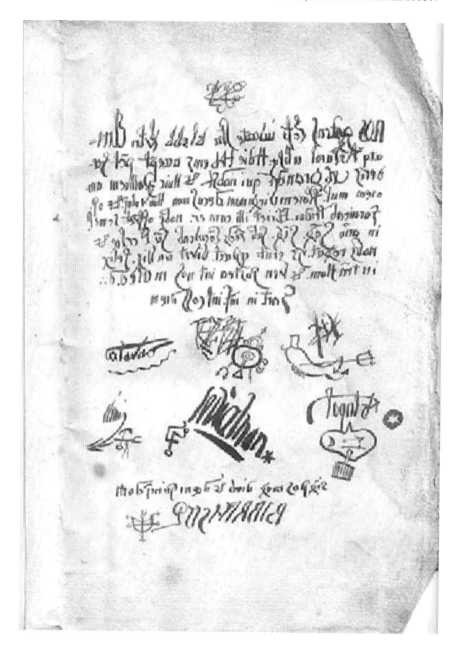

Figure 56: The Pact reputedly signed by Urbain Grandier and Lucifer, Astaroth, and other demons, 1634, Public Domain

Figure 57: The Devil as a bull in the front of some editions of the Red Dragon, Public Domain

Figure 58: Lucifuge Rofocale from an edition of the Grand Grimoire, Public Domain

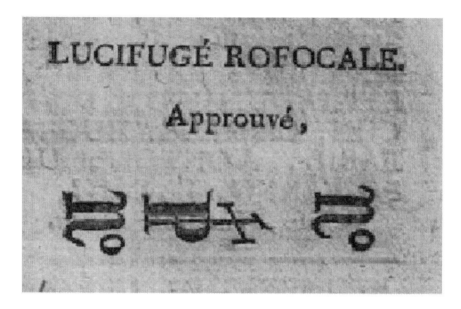

Figure 59: Lucifuge Rofocale's alleged signature, from Urbain Grandier's pact, in some editions of the Grand Grimoire, Public Domain

Figure 60: Lucifuge Rofocale, from an Italian edition of the Grand Grimoire, Public Domain

Figure 61: Frontispiece of a French Edition of the Grand Grimoire, Public Domain

Figure 62: Allium Victorialis, or the Herb of the Nine Shirts, Curtis' Botanical Magazine, Vol 29-30, Public Domain

822. Verbena officinalis L.

Vervain.

Figure 63: Verbena Officinalis, or vervain, Public Domain

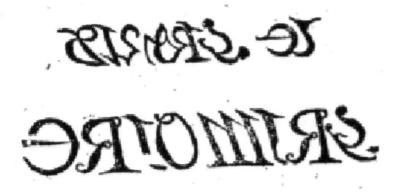

Figure 64: The Grand Grimoire written backwards to show the sinister nature of the work. In the front of some editions, Public Domain

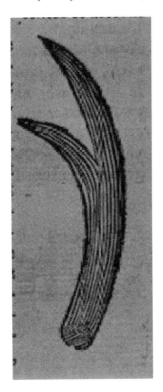

Figure 65: The Blasting Rod, from an edition of the Grand Grimoire, Public Domain

Figure 66: The Triangle of Pacts from an edition of the Grand Grimoire, Public Domain

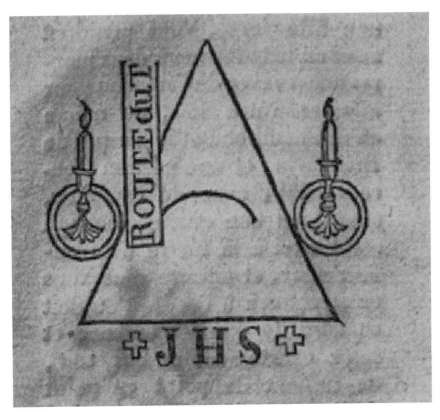

Figure 67: Another view of the Triangle of Pacts from an edition of the Grand Grimoire, Public Domain

Figure 68: The Signs and Characters of the Major Spirits of the Grand Grimoire, Public Domain

Des jours heureux et malheureux.

JOURS HEUREUX.	MOIS.	JOURS MALHEUREUX.
le 3. 10. 27. 31.	Janvier	le 13. et 23.
le 7. 8. et 18.	Février	2. 10. 17. 22.
3. 9. 12. 14. 16.	Mars	13. 19 23. 28.
5. — et le 27. —	Avril.	18. 20. 29. 30.
1. 2. 4. 6. 9. 14.	Mai.	10. 17. 20.
3. 5. 7. 9. 12. 23.	Juin.	le 4. et le 20.
2. 6. 10. 23. 30.	Juillet.	le 5. 13. 27.
5. 7. 10. 14. 19.	Août.	2. 13. 27. 31.
6. 10. 13. 18. 30.	Sept.	13. 16. 12. 15.
13. 16. 23. 31.	Octob.	le 3. 9. 27.
8. 13. 23. 30.	Novem	le 6. et 15.
le 10. 20. et 29.	Décem.	15. 28. 31.

REMARQUES.

Plusieurs Savans prétendent que cette Table fut donnée à Adam par un Ange; aussi étoit-ce la règle de sa conduite; il ne semoit ni ne transplantoit rien, que dans les jours heureux, et tout lui arrivoit à bon port; si nos cultivateurs suivoient ses traces, l'abondance combleroit nos vœux.

Figure 69: Table of Fortunate & Unfortunate Days from an edition of the Grand Grimoire, Public Domain

Figure 70: Necromantic Images, Grand Grimoire, Public Domain

Note the alchemical nature of these images.

THE INTER-LINEAR TEXT OF THE GRAND GRIMOIRE

LE DRAGON ROUGE, Ou Le Grand Grimoire

THE RED DRAGON, Or The Grand Grimoire

OU L'ART DE COMMANDER LES ESPRITS CELESTES, AERIENS, TERRESTRES, INFERNAUX

OR THE ART OF CONTROLLING CELESTIAL, AERIAL, TERRESTRIAL, AND INFERNAL SPIRITS

AVEC LE VRAI SECRET De faire parler les morts, de gagner toutes les fois qu'on met aux loteries, de découvrir les Trésors cachés, etc., etc.

With the TRUE SECRET of speaking with the dead, winning the lottery every time, discovering hidden treasure, etc., etc.

PRELUDE

L'homme qui gémit sous le poids accablant des préjugés de la présomption, aura peine à se persuader qu'il m'ait été possible de renfermer dans un si petit recueil l'essence de plus de vingt volumes, qui par leurs dits, redits et ambiguïtés, rendaient l'accès des opérations philosophiques presque impraticable : mais que l'incrédule et le prévenu se donnent la peine de suivre pas à pas la route que je leur trace, et ils verront la vérité bannir de leur esprit la crainte que peut avoir occasionné un tas d'essais sans fruits, étant faits hors de saison, ou sur indices imparfaits.

C'est encore en vain qu'on croit qu'il n'est pas possible de faire de semblables opérations sans engager sa conscience, il ne faut pour être convaincu du contraire, que jeter un clin d'œil sur la vie de Saint Cyprien.

PRELUDE

The man who groans under the overwhelming weight of prejudice & presumption will scarcely convince himself that I have been able to contain in this little compendium the essence of more than twenty volumes, which by their expressions and ambiguities, make philosophical operations hardly possible : but the disbeliever and cautious person who takes the pains to follow step by step the route that I guide them on will see for themselves the true banishing from their spirit of the occasional fear one might have from a series of efforts attempted through trial and error, be done out of season, or imperfect circumstances.

One can perform these operations and still be true to one's conscience, the evidence of which is visible by a glimpse at the life of St. Cyprian.

J'ose me flatter que les savants attachés aux mystères de la science divine, surnommé occulte, regarderont ce livre comme le plus précieux trésor de l'univers.

I might dare flatter myself by noting that the scholars of the mysteries of the Divine Science called Occultism will consider this book one of the most precious treasures of the universe.

CHAPITRE I

CHAPTER ONE

Ce grand livre est si rare, si recherché dans nos contrées, que pour sa rareté on peut appeler, d'après les rabbins, le véritable Grand Œuvre, et c'est eux qui nous ont laissé ce précieux original que tant de charlatans ont voulu contrefaire inutilement en voulant imiter le véritable, qu'ils n'ont jamais trouvé, pour pouvoir attraper de l'argent des simples qui s'adressent au premier venu sans rechercher la véritable source.

This great book is so rare and sought after that one might, as the Rabbis say, call this the Great Work. It is they who have left us the precious original of which so many charlatans make useless forgeries, wanting to imitate the truth, which they have never discovered, and which they lack the capacity to grasp, while trying to grab the money of the common people, who approach them without searching for the true source.

On a copié celui-ci d'après les véritables écrits du grand roi Salomon, que l'on a trouvés, par un pur effet du hasard, ce grand roi ayant passé tous les jours de sa vie dans les recherches les plus pénibles et dans les secrets les plus obscurs et les plus inespérés ; mais enfin il a réussi dans toutes ses entreprises, et il est venu à bout de pénétrer jusqu'à la demeure la plus reculée des esprits, qu'il a tous fixés et forcés de lui obéir, par la puissance de son Talisman ou Clavicule.

This book is based on the true writings of the great King Solomon that were discovered by chance efforts. The great king spent his lifetime searching for the hardest, most obscure and unexpected secrets; but he finally succeeded in all his enterprises, commanding and forcing obedience from even the most secluded spirits by the power of his Talisman or Key.

Car quel autre homme que ce puissant génie aurait eu la hardiesse de mettre au jour les foudroyantes paroles dont Dieu se servit pour consterner et faire obéir les esprits rebelles, à sa première volonté ; ayant pénétré jusqu'aux voûtes célestes pour approfondir les secrets et les puissantes paroles qui font toute la force d'un Dieu terrible et respectable.

What other man would have the powerful spirit and audacity to express the devastating words which serve God for commanding obedience and dismay from the rebellious spirits, by the force of his will, penetrating unto the vaulted ceilings of heaven by examining the secrets and powerful words that express the force of a terrible and honorable God?

Il a ce grand roi, pris l'essence de ces réservés secrets, dont s'est servi la grande divinité, puisqu'il nous a découvert les influences des astres, la constellation des planètes, et la manière de faire paraitre toutes sortes d'esprits, en récitant les grandes appellations que vous trouverez ci-après dans ce livre, de même que la véritable composition de la Verge Foudroyante, et les effets qui font trembler les esprits, et dont Dieu s'est servi pour armer son ange qui chassa Adam et Eve du paradis terrestre, et de laquelle Dieu frappa les anges rebelles, précipitant leurs orgueils dans les Abymes les plus épouvantables, par la force de cette Verge qui forme des nuées, qui disperse et brise les tempêtes, les orages, les ouragans, et les fait tomber sur

It is this great king, who has captured the most guarded secrets, that serve the grand divinity, since it reveals the influence of the stars, the position of the planets, and the means to manifest all types of spirits, by reciting the great names that you will find later in this book, those which constitute the commanding & powerful Blasting Rod, and the effects that make the spirits tremble, and which God served to arm the angels who chased Adam & Eve from the earthly paradise, and struck the rebel angels, thrown by their pride into the dreadful Abyss. The strength of this Rod forms clouds, disperses tempests, powerful thunderstorms, hurricanes, and makes them fall on any part of the earth

quelle partie de la terre que vous voulez.

Voici donc ci-après, les véritables paroles sorties de sa bouche que j'ai suivies de point en point, et dont j'ai eu tout l'agrément de toute la satisfaction possible, puisque j'ai eu le bonheur de réussir dans mes entreprises.

Signé
Antonio Venitiana del Rabina

These are therefore the true words expressed by him that I have followed step by step, and with which I have complete agreement and satisfaction, having had the good fortune to experience success in my endeavors.

(Signed)
Antonio Venitiana del Rabina

CHAPITRE II

CHAPTER TWO

Oh HOMMES ! faibles mortels! tremblez de votre témérité, lorsque vous pensez aveuglément de posséder une science assez profonde

Oh men! Feeble mortals! Tremble in your rashness when you blindly think of possessing such a profound science.

Apportez votre esprit au-delà de votre sphère, et apprenez de ma part qu'avant de rien entreprendre, il faut être fermes et inébranlables, et très attentif à observer exactement de point en point tout ce que je vous dis, sans quoi tout tournera à votre désavantage, confusion et perte totale; et si au contraire vous observez exactement ce que je vous dis, vous sortirez de votre bassesse et de votre indigence, ayant pleine victoire dans toutes vos entreprises.

You must direct your spirit beyond this realm and learn from me before undertaking anything to be firm and steadfast. Be very attentive and observe rigorously all that I say, point by point, otherwise everything will turn against you, you will suffer confusion and total loss; yet if you follow precisely what I tell you, you will rise out of your wretchedness and your poverty, achieving victory in all your endeavors.

Armez-vous donc d'intrépidité, de prudence, de sagesse et de vertu pour pouvoir entreprendre ce grand et immense ouvrage, dans lequel j'ai passé soixante-sept ans travaillant jours et nuits, pour arriver à la réussite de ce grand but ; il faut donc faire exactement tout ce qui est indiqué ci-après.

Fortify yourself therefore with a dauntless character, prudence, wisdom and the virtue to undertake this grand and immense work, in which I have spent sixty-seven years, working day and night, to arrive at a successful goal. One must therefore do precisely everything that is indicated hereafter.

PRIMO.

Vous passerez un quart de lune entier, sans fréquenter aucune compagnie de femmes ni de filles afin de ne pas tomber dans l'impureté.

Ensuite vous commencerez votre quart de lune dans le moment que le quartier commencera promettant au grand Adonay, qui est le chef de tous les Esprits, de ne faire que deux repas par jour, ou toutes les vingt-quatre heure dudit quart de lune, lesquels vous prendrez â midi et à minuit, ou si vous aimez mieux à sept-heures du matin et à sept heures du soir, en faisant la prière ci-après, avant que de prendre vos repas, pendant tout ledit quartier.

PRIÈRE

Je t'implore, ô grand et puissant Adonay, maître de tous les esprits, je t'implore, ô Eloïm. Je t'implore, ô Jehovam. O grand Adonay ! je te donne mon âme, mon cour, mes entrailles, mes mains, mes pieds, mes soupirs et mon être : ô grand ADONAY ! daigne m'être favorable, Ainsi soit-il, Amen.

FIRST,

You must spend a week without socializing with either women or girls, to avoid any moral corruption.

Then, you must begin a week in the period dedicated to the great Adonai, who is the chief of the spirits, by having no more than two meals a day, at noon and midnight, or if you prefer, at seven in the morning and in the evening, offering the following prayer before your meals during the whole week.

PRAYER

I beseech you, great and powerful Adonai, master of all the spirits, I beseech you, O Elohim, I entreat you, O Jehovah, O great Adonai! I give you my soul, my heart, my vitals, my hands, my feet, my breath and my being: O Great Adonai, favor me, so mote it be, Amen!

Prenez ensuite votre repas et ne vous déshabillez ni ne dormez que le moins qu'il vous sera possible pendant tout ledit quartier de lune, pensant continuellement à votre ouvrage, et fondant toute votre espérance dans l'infinie bonté du grand Adonay.

Après quoi le lendemain de la première nuit dudit quart de lune, vous irez chez un droguiste pour acheter une pierre sanguine dite ématille, que vous porterez continuellement avec vous crainte d'accident, attendu que dès lors l'esprit que vous avez en vue de forcer et de contraindre, fait tout ce qu'il peut pour vous dégoûter par la crainte, pour faire échouer votre entreprise, croyant par cette voie se dégager des filets que vous commencez à lui tendre;

Il faut observer qu'il ne faut être qu'un, ou trois, y compris le Karcist, qui est celui qui doit parler à l'esprit, tenant en main la Verge foudroyante ; vous aurez soin de choisir pour l'endroit de l'action un lieu solitaire et écarté du monde, afin que le Karcist ne soit pas interrompu.

Then have your meal and disrobe or sleep as little as possible throughout this week but think continuously about your Great Work and unite your entire hopes on the infinite goodness of the great Adonai.

On the second day of the week, you must purchase a bloodstone that you must carry continuously with you, since from then on the Spirit you intend to force and compel will do all that it can to disgust you and fill you with fear, to induce you to abandon your enterprise, believing by these means to be able to disengage itself from the nets that you begin to cast around it.

It must be noted that there should be one or three people in this evocation of the spirit, including the Karcist, holding in his hand the Blasting Rod. Carefully choose a solitary and remote place for the operation, where the Karcist will be undisturbed.

Après quoi vous achèterez un jeune chevreau vierge, que vous décorerez le troisième jour de la lune, d'une guirlande de verveine, que vous attacherez à son col, au-dessous de sa tête, avec un ruban vert.

After purchasing a young virgin goat, which you shall decorate on the third day of the month with a garland of verbena, that you attach to its collar, below its head, with a green ribbon.

Ensuite le transporterez à l'endroit marqué pour l'apparition, et la le bras droit nu jusqu'à l'épaule, armé d'une lame de pur acier, le feu étant allumé avec du bois blanc, vous direz les paroles suivantes avec espérance et fermeté

Then take this goat to the place identified for the evocation, and there, the right arm naked to the shoulder, armed with a sword of pure steel, and a fire of white wood, you must utter the following words with hope and determination:

PREMIERE OFFRANDE

INITIAL OFFERING

Je t'offre cette victime, o grand Adonay, Eloïm, Ariel et Jehovam, et cela à l'honneur gloire et puissance de ton être supérieur à tous les esprits ; daigne, ô grand Adonay! le prendre pour agréable.
Amen.

I offer you this victim, great Adonai, Elohim, Ariel and Jehovah, for your honor, glory and power, the highest of all the spirits, accept this offering, great Adonai!
Amen

Ensuite vous égorgerez le chevreau et lui ôterez la peau, et mettrez le reste dessus le feu, pour y être réduit en cendres que vous ramasserez et les jetterez du côté du soleil levant, en disant les paroles suivantes :

Then you must cut the throat of the kid, skin it, immolate the body and reduce it to ashes, which you must collect and cast towards the rising sun, while saying the following words:

C'est pour l'honneur, gloire et puissance de ton nom , ô grand Adonay, Eloïm , Ariel et Jehovam ! que je répands le sang de cette victime ; daigne , ô grand Adonay! recevoir ces cendres pour agréables.

This is for the glory, honor and power of your name, great Adonai, Elohim, Ariel and Jehovah, that I spill the blood of this victim. Accept this offering, great Adonai and deem it worthy.

Pendant que la victime brûle, vous pouvez vous réjouir en l'honneur et gloire du grand Adonay, Eloïm, Ariel et Jehovam, ayant soin de conserver la peau de chevreau vierge , pour former le rond ou le grand cercle cabalistique , dans lequel vous vous mettrez le jour de la grande entreprise.

After which, as the victim burns, rejoice in the glory and honor of the great Adonai, Elohim, Ariel and Jehovah. Preserve the skin of the virgin goat to form the great Kabbalistic circle, within which you will place yourself on the day of the great work.

CHAPITRE III

Contenant la véritable composition de la Baguette mystérieuse, ou Verge foudroyante, telle qu'elle est représentée ci-dessous.

La veille de la grande entreprise, vous irez chercher une baguette ou verge de noisetier sauvage, qui n'aye jamais porté, et qu'elle soit précisément semblable à celle que vous voyez ci-contre ; ladite baguette devant faire fourche en-haut, c'est-à-dire, du côté des deux bouts ; sa longueur doit être de dix-neuf pouces et demi ;

après que vous aurez trouvé une baguette de même forme, vous ne la toucherez que des yeux, attendant jusqu'au lendemain, jour de l'action, que vous irez la couper positivement au lever du soleil, et alors vous la dépouillerez de ses feuilles et petites branches, si elle en a, avec la même lame d'acier qui a servi à égorger la victime, qui sera encore teinte de son sang, attendu que vous devez faire attention de ne point essuyer la dite lame, en commençant à la couper quand le soleil commencera à paraître sur cet hémisphère en prononçant les paroles suivantes :

CHAPTER THREE

Containing the true composition of the Mysterious Wand or Blasting Rod, which is represented below.

On the eve of the Great work, you must search for a wand or rod from a wild hazel bush, that has never borne fruit, and when you have found one, look for a rod ending in a fork, the length of which should be precisely nineteen and a half inches.

Having espied such a forked branch, do not touch it save with your eyes until the next day, the day of action, when you must cut it precisely at sunrise, and then strip the leaves and little branches, if any are present, with the same blade of steel which you used to cut the throat of the victim, stained with its blood, making sure not to have wiped the blade. Begin cutting the rod when the sun is first rising, saying the following words:

Je te recommande, ô grand Adonay, Eloïm , Ariel et Jehovam ! de m'être favorable, et de donner à cette baguette que je coupe, la force et la vertu de celle de Jacob , de celle de Moïse.et de celle du grand Josué ; je te recommande aussi , ô grand Adonay, Eloïm, Ariel et Jehovam! de renfermer dans cette baguette toute la force de Samson , la juste colore d'Emmanuel et les foudres du grand Zariatnatmik , qui vengera les injures des hommes au grand jour du jugement.

Amen.

Après avoir prononcé ces grandes et terribles paroles, et ayant toujours la vue du côté du soleil levant, vous achèverez de couper votre baguette, et l'emporterez dans votre chambre; ensuite vous chercherez un morceau de bois que vous rendrez de même grosseur que les deux bouts de la véritable, que vous porterez chez un serrurier, pour faire ferrer les deux petites branches fourchues avec la lame d'acier qui a servi à égorger la victime, faisant attention que les deux bouts soient un peu aigus lorsqu'ils seront posés sur le morceau de bois:

I urge you, O Great Adonai, Elohim, Ariel and Jehovah! Favor me and grant this rod, that I cut, with the power and virtue of Jacob, of Moses and of the great Jesus; I request you also, O Great Adonai, Elohim, Ariel and Jehovah! Contain within this rod all the force of Samson, the righteous wrath of Emmanuel and the lightning of the great Zariatnatmik, who will avenge the injuries of mankind on the great day of Judgement.

Amen.

After having pronounced these great and terrible words, and viewing the rising sun, complete the cutting of the rod, and then bring into your room a block of wood of the same thickness as the two pieces of the Veritable Rod, and take it to a locksmith to fuse the two small forked branches with the blade of steel that you used to cut the throat of the victim, making sure that the two pieces are a bit pointed when placed over the block of wood.:

Le tout étant ainsi exécuté, vous retournerez à la maison et mettrez ladite ferrure vous-même à la véritable baguette ; vous, prendrez ensuite une pierre d'aimant que vous ferez chauffer pour aimanter les deux pointes de votre baguette, en prononçant les paroles suivantes:

When all is completed, return to the house and fix this hinge to the Veritable Rod; take a lodestone that you have warmed up to magnetize the two points of your rod, and state the following words:

Par la puissance du grand Adonay, Eloïm, Ariel et Jehovam, je te commande d'unir et d'attirer toutes les matières que je voudrai : par la puissance du grand Adonay, Eloïm, Ariel et Jehovam, je te commande, par l'incompatibilité du feu et de l'eau, de séparer toutes matières, comme elles furent séparées le jour de la création du monde.
Amen.

By the power of the great Adonai, Elohim, Ariel and Jehovah, I command you to unite and attract all the materials that I desire. By the power of the great Adonai, Elohim, Ariel and Jehovah, I order you by the incompatibility of fire and of water, of separating all materials, like they were separated on the day of creation of the world.
Amen.

Ensuite vous vous réjouirez en l'honneur et gloire du grand Adonay, étant sûr que vous possédez le plus grand trésor de lumière : le soir ensuite, vous prendrez votre baguette, votre peau de chevreau, votre pierre ématille et deux couronnes de verveine, de même que deux chandeliers et deux cierges de cire vierge, bénits et faits par une fille vierge. Vous prendrez aussi un batte-feu neuf, deux pierres

Then, you must rejoice in the honor and glory of the great Adonai, being certain that you possess the great treasure of light. In the evening, take your rod, the skin of the kid, your bloodstone and two verbena garlands, as well as two candlesticks and two candles of virgin wax, consecrated and made by a virgin girl. Take also a new fire brush, two new fire-stones with the tinder to light your fire, a half-bottle of brandy,

neuves avec de l'amadou pour allumer votre feu, de même qu'une demi-bouteille d'esprit de brandevin, avec du camphre, aussi bien que quatre clous qui aient servi à la bière d'un enfant mort, et ensuite vous vous transporterez à l'endroit où doit se faire le grand-œuvre, et ferez exactement ce qui suit, en imitant de point en point le grand cercle cabalistique, tel qu'il est démontré ci-après.

with camphor, as well as four nails that were used in the coffin of a dead child, and then take these items to the place of your Great Work. Now follow exactly what I am about to say and prepare the great Kabbalistic Circle that I will demonstrate henceforth.

CHAPITRE IV

Contenant la véritable représentation du grand cercle cabalistique.

Vous commencerez par former un cercle avec la peau du chevreau, tel qu'il est indiqué ci-devant , que vous clouerez avec vos quatre clous ; vous prendrez ensuite votre pierre ématille et tracerez un triangle au-dedans du cercle, tel qu'il est représenté , en commençant du côté du levant ; vous tracerez aussi avec la pierre ématille le grand A , le petit E le petit A , et le petit J , de même que le saint nom de Jésus au milieu de deux croix (+JHS+) , afin que les esprits ne vous puissent rien par derrière;

Après quoi Karcist fera entrer ses confrères, dans le triangle à leur place telle qu'elle est marquée, et y entrera lui-même sans s'épouvanter, quel bruit qu'il entende, plaçant les deux chandeliers avec les deux couronnes de verveine à la droite et à la gauche du triangle intérieur:

Cela fait, vous commencerez à allumer vos deux cierges et aurez un vase neuf devant vous, c'est-à-

CHAPTER FOUR

Containing the true representation of the great Kabbalistic Circle

Start by creating a circle with the virgin kid skin, that is indicated herein, pinning it down with the four coffin nails. Then take the bloodstone and trace a triangle inside the circle to the east of the circle. Also, with the bloodstone, trace Aeaj *(by Adonai, by Elohim, by Ariel, by Jehovah),* and +JHS+, the Holy Name of Jesus in the middle of two crosses, so that the spirits are unable to harm you from behind.

After this, the collaborators of the Operator enter the triangle that has been marked and he himself enters into it fearlessly, ignoring any noise that he hears, placing the two candlesticks with the two garlands of verbena to the right and the left of the interior triangle.

Having done so, start by lighting the two candles and have a new brazier before you, that is,

dire, devant le Karcist, rempli de charbons de bois de saule, que l'on aura fait brûler le même jour, que le Karcist allumera ; y jetant une partie de l'esprit de brandevin, et une partie de l'encens et du camphre que vous avez, réservant le reste pour entretenir un feu continuel, convenablement à la durée de la chose : tout ce qui est marqué ci-dessus étant fait exactement, vous prononcerez les paroles suivantes :

Je te présente, O grand Adonay ! cet encens comme le plus pur : de même je te présente ces charbons comme sortant du plus léger bois. Je l'offre au grand et puissant Adonay, Eloïm, Ariel et Jehovam, de toute mon amé et de tout mon cœur ; daigne, O grand Adonay ! le prendre pour agréable.

Amen.

Vous ferez aussi attention de n'avoir sur vous aucun métal impur, sinon de l'or ou de l'argent pour jeter la pièce à l'esprit, la ployant dans un papier que vous lui jetterez, afin qu'il ne vous puisse faire aucun mal, quand il se présentera devant le cercle : et pendant qu'il ramassera la pièce, vous commencerez la prière suivante, en vous armant de

before the Operator, filled with willow charcoal, that you have burned the same day yourself. Kindle this brazier with a part of the brandy and a part of the incense and camphor, keeping the rest to maintain a continuous fire throughout the operation. Once all this is done precisely as stated, state the following words:

O Great Adonai! I offer to you this purest incense. I also offer this charcoal from the lightest wood. I offer this to the great and powerful Adonai, Elohim, Ariel and Jehovah with all my soul and all my heart; deem what I offer acceptable, O Great Adonai.

Amen

Be careful not to have any impure metal on you, other than a gold or silver coin to offer before the spirit, folded in a paper, so that he does you no harm, when he appears before the circle. While he picks up the coin, begin the following prayer, arming yourself with courage, strength and prudence, ensuring that none but the Operator speak, the others

courage, de force et de prudence ; faites aussi attention qu'il n'y ait que le Karcist qui parle, les autres doivent garder le silence, quand même l'esprit les interrogerait, les menacerait.

keeping silent, even when the spirit questions or threatens them.

PREMIERE PARTIE

O grand Dieu vivant en une seule et même personne, le Père, le Fils et le Saint Esprit, je vous adore avec le plus profond respect, et me soumet sous votre sainte et digne garde avec la plus vive confiance : je crois, avec la plus sincère foi que vous êtes mon créateur, mon bienfaiteur, mon soutient et mon maître, et je vous déclare n'avoir d'autres volontés que celle de vous appartenir pendant toute l'éternité.

FIRST PART:

O Great and Living God! In one person, the Father, the Son and the Holy Ghost, I adore you with the most profound respect, and I submit to your holiness and gracious care with the most living confidence : I sincerely believe that you are my creator, my benefactor, my support and my master, and I declare to you that I have no will other than to belong to you for all eternity.

SECONDE PARTIE

O grand Dieu vivant qui as créé l'homme pour être bienheureux dans cette vie, qui as formé toutes choses pour ses besoins, et qui as dit tout sera soumis à l'homme, sois-moi favorable, et ne permets pas que des esprits rebelles possèdent des trésors qui ont été formés par tes mains pour nos besoins temporels. Donne-moi, ô

SECOND PART

O Great and Living God who has created man to be blissful in this life, who has made all things for his needs, and who said: All is subservient and favorable to man, and the rebel angels are not allowed to possess the treasures made by thy hands for our temporal needs. O Great God! Grant me the power to dispose of

grand Dieu ! la puissance d'en disposer par les puissantes et terribles paroles de ta clavicule, Adonay, Eloïm, Ariel, Jehovam, Tagla, Mathon, soyez-moi favorables.

Ainsi soit-il.

Amen.

Vous aurez soin d'entretenir votre feu avec de l'esprit de brandevin, l'encens et le camphre ; et direz ensuite la prière de l'offrande comme suit :

OFFRANDE

Je t'offre cet encens comme le plus pur que j'aie pu trouver, ô grand Adonay, Eloïm, Ariel et Jehovam! daigne le prendre pour agréable ; ô grand Adonay! sois-moi favorable par ta puissance, et fais-moi réussir dans cette grande entreprise.

Ainsi soit-il.

Amen

them by these powerful and terrible words of your Key, Adonai, Elohim, Ariel, Jehovah, Tagla, Mathon, be favorable unto me!

So mote it be!

Amen!

Continue to nourish the flame with brandy, incense and camphor, and offer the following prayer:

OFFERING:

I offer you this incense with the utmost power, O Great Adonai, Elohim, Ariel and Jehovah! O Great Adonai! Deem me favorable by your power and grant me success in this great enterprise.

So Mote it Be!

Amen!

PREMIÈRE APPELLATION A L'EMPEREUR LUCIFER

FIRST INVOCATION ADDRESSED TO THE EMPEROR LUCIFER

Empereur Lucifer, prince et maître des esprits rebelles, je te prie de quitter ta demeure dans quelle partie du monde qu'elle puisse être, pour venir me parler; je te commande et conjure de la part du grand Dieu vivant, le Père, le Fils et le St-Esprit, de venir sans faire aucune mauvaise odeur, pour me répondre à haute et intelligible voix, article par article, sur ce que je te demanderai, sans quoi tu y seras contraint par la puissance du grand Adonay, Eloïm, Ariel, Jehovam, Tagla, Mathon et de tous les autres esprits supérieurs qui t'y contraindront malgré toi.

Emperor Lucifer, prince and master of the rebel angels, I ask you to leave whichever part of the world you consider home to come and speak with me. I command and conjure you by the great living God, the Father, the Son and the Holy Ghost, to come without any foul odor, to answer me in a high and clear voice, point by point, whatever I ask you, for which you are constrained by the power of the great Adonai, Elohim, Ariel, Jehovah, Tagla, Mathon and all the other superior spirits who compel you.

Venite. Venite Submiritillor LUCIFUGE, ou tu vas être tourmenté éternellement par la grande force de cette baguette foudroyante. In subito.

Come. Come Appear Before Me LUCIFUGE, or you are tormented eternally by the great force of this Blasting Rod. Immediately!

SECONDE APPELLATION

Je te commande et conjure, empereur Lucifer, de la part du grand Dieu vivant, et par la puissance d'Emmanuel son fils unique, ton maître et le mien, et par la vertu de son sang précieux qu'il a répandu pour arracher les hommes de tes chaînes; je t'ordonne de quitter ta demeure dans quelque partie du monde qu'elle soit, jurant que je ne te donne qu'un quart d'heure de repos, si tu ne viens me parler au plutôt à haute et intelligible voix; ou si tu ne peux venir toi-même, m'envoyer ton messager Astarot en signe humain, sans bruit et mauvaise odeur, sans quoi je te vais frapper, toi et toute ta race, de la redoutable Baguette Foudroyante jusqu'au fond des abymes, et ce, par la puissance de ces grandes paroles de la clavicule: Par Adonay, Eloïm, Ariel, Jehovam, Tagla, Mathon, Almouzin, Arios, Pythona, Magots, Silphae;, Cabost, Salamandrae;, Gnomus, Terræ, Coelis, Godens, Aqua. In subito

SECOND INVOCATION

I command and conjure you, Emperor Lucifer, by the great Living God, and by the power of his unique son Emmanuel, your master and mine, and by the virtue of his precious blood which he has shed to free men from your chains; I order you to leave your home in whichever part of the world you may be, swearing that I will give you not even a quarter-hour of rest if you do not speak with me in a clear and intelligible voice, or if you do not appear yourself, to send me your messenger Astaroth in human form, without noise or terrible odor, failing which I will strike you and all your race with this fearsome Blasting Rod to the bottom of the abyss, and this, by the power of these great words of the Key:

By Adonai, Elohim, Ariel, Jehovah, Tagla, Mathon, Almouzin, Arios, Pythona, Magots, Silphae, Cabost, Salamdrae, Gnomus, Terrae, Coelis, Godens, Aqua. Immediately

AVERTISSEMENT

Avant que de lire la troisième appellation, si l'esprit ne comparaît pas, vous lirez la clavicule, telle qu'elle est ci-après, et frapperez tous les esprits en mettant les deux bouts fourchus de votre baguette dans le feu, et dans ce moment ne vous épouvantez pas des hurlements effroyables que vous entendrez, car pour lors tous les esprits paraîtront ; alors avant que de lire la clavicule, pendant le bruit que vous entendrez, vous direz encore la troisième appellation.

TROISIÈME APPELLATION

Je t'ordonne, empereur Lucifer, de la part du grand Dieu vivant, de son cher fils et du Saint-Esprit, et par la puissance du grand Adonay, Eloïm, Ariel et Jehovam, de comparaitre dans la minute, ou de m'envoyer ton messager Astarot, t'obligeant de quitter ta demeure dans quelque partie du monde qu'elle soit, te déclarant que si tu ne parois pas dans ce moment, je vais te frapper derechef toi et toute ta race, avec la baguette foudroyante du grand Adonay,

CAUTION

Before you read the third invocation, if the spirit refuses to appear, read the key that is provided later, and strike your rod in the fire, and do not be afraid of the horrible and awful howls that you hear, since it is by these that all the spirits appear; then before reading the Key, during the noise and commotion, recite the Third Invocation.

THIRD INVOCATION

I order you, emperor Lucifer, by the great living God, and his son and the Holy Ghost, and by the power of the great Adonai, Elohim, Ariel and Jehovah, to appear this very minute or to send me your messenger Astaroth, to be compelled to leave your home in whichever part of the world you may be, I declare to you that if you do not appear this moment, I will strike you and all your race once again with this Blasting Rod of the great Adonai, Elohim, Ariel and

Eloïm, Ariel et Jehovam.

Jehovah.

Si l'esprit ne parait pas jusqu'ici, mettez encore les deux bouts de votre baguette au feu, et lisez les puissantes paroles ci-après de la grande clavicule de Salomon

If the spirit does not appear immediately, plunge the two ends of your rod into the fire and read these powerful words of the Great Key of Solomon:

GRANDE APPELLATION

Tirée de la véritable clavicule

GREAT INVOCATION

Derived from the Veritable Key

Je te conjure, ô esprit! de paraître dans la minute, par la force du grand Adonay, par Eloïm, par Ariel, par Jehovam, par Agla, Tagla, Mathon, Oarios, Almouzin, Arios, Menbrot, Varios, Pithona, Magots, Silphæ, Cabost, Salamandræ, Tabots, Gnomus, Terræ, Goelis, Godens, aqua Gingua, Janua, Etituamus, Zariatnatmik, etc. A.. E.. A.. J.. A.. T.. M.. O.. A.. A.. M.. V.. P.. M.. S.. C.. S.. T.. G.. T.. C.. G.. A.. G.. J.. E.. Z... etc.

I conjure you, o spirit! To appear this very minute, by the force of the great Adonai, by Elohim, by Ariel, by Jehovah, by Agla, Tagla, Mathon, Oarios, Almouzin, Arios, Menbrot, Varios, Pithona, Magots, Silphae, Cabost, Salamandre, Tabots, Gnomus, Terrae, Goelis, Godens, aqua Gingua, Janua, Etituamus, Zariatnatmik,
A.. E.. A.. J.. A.. T.. M.. O.. A.. A.. M.. V.. P.. M.. S.. C.. S.. T.. G.. T.. C.. G.. A.. G.. J.. E.. Z... *(The initials of the names above)*

Après avoir répété deux fois ces grandes et puissantes paroles, vous êtes sûr que l'esprit paraîtra comme suit.

After having repeated twice these great and powerful words, you are sure to see the spirit appear immediately and respond in the following manner:

DE L'APPARITION DE L'ESPRIT

Me voici, que me demandes-tu ? pourquoi troubles-tu mon repos ? Ne me frappe plus de cette terrible baguette.

LUCIFUGE ROFOCALE

BY THE APPARITION OF THE SPIRIT:

I am here, what do you ask of me? Why do you disturb my rest? Do not strike me any more with this terrible Rod.

LUCIFUGE ROFOCALE

DEMANDE A L'ESPRIT

Si tu eusses paru quand je t'ai appelé, je ne t'aurais point frappé, pense ce que si tu ne m'accorde ce que je vais te demander, je te vais tourmenter éternellement.

SALOMON

TO THE SPIRIT:

If you had appeared when I called you first, I would not have had need to strike you, but if you do not agree with what I am going to ask you, I will torment you eternally.

SOLOMON

REPONSE DE L'ESPRIT

Ne m'amuse point ici et ne me tourmente plus ; dis-moi au plus tôt ce que tu me demandes.

LUCIFUGE ROFOCALE

RESPONSE BY THE SPIRIT:

Do not entertain me here and do not torment me anymore: Tell me immediately what you ask me.

LUCIFUGE ROFOCALE

DEMANDE A L'ESPRIT

Je te demande que tu me viennes parler deux fois tous les jours de la semaine, pendant la nuit, à moi ou à ceux qui auront mon présent livre, que tu approuveras et signeras, te laissant la volonté de choisir les heures qui te conviendront, si tu n'approuves

ASK OF THE SPIRIT:

I ask you to come and speak with me twice every day of the week, during the night, to me or to those who will present my book, which you will agree and sign, voluntarily and at your choice of time that may be convenient to you, if you do not approve of those marked

pas celles qui sont marquées ci-dessous.

Sçavoir :
Le lundi, à neuf heures et à minuit
Le mardi, à dix heures et à une heure
Le mercredi, à onze heures et à deux heures
Le jeudi, à huit heures et à dix heures
Le vendredi, à sept heures du soir et à minuit
Le samedi, à neuf heures du soir et à onze heures

De plus, je te commande de me livrer le trésor le plus près d'ici, te promettant pour récompense la première pièce d'or ou d'argent que je toucherai tous les premiers jours de chaque mois : voilà ce que je te demande.

SALOMON

below:

To wit:
On Monday, at 9 PM and at midnight.
On Tuesday, at 10 PM and 1 AM.
On Wednesday, at 11 PM and 2 AM
On Thursday, at 8 PM and 10 PM
On Friday, at 7 PM and midnight
On Saturday, at 9 PM and 11 PM.

Further, I order you to deliver me the greatest treasure near here, I promise you for your reward the first piece of gold or silver that I will touch the first day of each month. This is what I demand of you.

SOLOMON

REPONSE DE L'ESPRIT

Je ne puis t'accorder ce que tu me demandes sous ces conditions ni sous aucune autre, si tu ne te donnes à moi dans cinquante ans, pour faire de ton corps et de ton âme ce qu'il me plaira.

LUCIFUGE ROFOCALE

THE SPIRIT'S REPLY:

I cannot agree to what you demand of me under these conditions nor on any others, unless you give yourself to me in fifty years, to do with your body and soul as I please.

LUCIFUGE ROFOCALE

DEMANDE A L'ESPRIT

Je vais te frapper toi et toute ta race, par la puissance du grand Adonay, si tu ne m'accorde au plutôt ce que je te demande.

SALOMON

AVERTISSEMENT

Vous remettrez ici le bout de la Baguette Foudroyante au feu, et relirez la grande appellation de la clavicule, jusqu'à ce que l'esprit se soumette à vos désirs.

REPONSE ET CONVENTION DE L'ESPRIT

Ne me frappe pas davantage, je te promets de faire tout ce que tu voudras, deux heures de nuit de chaque jour de la semaine.

Sçavoir :
Le lundi à dix heures et à minuit Le mardi à onze heures et à une heure Le mercredi, à minuit et à deux heures Le jeudi, à huit heures et à onze heures Le vendredi, à

SAY TO THE SPIRIT:

I will strike you and all your race, by the power of the great Adonai, if you do not grant all my wishes.

SOLOMON

CAUTION

Now plunge the tip of the Blasting Rod into the fire and repeat the great Invocation of the Key, until the spirit surrenders to your desires.

RESPONSE AND COMPACT OF THE SPIRIT:

Do not strike me anymore, I promise you to do all that you wish, for two hours each night of the week.

To wit:
On Monday at 10 PM and at midnight, on Tuesday at 11 PM and at 1 AM, On Wednesday, at midnight and at 2 AM, On Thursday, at 8 PM and at 11 PM,

neuf heures et à minuit Le samedi, à dix heures et à une heure.

On Friday, at 9 PM and at midnight, On Saturday, at 10 PM and at 1 AM.

J'approuve aussi ton livre, et te donne ma véritable Signature en Parchemin, que tu y attacheras à la fin, pour t'en servir au besoin, me soumettant aussi d'y comparaitre devant toi toutes les fois que j'y serai appelé lorsque tu ouvriras le livre, que tu te seras purifié, que tu auras la terrible Baguette Foudroyante, et que tu auras composé le grand cercle cabalistique, et que tu prononceras le mot de ROFOCALE ; te promettant de comparaitre et traiter à l'amiable avec ceux qui seront munis dudit Livre, où est ma véritable signature, pourvu qu'ils m'appellent en règle, la première fois qu'ils auront besoin de moi

I also approve your book, and I give you my true Signature on Parchment, which you will place at the end, to serve you in your need, I will submit myself also and appear before you every time that you call my name or when you open the book, being purified, and when you will have the terrible Blasting Rod, and have constructed the great Kabbalistic Circle, and when you will pronounce the Word ROFOCALE; I promise to appear in a pleasing form to those who provide this book, where is my true signature, provided they call me in good standing and according to the rule, the first time that they have need of me

Je m'engage aussi à te livrer le trésor que tu me demandes, pourvu que tu gardes le secret pour toujours, que tu sois charitable envers les pauvres, et que tu me donnes une pièce d'or ou d'argent tous les premiers jours de chaque mois : si tu y manques, tu seras à moi pour toujours.

I also promise to deliver to you the treasure that you have demanded of me, provided that you keep this secret always, that you are charitable towards the poor, and that you grant me one piece of gold or silver on the first day of every month, if you miss this, you will be mine forever.

LUCIFUGE ROFOCALE
Approuvé

LUCIFUGE ROFOCALE,
Approved

REPONSE A L'ESPRIT :

REPLY TO THE SPIRIT:

J'acquiesce à ta demande.
SALOMON

I agree to your conditions.
SOLOMON

CENTUM REGNUM CHIAMTA DI LUCIFERO

LUCIFER, OUIA, KAMERON, ALISCOT, MANDESUMINI, POEMI, ORIEL, MAGREUSE, PARINOSCON, ESTIO, DUMOGON, DIVORCON, CASMIEL, HUGRAS, FABIEL, VONTON, ULI, SODIERNO, PETAN! Venite, Lucifer. Amen.

PROMESSE DE L'ESPRIT

CAPO PRIMO

Io Lucifero Imperatore potentissimo, supremo ed indipendente, libero ed assoluto ,padrone di tutto il Regno sotteraneo, dispotico Signor in tutte le mi giuridizione, formidabile, terribile, nobilissimo, al cui Impero tuto regolatissimo, si muove e governa, arbitro di tutte le fortune, di tutte le siagure, sapiente à sagace, è fornito d'ogni più sublime luminoso caratere Dominatore dell'Europa è di tutte

CENTUM REGNUM CHIAMTA DI LUCIFERO

(One hundred kingdoms call unto Lucifer) LUCIFER, OUIA, KAMERON, ALISCOT, MANDESUMINI, POEMI, ORIEL, MAGREUSE, PARINOSCON, ESTIO, DUMOGON, DIVORCON, CASMIEL, HUGRAS, FABIEL, VONTON, ULI, SODIERNO, PETAN! Come Lucifer. Amen.

PROMISE OF THE SPIRIT

ARTICLE ONE

I, Emperor LUCIFER, am powerful, supreme and independent, free and absolute, master of all the subterranean kingdoms, despotic Lord in all my jurisdiction, formidable, terrible, very noble, who governs all fortune, all sages, wise, sagacious, equipped with every sublime luminous characteristic. I am the dominator of Europe and all misfortunes of Asia in particular.

le siagure ed Asia in particolare.

CAPO SECUNDO

PROMETTO è giuro al nome di Dio da viventi obedienza, prontezza, è sommissione al padrone di questo libro firmato, è giuratto al nome suddetto, è de Miei Suddetti carateri, ed in virtù di tal giuramento e sotto signassione, giuro d'adedire à tutto quello che più sarà in piacero del padrone di questo libro.

CAPO TERTIO

Piu, prometto è giuro per parte dei miei sudite l'istesso; Onde al solo legere che si sarà della mia chiamata al capo primo di questo libro, di comparir subitto prontamente in forma di bel garzone, ô giovine, in aria piacouele, sensa sterpitto, rumore, o altro che possa offendere, o intimorire il padrone di questo libro, rispondendo giustamente con chiarezza, senza anfibologia alle sue interrogazioni, ed esequendo quanto mi verà commandatto, con tutta realtà, e sinceritià, sensa che de bono precedere profumi o altre invocasioni, magiche azioni, ô

ARTICLE TWO

I SWEAR in the name of the living God obedience, readiness and submission to the master of this book, signed and sworn to the aforementioned name, and my named characters, and by virtue of this oath and my signature below, I swear to accept everything that will please the owner of this book.

ARTICLE THREE

Additionally, I promise that all my subjects, on reading my summons from the first Article, will cause them to appear at once in the guise of a handsome young man, with a pleasing appearance and without making any uproar or noise or any action that would offend or intimidate the master of this book, and respond with clarity and without ambiguity to his questions, without need for any incense or any other magical invocations, actions or ceremonies, but rather to appear instantly ready for your commands.

circoli, o ceremonie, ma pensi instentamente ofermi pronto esequitore de' suoi commandi.

CAPO QUARTO

Senso che in tali occasioni maimai offenda le compagne, ô altre cose del mondo, è compito il mio servisio di subitamente partire sensa strepito alenno.

CAPO QUINTO

Piu, prometto è giuro nella forma predetta, sua universalissima servitù di tutti i miei sudditi al padrone di questo libro sensa diferensa digre de dignità od altre regioni, ma ogni quale volta, tempo, stagione, anno, meso, settimana, giorno, ora, è quarto est instante che rara letta la mia chiamata, di compartre in forma di bel giovine, e di somministrali qualsisia de' miei rudetti in servizion al padrone di questo libro, e di non partire se prima non sarà ô sara licensiato colla semplice formola o di me, o delli altri.

ARTICLE FOUR

On such occasions to not harm or offend the companions, or other things of the world, and after completing my service, I will depart at once without making any noise.

ARTICLE FIVE

Also, I swear the universal servitude of all my subjects to the master of this book without distinction to the dignity of other regions. At any time, in any weather, season, year, month, week, day, hour or quarter, at the moment my invocation is read, to appear in the form of a handsome boy, and to perform any of my qualities to the master of this book, and not to leave until it be permitted by the simple formula, either from the owner of the book, or whoever may have it.

CAPO SEXTO

Piu, prometto è giuro per me e tutti li altri al nome di Dio è delli nostri misteriori carateri, segretessa, fedeltà inviolabile, sensa ponto maimai contravenire al mio giuramento e promessa.

CAPO SEPTIMO

Piu, prometto è giuro io in particolare per tutti i miei sudetti di protegere e di diffendere il padrone di questo libro da tutte le fiagure, pericoli, ed altre naturali ed accidentali vicende, ad in caso, per qualonque suo bisogno saro chiamato, di assisterlo, è provederlo di tutto il bisogneuole, abenchè non si inotato in questo libro.

MODO DI LICENZIARE

Ite in pace a loco vestro et pax sit inter vos redituri ad me cum vos invocavero, in nomine Patris, et Filii et Spiritus Sancti. Amen.

ORDRE DE L'ESPRIT

ARTICLE SIX

Also, I promise to swear for myself and everyone else in the name of God and the mysteries, to provide secrecy, inviolable loyalty and never breaking my oath and promise.

ARTICLE SEVEN

Also, I promise and swear on behalf of all my subjects to protect and defend the owner of this book from all fears, dangers, and other natural and accidental events, in case, for whatever reason I am called to assist him, or for anything not mentioned in this book.

LICENSE TO DEPART

Go your way in peace and return when I call you, in the name of the Father, the Son and the Holy Ghost. Amen

ORDER OF THE SPIRIT

Suis-moi et viens reconnaitre le trésor.

Follow me and come discover the treasure.

Alors le Karcist, armé de la Baguette Foudroyante et de la pierre ématille, sortira du cercle par l'endroit où est indiquée la route du trésor, qui est la porte du grand Adonay, et suivra l'esprit ; les autres ne bougeront absolument point du cercle, mais y resteront fermes et inébranlables, quels bruits qu'ils entendent et quelques visions qu'ils voient :

The Operator, armed with the Blasting Rod and the bloodstone, goes out of the circle from the door of mighty Adonai to the treasure, following the spirit. The others do not move at all from the circle, but they stay firm and unshakeable even when they hear noises and see strange visions.

L'esprit conduira alors le Karcist jusqu'à l'entrée du trésor: et il se pourra qu'alors le Karcist voie comme un grand chien cotonné qui en fermera l'entrée, avec un collier reluisant comme le soleil, ce qui sera un Gnome qu'il écartera en lui présentant le bout de sa baguette, lequel marchera vers le trésor;

The spirit guides the Operator to the vicinity of the treasure. The Operator may see a large woolly dog block the entrance, with a shining collar like the sun. This is a gnome, who leaves when the Rod is brandished and moves towards the treasure.

Le Karcist le suivra, et en arrivant auprès du Trésor, il sera surpris d'y voir la personne qui l'aura caché, qui voudra se jeter sur lui, mais elle ne pourra absolument pas l'approcher: le Karcist sera aussi pourvu d'un morceau de parchemin vierge, où

The Operator follows and when he arrives near the treasure, it will be surprising to see the guardian of the hiding place, who will jump at him, but it is absolutely impossible to approach the Operator, who is provided with a virgin parchment, where

sera écrite la grande conjuration de la clavicule, qu'il jettera sur le trésor en prenant en même temps une pièce pour gage et reconnaissance, et en jetant d'abord une pièce de son argent, qu'il aura mordue;

Après quoi il se retirera à reculons, emportant avec lui ce qu'il pourra du trésor, le reste ne pouvant pas lui échapper par les précautions prises ci-devant, faisant attention de ne se point tourner quelque bruit qu'il entende, car dans ce moment il lui semblera que toutes les montagnes du monde se renverseront sur lui; il faut pour lors s'armer d'intrépidité, ne point s'épouvanter et tenir ferme: faisant cela, l'esprit le reconduira jusqu'à l'entrée du cercle. Alors le Karcist commencera à lire le renvoi de l'esprit tel qu'il est ci-après.

CONJURATION ET RENVOI DE L'ESPRIT

Oh ! Prince Lucifer ! je suis content de toi pour le présent ; je te laisse en repos et te permets de te retirer où bon te semblera, sans

will be written the great invocation of the Key, which is cast on the treasure, while taking a piece for pledge and confirmation, but also throwing a coin that he has brought with him.

After this, he will withdraw, walking backwards and taking with him what he can of the treasure, the rest cannot be lost with the precautions mentioned earlier. He must be careful not to turn around even when hearing any sound, because at this moment, it will seem as if all the mountains in the world will fall on him. He must be fearless, not be terrified and hold firm, thus, the spirit will guide him back until the entrance of the circle. Then the Operator reads the following discharge of the spirit.

CONJURATION AND DISMISSAL OF THE SPIRIT:

Oh! Prince Lucifer! I am satisfied with you for this gift; I release you to your rest and allow you to withdraw wherever you may

faire aucun bruit ni laisser aucune mauvaise odeur. Pense aussi à ton engagement, car si tu y manques d'un instant, tu peut être sûr que je te frapperai éternellement avec la baguette foudroyante du grand Adonay, Eloïm, Ariel et Jehovam. Amen.

ACTIONS DE GRACES

O grand Dieu qui as créé toutes choses pour le service et l'utilité de l'homme, nous te rendons de très humbles actions de grâce de ce que, par ta grande bonté, tu nous as comblé pendant cette nuit de tes précieuses faveurs, et de ce que tu nous avons accordé tout ce que nous désirons: c'est à présent, ô grand Dieu, que nous avons connu toute la force de tes grandes promesses, lorsque tu nous as dit: cherchez et vous trouverez, frappez et l'on vous ouvrira; et comme tu nous as ordonné et recommandé de soulager les pauvres, nous te promettons, à la face du grand Adonay, d'Eloïm, d'Ariel et de Jehovam, d'être charitables et de répandre sur eux les rayons du soleil, dont ces quatre puissantes Divinités, viennent de nous combler.

please, without noise or any bad odor. Think of your actions, because if you fail for even a moment, you can be sure that I will eternally strike you with the Blasting Rod of the great Adonai, Elohim, Ariel and Jehovah. Amen.

BENEDICTIONS

O Omnipotent God Who has created everything for the service and use of mankind, we grant you these humble thanks that you have, by your great goodness, filled this night with your precious favor to us, and that you have granted us all our desires. In this moment, O Great God, we know the power of your great promises as you have said: Seek and ye shall find, Ask and it shall be given to you. As you have ordered and recommended to us to care for the poor, we promise you, before the great Adonai, Elohim, Ariel and Jehovah, to be charitable and to spread the rays of the sun on them, whose four powerful divinities have just filled us.

SECOND LIVRE

CONTENANT LE VERITABLE SANCTUM REGNUM DE LA CLAVICULE OU LA VERITABLE MANIERE DE FAIRE LES PACTES

Avec les Noms, Puissances et Talents, de tous les grands esprits supérieurs, comme aussi la manière de les faire paraitre par la grande Appellation du chapitre des Pactes de la grande clavicule, qui les force à obéir à quelle opération que l'on souhaite.

BOOK TWO

CONTAINING THE TRUE HOLY KINGDOM OF THE KEY OR THE TRUE METHOD OF MAKING PACTS

With the Names, Powers, and Abilities of all the great Superior spirits, with also the method of making them appear by the great Conjuration in the chapter of the Pacts of the Great Key, which commands them to obey any succeeding operation

LE SANCTUM REGNUM

Où la véritable manière de faire des PACTES, avec quels Esprits que ce soit, sans qu'ils vous faire aucun tort.

Le véritable *Sanctum Regnum* de la grande clavicule, autrement dit, le *Pacta Conventa Daemoniorum* dont on parle depuis si longtemps, est une chose fort nécessaire à expliquer ici, pour l'intelligence de ceux qui voulant forcer les esprits n'ont point la qualité requise pour composer la Verge Foudroyante et le cercle Cabalistique, dont il est parlé dans le livre précédent. Ils ne peuvent dis-je ; venir à bout de forcer aucuns Esprits de paraître s'ils n'exécutent de point en point tous ce qui est décrit ci-après, touchant la manière de faire des Pactes avec quels Esprits que ce puissant être ;

THE HOLY KINGDOM

Wherein is the true method of making PACTS with whichever spirits you choose, without them doing you any harm.

The true *Holy Kingdom* of the Great Key also called the *Daemonic Pact* that we have been discussing herein, is an important topic to explain, for those who want to command the Spirits but are unable to make the Blasting Rod and the Kabbalistic Circle, which is described in the preceding book. Such persons cannot succeed in making any spirit to appear if they do not execute all that I have described hereinafter step by step, regarding the method of making Pacts with these powerful Spirits.

soit pour avoir la jouissance des femmes et des filles et en avoir telle faveur que l'on souhaite, soit pour découvrir les secrets les plus cachés, dans toutes les cours, tous les cabinets du monde, soit de dévoiler les plus impénétrables secrets, soit pour faire travailler un esprit pendant la nuit à son ouvrage, soit pour faire tomber la grêle ou la tempête par tout où l'on souhaite, soit de vous rendre invisible, soit pour vous faire transporter partout où l'on veut, soit d'ouvrir toutes les serrures, de voir ce qui se passe dans les maisons et d'apprendre tous les tours et finesses des Bergers, soit pour acquérir la main de Gloire et pour connaitre toutes les qualités et vertus des métaux, des minéraux, des végétaux et de tous les animaux purs et impurs, et pour faire des choses si surprenantes qu'il n'y a aucun homme qui ne soit dans la dernière surprise de voir que par le moyen de faire pacte avec quelques esprits, que l'on puisse découvrir les plus grands secrets de la nature ; qui sont cachés aux yeux de tous les autres hommes.

C'est par le moyen de la clavicule du grand roi Salomon, que l'on a découvert la véritable

By means of such Pacts, it would be possible to have the company and pleasure of women and girls and to have such favor as one wish, to discover the most hidden secrets, success in all the courts, all the governments of the world, to be able to reveal the most impenetrable secrets, to be able to make a spirit work during the night on one's labors, to be able to cause hail or raise a storm wherever one wishes, to be able make oneself invisible, to be able to transport oneself wherever one wished, to be able to open all locks, to see what happens inside homes and to learn all the tricks and subtleties of the Shepherds, to be able to acquire the Hand of Glory and for understanding all the qualities and virtues of metals, minerals, plants and all pure & impure animals, to be able to perform such amazing actions that there would be no man able to see such and not be surprised that we could discover the greatest secrets of nature, which are hidden from the eyes of all other men.

This is by means of the Key of the Great King Solomon, who discovered the true method of

manière de faire les pactes, dont il s'est servi lui-même, pour acquérir tant de richesses, pour avoir la jouissance de tant de femmes, et pour connaitre les plus impénétrables secrets de la nature, par lequel l'on peut faire toute sorte de bien, et toute sorte de mal.

Enfin, nous commencerons par décrire les noms des principaux esprits avec leurs puissances et pouvoirs, et ensuite nous expliquerons le *Pacta Daemoniarum*, ou la véritable manière de faire les pactes, avec quels esprits que ce soit.

Voici ci-après les noms et signes des principaux esprits infernaux.

making Pacts, which he used himself, to acquire vast riches, to be able to have the company and pleasure of women, and to be able to understand the most impenetrable secrets of nature, by which one could do all kinds of good and evil acts.

We shall begin by describing the names of the Principal Spirits with their powers and abilities, and then we will explain the Demonic Pact, or the true method of making Pacts, with any spirit one chooses.

The following are the names and signs of the principal infernal spirits

LEURS SIGNES ET CARACTERES

THEIR SIGNS AND CHARACTERS

LUCIFER
Empereur

LUCIFER
Emperor

BELZEBUT
Prince

BELZEBUT
Prince

ASTAROT
Grand-Duc

ASTAROT
Grand Duke

Ensuite viennent les esprits supérieurs, qui sont subordonnés aux trois nommés ci-dessus.

Then we have the Superior Spirits, who are subordinate to the trinity above.

Sçavoir:

To wit:

LEURS SIGNES ET CARACTERES

THEIR SIGNS AND CHARACTERS

LUCIFUGE
Prem. Minis.
SATANACHIA
Grand General
AGALIAREPT
Aussi General
FLEURETY
Lieut. General
SARGATANAS
Brigadier
NEBIROS
Mal. De Camp.

LUCIFUGE
Prime Minister
SATANACHIA
Great General
AGALIAREPT
Also General
FLEURETY
Lt. General
SARGATANAS
Brigadier
NEBIROS
Camp Marshal

Les six grands esprits que je viens de donner ci-devant, dirigent leur pouvoir sur toute la Puissance Infernale qui est donnée aux autres esprits. Ils ont à leur service dix-huit autres esprits, qui leur sont subordonnés, sçavoir :

The six great Spirits that are named above have authority over all the Infernal powers which are given to the other spirits. They have at their service eighteen other spirits who are their subordinates, to wit:

1. Baël.
2. Agares
3. Marbas
4. Pruslas
5. Aamon
6. Barbatos

1. Baël.
2. Agares
3. Marbas
4. Pruslas
5. Aamon
6. Barbatos

7. Buer	7. Buer
8. Gusoyn	8. Gusoyn
9. Botis	9. Botis
10. Bathim	10. Bathim
11. Pursan	11. Pursan
12. Abigar	12. Abigar
13. Loray	13. Loray
14. Valefar	14. Valefar
15. Foraii	15. Foraii
16. Ayperos	16. Ayperos
17. Naberus	17. Naberus
18. Glasyabolas	18. Glasyabolas

Après vous avoir indiqué les noms des dix-huit esprits ci-dessus, qui sont inférieurs aux six premiers que j'ai décrit aussi ci-devant, il est bon de vous prévenir aussi de ce qui suit, sçavoir :

After enumerating the names of the eighteen spirits above, who are below the six Chiefs that I have described also earlier, it is advisable to caution you also on what follows. To wit:

Que LUCIFUGE, commande sur les trois premiers, qui se nomment *Baël, Agares et Marbas....*

That LUCIFUGE, commands the three Chiefs, who are named *Bael, Agares & Marbas.*

SATANACHIA, sur *Pruslas, Aamon et Barbatos.*

SATANACHIA over Pruslas, Aamon & Barbatos,

AGALIAREPT, sur Buer, Gusoyn et Botis

AGALIAREPT over Buer, Gusoyn & Botis.

FLEURETY, sur Bathim, Pursan et Abigar

FLEURETY over Bathim, Pursan & Abigar.

SARGATANAS, sur Loray, Valefar et Faraü

SARGATANAS over Loray, Valefar & Farau.

NEBIROS, sur Ayperos, Naberus et Glasyabolas.

NEBIROS over Ayperos, Naberus & Glasyabolas.

Et quoi qu'il y ait encore des millions d'esprits, qui sont tous subordonnés à ceux nommés ci-devant, il est inutile de les nommer, à cause que l'on ne s'en sert que quand il plaît aux esprits supérieurs de les faire travailler à leur place, parce qu'ils se servent de tous ces esprits inférieurs, comme si c'était leurs ouvriers ou leurs esclaves :

While there are millions of other subordinate spirits, it is unnecessary to name them, because they are employed only when it pleases the Superior Spirits in their own stead, because they use all these inferior spirits, as if they were workers or slaves.

Ainsi, en faisant le Pacte avec un des principaux dont vous avez besoin, il n'importe quel esprit qui vous serve ; néanmoins demandez toujours à l'esprit avec lequel vous faite votre pacte, que ce soit un des trois principaux qui lui sont subordonnés qui vous serve.

So, by making the Pact with one of the Principals that you have need of, it does not matter which spirit serves you. However, require of the Spirit with whom you make the Pact that you be served by one of the three Superiors among his many subordinates

Voici précisément les puissances, sciences, arts et talens des esprits surnommés, afin que celui qui veut faire un Pacte, puisse trouver dans chacun des talens des six esprits supérieurs, ce dont il aura besoin.

Here are the precise powers, sciences, arts and Abilities of the spirits, so that those who wish to make such a Pact, can find in each of the abilities of the six Superior Spirits, whatever is needed.

Le premier est le grand LUCIFUGE ROFOCALE, premier ministre infernal ; il a la puissance que LUCIFER lui a donnée sur toutes les richesses et sur tous les trésors du monde. Il a sous lui *Baël, Agares et Marbas*, et

The first is the great LUCIFUGE ROFOCALE, Infernal Prime Minister. He has the power that LUCIFER grants him over all the wealth and all the treasures of the world. He has under him *Bael, Agares and Marbas*, and thousands

plusieurs autres milliers de démons ou d'esprits qui lui sont tous subordonnés.

of spirits who are his subordinates.

Le second est le grand SATANACHIA, grand général ; il a la puissance de soumettre à lui toutes les femmes et toutes les filles, et d'en faire ce qu'il souhaite. Il commande la grande légion des esprits, il a sous lui *Pruslas, Aamon et Barbatos*, etc., etc.

The second is the great General SATANACHIA. He has the power to submit to himself all women and girls and make them do what he wishes. He commands the great spirit legion; he has under him *Pruslas, Aamon and Barbatos*, etc.

AGALIAREPT, aussi général, a la puissance de découvrir les secrets les plus cachés, dans toutes les cours et dans tous les cabinets du monde, il dévoile les plus grands mystères ; il commande la seconde légion des esprits, il a sous lui *Guer, Gusoan et Botis*, etc., etc.

The third is the great General AGALIAREPT, who has the power to discover the most hidden secrets, in all the Courts and Governments of the world, he reveals the greatest mysteries. He commands the second legion of spirits, he has under him *Guer, Gusoan & Botis*, etc.,

FLEURETY, lieutenant général, a la puissance de faire tel ouvrage que l'on souhaite pendant la nuit, il fait aussi tomber la grêle partout où il veut. Il commande un corps très considérable d'esprits, il a sous lui *Bathim, Parsan et Abigar*, etc., etc.

The fourth is the Lieutenant General FLEURETY, who has the power to perform any task he wishes during the night, he can also cause hail or raise a storm where he wishes. He commands a very considerable army of spirits, he has under him *Bathim, Parsan and Abigar*, etc.

SARGATANAS, brigadier, a la puissance de vous rendre invisible, de vous transporter partout,

The fifth is Brigadier SARGATANAS, who has the power to make one invisible, to

d'ouvrir toutes les serrures, de vous faire voir tout ce qui se passe dans les maisons, de vous apprendre tous les tours et finesses des bergers ; il commande plusieurs brigades d'esprits. Il a sous lui *Loray, Valefar et Faraü*, etc., etc.

NEBIROS, maréchal de camp et inspecteur général, a la puissance de donner du mal à qui il veut ; il fait trouver la main de gloire, il enseigne toutes les qualités des métaux, des minéraux, des végétaux et de tous les animaux purs et impurs ; c'est lui qui a aussi l'art de prédire l'avenir, étant un des plus grands nécromanciens de tous les esprits infernaux ; il va partout, il a inspection sur toutes les milices infernales ; il a sous lui, Ayperos, Nuberus et Glasyabolas., etc., etc. .

transport one anywhere, to open all locks, to grant the power to see what is happening inside homes, to teach all the tricks and subtleties of the shepherds. He controls several brigades of spirits. He has under him *Loray, Valefar and Farau*, etc.

The sixth Superior Spirit is NEBIROS, Major General and Inspector General, who has the power to harm whoever he pleases, he can reveal the Hand of Glory, he educates on all the qualities of Metals, Minerals, Plants and all pure & impure Animals. He also grants the art of predicting the future, being one of the greatest necromancers of all the infernal spirits. He can go anywhere and inspect all the infernal militias. He has under him *Ayperos, Nuberus & Glasyabolas*, etc.

AVERTISSEMENT

Quand vous voudrez faire votre pacte avec un des principaux esprits que je viens de nommer, vous commencerez l'avant-veille du pacte d'aller couper avec un couteau neuf qui n'ait jamais servi, une baguette de noisetier sauvage, qui n'aye jamais porté et qui soit semblable à la Verge Foudroyante, telle que celle qui est déjà décrite, et dont vous avez la figure dans le premier livre, positivement au moment que le soleil parait sur notre horizon ;

Cela fait, vous vous munirez d'une pierre ématille, et de deux cierges bénis, et vous choisirez ensuite un endroit pour l'exécution que personne ne vous incommode, vous pouvez même faire le pacte dans une chambre écartée ou dans quelque masure de vieux château ruiné, parce que l'esprit a le pouvoir d'y transporter quel trésor qu'il lui plaît.

Cela étant vous tracerez un triangle avec votre pierre ématille, et cela seulement la première fois que vous ferez votre pacte ; ensuite vous placerez les deux cierges bénis à côté et tels qu'ils

CAUTION
:

When you wish to make your Pact with one of the principal spirits that I have named, begin by cutting a rod of wild hazel that has never borne fruit, similar to the Blasting Rod described and depicted in Book One, with a new knife two days before the pact at precisely the moment that the sun appears on the horizon.

Having done so, equip yourself with a bloodstone and two consecrated candles, and select a location for the operation where you will be undisturbed. You can choose to make this pact in an isolated room or in some dilapidated ruin, because the spirit will bring the Treasure there.

Begin by tracing a triangle with your bloodstone and do this only the first time you make your Pact. Then place the two consecrated candles parallel to the two edges of the triangle and inscribe the

sont placés vers le triangle des pactes que vous voyez ci-après, y plaçant le S. N. de Jésus derrière, afin que les esprits ne vous puissent faire aucun mal ; ensuite vous vous placerez au milieu du dit triangle, ayant en main la baguette mystérieuse, avec la grande appellation à l'esprit, avec le pacte et le renvoi de l'esprit, tel qu'il est marqué ci-après au modèle du triangle cabalistique des pactes.

Sacred Name of Jesus at the base of the triangle so that the spirits are unable to harm you from behind. Then enter the triangle, holding the mysterious Rod, along with the great conjuration of the Key, the pact and the discharge of the spirit, as indicated below in the model of the Kabbalistic Triangle of Pacts. Having followed these steps precisely, begin to recite the following conjuration with confidence and determination.

GRANDE APPELLATION DES ESPRITS AVEC LESQUELS L'ON VEUT FAIRE PACTE, TIREE DE LA GRANDE CLAVICULE

GRAND CONJURATION OF THE SPIRITS WITH WHOM ONE WISHES TO MAKE A PACT, TAKEN FROM THE GREAT KEY

Empereur LUCIFER, maître de tous les esprits rebelles, je te prie de m'être favorable dans l'appellation que je fais à ton grand ministre LUCIFUGE ROFOCALE, ayant envie de faire pacte avec lui ;

Emperor LUCIFER, master of all the rebel spirits, I pray to you to consider my appeal favorable which I make to your Prime Minister LUCIFUGE ROFOCALE, wishing to make a Pact with him.

Je te prie aussi Prince BELZEBUT, de me protéger dans mon entreprise. O comte ASTAROT ! sois-moi propice, et

I pray to you also, Prince BELZEBUT, to protect me in my enterprise. O Count ASTAROT! Find me favorable and protect me

fais que je sois protégée dans mon entreprise. O comte ASTAROT ! sois moi propice, et fais que dans cette nuit le grand LUCIFUGE m'apparaisse sous une forme humaine, et sans aucune mauvaise odeur, et qu'il m'accorde par le moyen du pacte que je vais lui présenter, toutes les richesses dont j'ai besoin.

O Grand Lucifuge ! Je te prie de quitter ta demeure, dans quelle partie du monde qu'elle soit, pour venir me parler, sinon je t'y contraindrai par la force du grand Dieu vivant, de son cher Fils et du Saint-Esprit ; obéis promptement, où tu vas être éternellement tourmenté par la force des puissantes paroles de la grande clavicule de Salomon, et dont il se servait pour obliger les esprits rebelles à recevoir son pacte ;

Ainsi parait au plutôt, ou je te vais continuellement tourmenter par la force de ces puissantes paroles de la clavicule,

Aglon, Tetragram, Vaycheon, Stimulamaton y ezpares retragrammaton olyoran irion esytion existion eryona onera erasym moym messias soter Emanuel Sabaoth Adonay, te

in my enterprise. O Count ASTAROT! Protect me and grant the great LUCIFUGE to appear before me in a human form, without bad odor and agreeable to grant all the wealth I desire through this Pact that I propose to him.

O Great LUCIFUGE! I pray you leave your current residence in any part of the world to speak with me, otherwise I will compel you by the power of the great living God, his dear Son, and the Holy Spirit; obey me promptly, or you will be tormented forever by the powerful words of the Great Key of Solomon, which he would use to compel the rebel spirits to accept his Pact.

Appear therefore or else I will continue to torment you by the force of these powerful words of the Key,

Aglon, Tetragram, Vaycheon, Stimulamaton y ezpares retragrammaton olyoran irion esytion existion eryona onera erasym moym messias soter Emanuel Sabaoth Adonai, I love

adore et invoco. Amen

& invoke you. Amen

Vous êtes sûr que d'abord que vous aurez lu les puissantes paroles indiquées ci-dessus, que l'esprit paraîtra, et vous dira ce qui suit :

You can be certain that before you have finished speaking these powerful words, the spirit will appear and tell you the following:

APPARITION DE L'ESPRIT.

APPEARANCE OF THE SPIRIT:

Me voici, que me demandes-tu ? pourquoi troubles-tu mon repos ? réponds-moi.
LUCIFUGE ROFOCALE

I say, what do you ask of me? Why do you trouble my rest? Answer me
LUCIFUGE ROFOCALE

DEMANDE A L'ESPRIT

ASK OF THE SPIRIT:

Je te demande pour faire pacte avec toi, et enfin que tu m'enrichisses au plutôt, sinon je te tourmenterais par les puissantes paroles de la clavicule.
N.N.

I ask you to make a pact with me, and to grant me wealth as soon as possible, or else I will torment you by the powerful words of the Key
<YOUR NAME>

REPONSE DE L'ESPRIT

THE SPIRIT'S REPLY

Je ne puis t'accorder ta demande, qu'a condition que tu te donnes à moi dans vingt ans, pour faire de ton corps et de ton amé ce qu'il me plaira.
LUCIFUGE ROFOCALE.

I cannot agree to your demands unless you agree to surrender yourself to me in twenty years, to do with your body and soul as I please.
LUCIFUGE ROFOCALE

Alors vous lui jetterez votre pacte, qui doit être écrit de votre propre main, sur un petit morceau de Parchemin vierge, qui consiste à ces peu de mots ci-après, en y mettant votre signature avec votre véritable sang.

Then cast before him your Pact that you have written yourself on a sheet of virgin parchment, consisting of the following words, signed by you with your own blood:

VOICI LE PACTE

HERE IS THE PACT:

Je promets au grand LUCIFUGE de le récompenser dans vingt ans de tous les trésors qu'il me donnera. En foi de quoi je me suis signé.

N.N.

I promise the great LUCIFUGE that I will repay him in twenty years for all the treasure that he grants me. In Witness Whereof I sign this myself

<YOUR NAME>

Je ne puis t'accorder ta demande.
LUCIFUGE ROFOCALE.

I cannot grant your request.
LUCIFUGE ROFOCALE

Alors pour forcer l'esprit à vous obéir, vous relirez la grande appellation avec les terribles paroles de la clavicule, jusqu'à ce que l'esprit reparaisse et vous dise ce qui suit :

Then to force the spirit to obey you, read once again the Great Conjuration with the terrible words of the Key, until the spirit reappears and tells you the following:

SECONDE APPARITION DE L'ESPRIT

SECOND APPEARANCE OF THE SPIRIT

Pourquoi me tourmentes-tu davantage ? Si tu me laisses en repos, je te donnerai le plus

Why do you torment me more and more? If you allow me to rest, I will grant you the nearest treasure,

prochain trésor, à condition que tu m'en consacreras une pièce tous les premiers lundis de chaque mois, et que tu ne m'appelleras qu'un jour de chaque semaine, sçavoir ; depuis les dix heures du soir jusqu'à deux heures après minuit.

Ramasse ton pacte, je l'ai signé ; et si tu ne tiens pas ta parole, tu seras à moi dans vingt ans.

LUCIFUGE ROFOCALE

on the condition that you consecrate me one coin the first Monday of every month, and that you do not summon me more than one day a week, from 10 PM to 2 AM.

Pick up your Pact that I have signed, and if you do not keep your word, you will be mine in twenty years.

LUCIFUGE ROFOCALE

REPONSE A L'ESPRIT :

J'acquiesce à ta demande, à condition que tu me feras paraître le plus prochain trésor que je pourrai emporter tout de suite.

N.N.

REPONSE DE L'ESPRIT

Suis-moi, et prends le trésor que je vais te montrer.

Alors vous suivrez l'esprit par la route du trésor qui est indiquée au triangle des pactes, sans vous épouvanter, et jetterez votre pacte tout signé sur le trésor, en le touchant avec votre baguette ; vous en prendrez tant que vous pourrez, et vous vous en retournerez dans le triangle, en

REPLY TO THE SPIRIT:

I agree to your demands, on the condition that you take me to the nearest treasure immediately.

<YOUR NAME>

THE SPIRIT'S REPLY

Follow me and take the treasure that I am going to show you.

Then follow the spirit by the route to the treasure that he indicates from the Triangle of Pacts, without fear, and cast your signed pact on the treasure, touching it with your Rod. Take as much of it as you can, and then return into the Triangle, walking backwards and place your treasure before you

marchant à reculons ; vous y poserez votre trésor devant vous et vous commencerez tout de suite à lire le renvoi de l'esprit, tel qu'il est marqué ci-après.

and immediately beginning to read the discharge of the Spirit, which is provided hereafter.

CONJURATION
& renvoi de l'Esprit avec lequel l'on a fait un pacte

CONJURATION
& Discharge of the Spirit with whom the Pact has been made

O Grand LUCIFUGE ! je suis content de toi pour le présent, je te laisse en repos et te permets de te retirer où bon te semblera, sans faire aucun bruit ni laisser aucune mauvaise odeur. Pense aussi à ton engagement de mon pacte, car si tu y manques d'un instant, tu peux être sûr que je te tourmenterai éternellement avec les grandes et puissantes paroles de la clavicule du grand roi Salomon, par lequel l'on force tous les esprits rebelles d'obéir.

O Great LUCIFUGE! I am pleased with you for your gift, I release you to your rest and allow you to leave, without any noise or bad odor. Think also of your commitment to my Pact, because if you fail for even a moment, you may be assured of eternal torment with the great and powerful words of the Key of the Great King Solomon, which he used to command obedience of all the rebel spirits.

PRIERE AU TOUT-PUISSANT EN FORME D'ACTION DE GRACE

PRAYER TO THE OMNIPOTENT IN THANKSGIVING

Dieu Tout-Puissant, père céleste, qui as créé toutes choses pour le service et l'utilité des hommes, je te rends de très humbles actions de grâces de ce que par ta grande bonté tu as permis que sans risque,

Omnipotent God, Heavenly Father, who has created all things for the service and use of mankind, I offer the humblest thanks for the great kindness you have granted me to make this Pact

je puisse faire pacte avec un de tes esprits rebelles, et le soumettre à me donner tout ce dont je pourrais avoir besoin. Je te remercie, ô Dieu Tout-Puissant, du bien dont tu m'as comblé pendant cette nuit ; daigne accorder à moi, chétive créature, tes précieuses faveurs : c'est à présent, ô grand Dieu ! que j'ai connu toute la force et la puissance de tes grandes promesses, lorsque tu nous a dit : cherchez et vous trouverez ; frappez et l'on vous ouvrira ; et comme tu nous as ordonné et recommandé de soulager les pauvres, daigne, grand Dieu, m'inspirer de véritables sentiments de charité, et fais que je puisse répandre sur une aussi sainte œuvre une grande partie des biens dont la grande divinité a bien voulu que je fusse comblé ;

without risk with one of your rebel spirits, and to have him grant me all that I need. I thank you for the goodness you have shown me tonight; Deem me, a puny creature, worthy of your precious favor. O Great God! This is the moment that I have known all the force and power of your great promises, when you said to us, Seek and Ye Shall Find; Knock and the Door shall be opened! And as you ordered us to ease the burden of the poor, great God, inspire in me the true feelings of charity, so that I spend a great portion of the bountiful gifts I have received on holy works to favor your great Divinity, O Great God, allow me to peacefully enjoy these great riches that I possess, and do not let any rebellious spirit to harm me in the enjoyment of these precious treasures that you have permitted me to possess. O Great God inspire me with the necessary emotions to free myself from the claws of the devil and all evil spirits. I am under your saintly protection, great God the Father, God the Son and the Holy Spirit, Amen.

ORAISON

Pour se garantir des mauvais Esprits

PRAYER

To protect oneself from evil spirits

O père Tout Puissant ! O Mère, la plus tendre des Mères ! O Exemplaire admirable des sentiments et de la tendresse des mères ! O Fils, la fleur de tous les fils, ! O forme de toutes les formes ! Âme, esprit, harmonie et nombre de toutes choses, conservez-nous, protégez-nous, conduisez-nous, et soyez-nous propice. Amen.

O Omnipotent God! O Mother, the most caring of Mothers! O admirable example of sentiments and tenderness of mothers! O Son, the flower of all sons! O form of all forms! Soul, Spirit, Harmony and Name of all things! Keep me, protect me, lead me and be propitious unto me. Amen

CITATIO PRAEDICTORUM SPIRITUUM

SUMMONING THE AFORESAID SPIRITS

Ubi quem volueris Spiritum, cujus nomen et officium supra cognosces: imprimis autem ab omni pollutione minimùm tres vel quatuor dies mundus esto in primà citatione, sic et spiritus posteà obsequentiores erunt: fac et circulum, et voca spiritum cum multâ intentione, primùm verò annulum in manu continetur: indè hanc recitato benedictionem, tuo nomine et socii, si præsto fueris, et affectum tui instituti sortieris, nec detrimentum à spiritibus sancies: imò tuæ animæ perditionem.

Before calling the Spirit, whose name and Office you know, you must fast and be free of all pollution for three or four days so the spirits will be more obedient to you. Make the circle and call the spirit with the proper intention, with a ring in your hand. Say the following prayer on this day in your name and your companions, for they must always be with you, that you are granted your wishes, with no harm from the Spirit, and no destruction of your soul:

§ 2. In nomine Domini nostri Jesu Christi, Patris et Filii et Spiritûs Sti, sancta trinitas et inseparabilis

§ 2. In the name of God and Jesus Christ, Father, Son and Holy Ghost, holy trinity and indivisible,

THE COMPLETE ILLUSTRATED GRAND GRIMOIRE, INTERLINEAR EDITION

unitas te invoco, ut sis mihi salus et defensio, et protectio corporis et animæ meæ, et omnium rerum mearum. Per virtutem sanctæ crucis et per virtutem passionis tuæ deprecor te, Domine Jesu-Christe, per merita beatissimæ Mariæ Virginis et matris tuæ atque omnium sanctorum tuorum, ut mihi concedas gratiam et potestatem divinam super omnes malignos spiritus, ut quocumque nominibus invocavero, statim ex omne parte conveniant, et voluntatem meam perfectè adimpleant quod mihi nihil nocentes neque timorem inferentes sed potiùs obedientes, et ministrantes, tuâ districtè virtute præcipientes, mandata mea perficient. Amen;

I call to you for my safety and protection, and the protection of my body and soul, and all my possessions through the virtue of the Holy Cross and by the power of your passion, I beg you, Lord Jesus Christ, and by the blessed Virgin Mary and all the saints and all thy brethren, to minister unto me, and give me grace and divine power over all the wicked spirits, so that whichever of them I call by their name, they may come from wherever they are and voluntarily accomplish what I wish, with no harm, and be fearful and obedient to me, and through thy virtue commanding them, let them fulfil my commandments. Amen.

Sanctus, sanctus Dominus Deus sabaoth, qui venturus est judicare vivos et mortuos: tu es A et a primus et novissimus, rex regnum et dominus dominantium,

Holy, Holy is the Lord God of Hosts, who will come to judge the living and the dead. From you and from the First and the Last, King of Kings and Lord of Lords,

Joth, Aglanabrath El Abiel anathi Enatiel Amazin sedames hayes tolima Elias ischiros arganatos ymas heli Messias,

Joth, Aglanabrath, El Abiel, anathi Enatiel Amazin sedamas hayes tolima Elias ischiros arganatos ymas heli Messias,

per hæc tua S. nomina, et per omnia alia in voco te et obsecro te, Domine, Jesu Christe, per tuam

By these holy Names, and by all other holy names I call on thee, Lord, Jesus Christ, by your

nativitatem, per baptismum tuum, per passionem et crucem tuam per ascensionem tuam, per adventum Spiritûs Sancti paracleti, per amaritudinem animæ tuæ quando exivit de corpore tuo per quinque vulnera tua, per sanguinem et aquam quæ exierunt de corpore tuo, per sacramentium quod dedisti discipulis tuis pridiè quam passus fuisti per sanctam Trinitatem, per individuam unitatem, per beatam Mariam matrem tuam, per Angelos et Archang., per prophetas et patriarchas et per omnes sanctos tuos: et per omnis sacramenta quæ fiunt in honore tuo: Adoro te, et obsecro te, benedico tibi et rogo, ut accipias orationes has et conjurationes et verba oris mei, quibus uti voluero. Peto, Domine Jesu Christe, da mihi virtutem et potestatem tuam super omnes Angelos tuos qui de coelo ejecti sunt ad decipiendum genus humanum, ad attrahendum eos, ad constringendum, ad ligandum eos pariter et solvendum, Et congregandum eos coram me, et ad præcipiendum eis ut omnia, quæ possunt, faciant ert verba mea vocemque meam nullo modo contemnant: sed mihi et dictis meis obediant, et me timeant; per humanitatem et misericordiam et

nativity, by your baptism, by your passion and crucifixion, by your ascension, by the advent of the Holy Ghost, the comforter, when you went out of your body through the bitterness of the five wounds, by the blood and water that came out of your body, by the Blessed Sacrament you gave your disciples on the eve of your suffering, by the Holy Indivisible Trinity, by the blessed Mary, your mother, by the Angels and Archangels, by the prophets and patriarchs and by all your saints, and by all the sacraments which were made in your honor, I worship you and beseech you, and ask you to accept my prayers and conjurations, and the words from my mouth. I beseech thee, O Lord Jesus Christ, to give me strength, over all angels that you cast out of heaven who seek to deceive mankind, to draw them to me, to tie them and bind them, and also to loosen them and gather them in front of me, to command them and not have them disrespect me, but obey me and my words, and fear me; through thy grace, through Christ's humanity, and make supplication to thee, and show mercy, and I beseech *Adonai, Amay Horta Videgoram Mitey Hel Surana & Syon & Svesy*

gratiam tuam deprecor et pero te Adonay amay horta videgoram mitey hel surana y syon y svesy, et per omnia nomina tua sancta, per omnes sanctos et sanctos tuos, per Angelos et Archangelos, Potestates, Dominationes et Virtutes, et per illud nomen per quod Salomo constringebat dæmones, et conclusit ipso Elh rocobem her agle goth joth othie venochnabrat, et per omnia sacra nomina quæ scripta sunt in hoc libro, et per virtutem eorumdem, quatenùs me potentem facias, congregare, constingere omnes tuos spiritus de cœlo depulsos ut mihi veraciter de omnibus meis interrogatis, de quibus quæram, responsionem veracem tribuant, et omnibus meis mandatis illis satisfaciant, sine læsione corporis et animæ meæ et omnium ad me pertinentium, per Dominum nostrum Jesum Christum filium tuum, qui tecum vivit et regnat in unitate Spiritûs Sancti Deus, per omnia sæcula.

and by all your holy names, by all your saints, by the Angels and Archangels, the Powers, Principalities and Virtues, and by that Name which Solomon used to bind the demons, and he concluded therefore *Elroch Ebanher Agla Goth Joth Othie Venochnabrat*, and by all the holy names which are written in this book, and by virtue of the same, by my powers make them congregate, bind all your spirits driven from heaven to give me a true answer to all my demands, and that they satisfy all my requests, without harm to my body or soul, of all that concerns me, by our Lord Jesus Christ thy son, who lives and reigns in unity with the Holy Ghost, one God, forever and ever!

§ 3. O Pater omnipotens! ô Fili sapiens! ô Spiritus Sancte! corda hominum illustrans, ô vos tres in personis, una vero deitas in substantia qui Adamæ et Evæ in peccatis eorum pepercisti, et

§ 3. O Omnipotent Father! O Wise son! O Holy Spirit! Lighting the hearts of men, the threefold person, one in substance, who did spare Adam and Eve their sins, and of thy son, who you sustained

propter eorum peccata morte subjecti, tuum filium turpissima, in lignoque sanctæ crucis sustinuisti; ô misericordissime, quando tuam confugio misericordiam, et supplico modis omnibus quibus possum, per hæc nomina sancta tua filii, scicilet A et v et per omnia alia sua nomina, quatenus concedas mihi virtutem et potestatem tuam, ut valeam tuos spiritus qui de cœlo ejecti sunt ante me citare, et ut ipsi mecum loquentur, et mandata mea perficiant statim et sine mora cum eorum voluntate, sine omni læsione corporis, animæ et bonorum meorum, etc. Continua ut libro Annuli Salomonis continetur.

as he died a most shameful death on the holy wooden cross. O Most merciful, grant kindness and mercy in every way possible, by the holy name of your son, the beginning and the end, and all other holy names, grant me power and authority of all your spirits which you cast out of heaven, to speak with me and be diligent unto me immediately and without delay of their own will, with no harm to my body, soul or possessions, etc. as is continued in the book Solomon's Ring

§ 4. O summa et æterna virtus Altissimi, quæ, te disponente, his judicio vocatis
Vaycheon stimulamaton esphares tetragramaton ilioram rion esytio existioneriona onera brasym moyn messias sodxer, Emmanuel, Sabaoth, Adonay
te adoro, te invoco, totius mentis, viribus meis imploro, quatenus per te præsentes orationes et consecrationes et conjurationes consecrantur; videlicet, et ubicumque maligni spiritus in virtute tuorum nominum sunt

§ 4. O Great and eternal power, most high, which calls to judgement
Vaycheon stimulamaton esphares tetragrammaton ilioram rion estyio existioneriona onera brasym moyn messiah Soter Emmanuel Sabaoth Adonai
I worship you, invoke you with all my power, mind and heart, that by you, these prayers and consecrations and conjurations be hallowed unto thee, namely, (to control) these malignant spirits, and wherever the virtue of your

vocati, et omni parte conveniant, et voluntatem meam exorcismis diligenter adimpleant, fiat, fiat, fiat. Amen

holy names are called, that they come together from everywhere, that thy names are suitable for each spirit and that they diligently fulfill the will of me, the exorcist.

LE SECRET MAGIQUE

Où le Grand ART de pouvoir parler aux Morts

Il est absolument nécessaire d'assister à la Messe de Noel, à minuit précis, pour avoir une conversation familière avec les habitants de l'autre Monde. C'est au moment où le Prêtre levé la Sainte Hostie, qu'il s'incline intérieurement & dire d'une voix contrainte :

Exsurgent mortui, et ac me veniunt.

A peine aurez-vous prononcé ces fix mots Latins, qu'il faut gagner le cimetière, & a la première tombe qui peut s'offrir à vos regards : vous ferez ces prières :

Puissances Infernales ; vous qui portez le trouble dans tout l'univers, abandonnez vos demeures sombres, & allez-vous confiner au-delà du Fleuve Styx.

Vous ajouterez ensuite après quelques moments de silence :

THE MAGICAL SECRET

Wherein is the great ART of speaking with the Dead

It is necessary to attend the Christmas Mass, precisely at midnight, to have a familiar conversation with the residents of the other World. When the Priest raises the Holy Host, the sorcerer makes a covert bow and in a constrained voice intones:

Arise ye dead and come to me

As soon as you have pronounced these fixed Latin words, go to the cemetery and at the first tomb you espy, make these prayers:

Infernal Powers, you who bring trouble into all the universe, abandon your dark dwellings and go beyond your abode by the River Styx.

After a few moments of silence, add:

Si vous tenez sous votre puissance, celui ou celle pour qui je m'intéresse, je vous conjure au nom du Roi des Rois de me le faire apparaitre à l'heure & au moment que je vois invoquerai.

If you have under your domain of control, the one whom I am interested in, I conjure you in the name of the King of Kings to have it appear before me at this hour and moment of my invocation

Après cette cérémonie, qu'il est indispensable de faire, vous prendrez une poignée de terre & la disperserez, comme on disperse le grain dans un champ, en disant – d'une voix basse –

After this ceremony, which is essential to perform, take a handful of graveyard dirt and scatter it, like one might scatter grain in the field, saying, in a low voice,

« Que celui qui n'est que poussière, se réveille de son tombeau, qu'il force de sa cendre, & qu'il réponde aux objections que je vais lui faire au nom du Père de tous les hommes. »

"He who is only dust, rise from thy tomb, from thy ashes, and answer the questions I will make of him in the name of the Father of all men"

Vous fléchirez alors un genou contre terre, en tournant les yeux du côté de l'Orient, lorsque vous verrez que les portes du Soleil s'ouvriront, vous vous armerez de deux os de Mort que vous mettrez en sautoir, & incontinent les jetterez sur le premier Temple ou la première Eglise qui frappera votre vue.

Then bend a knee to the ground, turning your eyes to the East, when you see the sun open the gates of dawn, take two bones of the dead enchained in the form of a cross and immediately throw them away towards the first Temple or Church that you see.

Toutes les dispositions ainsi prises, vous vous acheminerez du côté de l'Occident, & lorsque vous aurez fait quatre mille dix-neuf

All arrangements thus made, turn towards the West, and when some time has passed, lie flat on the ground, pressing your palms

cents pas vous vous coucherez par terre tout allonge, les deux pommes des mains contre cos cuisses, les yeux au ciel ; & un peu tourne du côté de la Lune. C'est dans cette posture, que vous appellerez, par son nom, celui ou celle que vous défierez de voir, en faisant attention de ne point se troubler ; lorsque vous verrez paraitre le Spectre, & vous solliciterez sa présence par les terres qui suivent :
Ego sum, te peto, et videre queo

Au moment même que vous aurez articule ces paroles, vos yeux satisfaits verront agréablement se repaitre de l'objet qui leur était le plus cher, & qui se soit leurs plus agréables délices.

Lorsque vous aurez obtenu de l'ombre que vous invoquez ce qui vous aura paru le plus propre à vous satisfaire, vous la renverrez, en lui disant :

Retourne dans le Royaume des Elus : je suis content de ta présence ;
Alors quittant la posture ou vous vous étiez mis, vous retournerez sur la même tombe, ou vous avez déjà fait une Prière, & sur laquelle

against the thighs, your eyes towards the sky, and a slight turn towards the moon. It is in this posture that you will call the name of the spirit you wish to see, being careful not to get confused when you see the apparition of the Specter and you appeal to its presence on the earth in the following words:

I am here, I seek you, & I cannot see you

At the very moment you speak these words, your eyes will be pleasantly satisfied by the appearance of that which you seek most dearly, and which was their most agreeable delight.

When you have obtained the shade you seek, and are satisfied, you may dismiss it, saying these words:

Return to the Kingdom of the Elect, I am pleased with your presence
Then, leaving your recumbent posture, return to the same tomb where you had made the Prayer, and cross yourself by the left hand

vous serez une croix de la main gauche avec la pointe de votre couteau.

with the point of your knife.

Le Lecteur n'oubliera point qu'il ne faut pas omettre la moindre circonstance de ce qui est ici préférait ; sans cela, on courrait risque de devenir soi-même la proie de toutes les puissances de l'enfer.

The reader will not forget that one must not omit a single point or slightest circumstance of what is described herein, without which we run the risk of becoming ourselves the prey of all the denizens of Hell.

DES JOURS HEUREUX ET MALHEUREUX

FORTUNATE AND UNFORTUNATE DAYS

JOURS HEREUX	MOIS	JOURS MALHEREUX
3, 10, 27, 31	Janvier	13 et 22
7, 8 et 18	Févier	2, 10, 17, 22
3, 9, 12, 14, 16	Mars	13, 19, 23, 28
5 et 27	Avril	18, 20, 29, 30
1, 2, 4, 6, 9, 14	Mai	10, 17, 20
3, 5, 7, 9, 12, 23	Juin	4 et 20
2, 6, 10, 23, 30	Juillet	5, 13, 27
5, 7, 10, 14, 19	Aout	2, 13, 27, 31
6, 10, 13, 18, 30	Sept.	13, 16, 12, 15
13, 16, 23, 31	Octob.	3, 9, 27
8, 13, 23, 30	Novem.	6 et 25
10, 20, 29	Decem.	15, 28, 31

Happy Days	Months	Unhappy Days
3, 10, 27, 31	January	13 and 22
7, 8 and 18	February	2, 10, 17, 22
3, 9, 12, 14, 16	March	13, 19, 23, 28
5 and 27	April	18, 20, 29, 30
1, 2, 4, 6, 9, 14	May	10, 17, 20
3, 5, 7, 9, 12, 23	June	4 and 20
2, 6, 10, 23, 30	July	5, 13, 27
5, 7, 10, 14, 19	August	2, 13, 27, 31
6, 10, 13, 18, 30	September	13, 16, 12, 15
13, 16, 23, 31	October	3, 9, 27
8, 13, 23, 30	November	6 and 25
10, 20, 29	December	15, 28, 31

REMARQUES

Plusieurs Savants prétendent que cette Table fut donnée à Adam par un Ange aussi était-ce la réglé de son conduit ; il ne semait ni ne transplantait rien, que dans les jours heureux, et tout lui arrivait à bon port ; si nos cultivateurs suivaient ses traces, l'abondance comblerait nos vœux.

REMARKS

Many scholars claim that this table was given by an angel to Adam, and that this was his mode of conduct, wherein he did not sow or transplant anything, except on the appropriate days, and everything had granted him. If our farmers followed in his footsteps, they would reap abundant rewards.

SECRETS DE L'ART MAGIQUE DU GRAND GRIMOIRE

SECRETS OF THE MAGICAL ART OF THE GRAND GRIMOIRE

COMPOSITION DE MORT, OU LA PIERRE PHILOSOPHALE.

THE COMPOSITION OF DEATH, OR THE PHILOSOPHER'S STONE

Rendez un pot de terre neuf, mettez-y une livre de cuivre rouge avec une demi chopine d'eau forte, que vous ferez bouillir pendant une demi-heure: après quoi vous y mettrez trois onces de vert de gris que vous ferez bouillir une heure; puis vous mettrez deux onces et demie d'arsenic que vous ferez bouillir une heure; vous y mettrez trois onces d'écorce de chêne, bien pulvérisée, que vous laisserez bouillir une demi-heure, une potée d'eau rose bouillir douze minutes, trois onces de noir de fumée que vous laisserez bouillir jusqu'à ce que la composition soit bonne; pour voir si elle est assez cuite, il faut y

Place a pound of red copper in a new earthenware pot with a half-pint of fortified water. Boil for half an hour, then add three ounces of verdigris and boil for another hour. Then add two and a half ounces of arsenic, boiled for an hour, followed by three ounces of powdered oak bark, that you will let boil for half an hour, a pot of rose water boiled for twelve minutes, three ounces of lamp black boiled until it is of a glossy composition. To check if it is well-cooked, soak a nail in the pot: If it cloys to the liquid, take it off the flame. This should produce a pound and a half of pure gold, and if it doesn't render any outcome, this indicates the liquor is not fully

tremper un clou: si elle y prend, ôtez-la; elle vous procurera une livre et demie de bon or; et si elle n'y prend point, c'est une preuve qu'elle n'est pas assez cuite; la liqueur peut servir quatre fois.

cooked. The liquor can be used to produce results four times before it is used up.

POUR FAIRE LA BAGUETTE DIVINATOIRE ET LA FAIRE TOURNER :

Dès le moment que le soleil parait sur l'horizon, vous prenez de la main gauche une baguette vierge de noisetier sauvage et la coupez de la droite en trois coups, en disant: Je te ramasse au nom d'Eloim, Mutrathon, Adonay et Semiphoras, afin que tu aies la vertu de la verge de Moïse et de Jacob, pour découvrir tout ce que je voudrai savoir; et pour la faire tourner, il faut dire, la tenant serrée dans ses mains par les deux bouts qui font la fourche: *Je te recommande au nom d'Eloim, Matrathon, Adonay et Semiphoras de me relever....*

TO PREPARE THE DIVINING ROD AND TO MAKE IT WORK

When the sun appears on the horizon, take in your left hand a branch of virgin wild hazel and cut in three strokes, while saying "I collect you in the name of Elohim, Metatron, Adonai and Semiphoras, so that you may have the virtue of the rod of Moses and of Jacob, to discover all that I wish to know. " To make it work, hold the rod tightly in your hands by the forked end and say, *"I command you in the name of Elohim, Metatron, Adonai and Semiphoras to reveal to me, etc."*

POUR GAGNER TOUTES LES FOIS QU'ON MET AUX LOTERIES

TO WIN ALL LOTTERIES THAT ONE MIGHT PLACE BETS ON

Il faut, avant de se coucher, réciter trois fois cette oraison, après quoi vous la mettrez sous l'oreille, écrite sur du parchemin vierge, sur lequel vous aurez fait dire une messe du St-Esprit, et pendant le sommeil le génie de votre Planète vient vous dire l'heure que vous devez prendre votre billet.

Before going to bed, recite the following prayer thrice, and place it under your ear, written on virgin parchment that has been blessed during a mass of the Holy Ghost. During sleep, the Genius of your Planet will tell you the hour in which you should buy your lottery ticket.

ORAISON

Domine Jesu Christe, qui dixisti ego sum via, veritas et vita, ecce enim veritatem dilexisti, incerta et occulta sapientiæ tuæ manifestasti mihi, adhuc quæ reveles in hac nocte sicut ita revelatum fuit parvulis solis, incognita et ventura unaque alia me doceas, ut possim omnia cognoscere, si et si sit; ita monstra mihi montem ornatum omni nivo bono, pulchrum et gratum pomarium, aut quandam rem gratam, sin autem ministra mihi ignem ardentem, vel aquarum currentem vel aliam quamcumque rem quæ Domino

PRAYER

O Lord Jesus Christ, who has said I am The Way, The Truth and The Life, behold, you desire truth in the inward parts, and in your occult wisdom that you have made manifest to me, and revealed to me like the sun, and along with other things, you have taught the unknown and revealed things to come, in order that I may know all things, if they exist. So, show me the mountain adorned with all good and pleasing things, like an orchard, and if they serve me, the flames or running water or whatever the Lord pleases and of the Angels Ariel, Rubiel and Barachiel, may I have many who

placeant, et vel Angeli Ariel, Rubiel et Barachiel sitis mihi multúm amatores et factores ad opus istud obtinendum quod cupio scire, videre cognoscere et prævidere per illum Deum qui venturus est judicare vivos et mortuos, et sæculum per ignem. Amen.

Vous direz trois Pater et trois Ave, Maria pour les amés du purgatoire.

love and work to grant me what I want to know and learn, through the providence of the living God who comes to judge the living and the dead, and everlasting fire, Amen

Say three Our Fathers and three Hail Mary's for the souls in purgatory

POUR CHARMER LES ARMES A FEU :

Il faut dire: Dieu y ait part et le diable la sortie, et lorsqu' on met en joue, il faut dire en croisant la jambe gauche sur la droite: non tradas Dominum nostrum Jesum Christum. Mathon. Amen.

TO ENCHANT FIREARMS:

Say: God has the power and the Devil does not, and when you fire, say the following while crossing your left arm over the right: You cannot pass our Lord, Jesus Christ. Mathon. Amen

POUR PARLER AUX ESPRITS LA VEILLE DE LA ST. JEAN-BAPTISTE :

Il faut se transporter depuis les onze heures jusqu'à minuit près d'un pied de fougère, et dire: Je prie Dieu que les esprits à qui je souhaite parler apparaissent à

TO SPEAK WITH SPIRITS ON THE EVE OF ST. JOHN THE BAPTIST:

Go near a stem of bracken fern between 11 PM and midnight and say: "I pray to God that the spirits with whom I wish to speak appear to me at midnight."

minuit précis; et aux trois-quarts vous direz neuf fois ces cinq paroles: *Bar, Kirabar, Alli, Alla Tetragamaton*

At 11:45 PM, say the following five words nine times: *Bar, Kirabar, Alli, Alla, Tetragrammaton*

POUR SE FAIRE AIMER DE TELLE FILLE OU FEMME QUE VOUS VOUDREZ

TO BE ABLE TO LOVE WHICHEVER GIRL OR WOMAN YOU WISH:

Il faut dire en ramassant l'herbe des neuf chemises, dite concorda: Je te ramasse au nom de Scheva pour que tu me serves à m'attacher l'amitié de (nommez la personne), et ensuite vous mettrez ladite herbe sur la personne, sans qu'elle ne le sache ni qu'elle s'en aperçoive, et aussitôt elle vous aimera.

While picking an Alpine Leek (Victory Onion or *allium victorialis*), say the following words: "I gather you in the name of Sheba so that you serve me by granting me the love of <Name>".
Then put this herb on the intended person, without her noticing it, and she will immediately love you.

POUR FAIRE DANSER TOUT NU :

TO COMPEL ONE TO DANCE NAKED:

Il faut ramasser la veille de la saint Jean-Baptiste, à minuit, trois feuilles de noyer, trois plantes de marjolaine, trois plantes de mirthe et trois plantes de verveine, faire sécher le tout à l'ombre, le mettre en poudre et en jeter comme une petite pincée de tabac en l'air dans la chambre où sont les personnes que l'on veut jouer.

On the eve of St. John the Baptist, at midnight, gather three walnut leaves, three marjoram plants, three myrtle plants and three verbena plants. Dry them in the shade and grind into a powder. Throw some into the air like a pinch of tobacco in the room with the people whom you wish to play with.

POUR SE RENDRE INVISIBLE :

Vous volerez un chat noir, et achèterez un pot neuf, un miroir, un briquet, une pierre d'agathe, du charbon et de l'amadou, observant d'aller prendre de l'eau au coup de minuit à une fontaine, après quoi vous allumez votre feu, mettez le chat dans le pot, et tenez le couvert de la main gauche sans bouger ni regarder derrière vous, quelque bruit que vous entendiez; et après l'avoir fait bouillir 24 heures vous le mettez dans un plat neuf; prenez la viande et la jetez pardessus l'épaule gauche, en disant ces paroles: *accipe quod tibi do, et nihil ampliùs*; puis vous mettrez les os un à un sous les dents du côté gauche, en vous regardant dans le miroir; et si ce n'est pas le bon, vous le jetterez de même, en disant les mêmes paroles jusqu'à ce que vous l'ayez trouvé; et sitôt que vous ne vous verrez plus dans le miroir, retirez-vous à reculons en disant: *Pater, in manus tuas commendo spiritum meum*

TO MAKE ONESELF INVISIBLE:

Steal a black cat, and buy a new pot, a mirror, a briquette, an agate stone, coal and tinder. Take water at the stroke of midnight from a fountain. Then light your fire, place the cat in the pot and hold it covered with your left hand without moving or looking behind you, no matter what sounds you might hear. Then boil it for 24 hours and place it on a new plate. Take the meat and throw it over your left shoulder, while saying the following words: Take what you need and do nothing else. Then place the bones under the teeth one by one, while looking at yourself in the mirror. If this does not seem right, throw them over your left shoulder, while saying the same words until you find it, and until your reflection disappears. Retreat backwards, saying: *Father, into your hands, I give my spirit.*

POUR FAIRE LA JARRETIERE DE SEPT LIEUES PAR HEURE

Vous achèterez un jeune loup au-dessous d'un an, que vous égorgerez avec un couteau neuf, à l'heure de Mars, en prononçant ces paroles : *Adhumatis cados ambulavit in fortitudine cibi ilius;* puis vous couperez sa peau en jarretières larges d'un pouce, et y écrirez dessus les mêmes paroles que vous avez dites en l'égorgeant, savoir, la première lettre de votre sang, la seconde de celui du loup, et immédiatement de même jusqu'à la fin de la phrase.

Après qu'elle est écrite et sèche, il faut la doubler avec un padoue de fil blanc, et attacher deux rubans violets aux deux bouts pour la nouer du dessus du genou au-dessous ; il faut aussi bien prendre garde qu'aucune femme ou fille ne la voie point: comme aussi la quitter avant de passer une rivière, sans quoi elle ne serait plus si forte.

TO MAKE THE SEVEN-LEAGUE GARTERS

Buy a young wolf, less than a year old, and cut its throat with a new knife, in the hour of Mars, while saying the following words: *Adhumatis cados ambulavit in fortitudine cibi ilius* (Adhumatis falls, walking luckily with food) Then skin the wolf and slice the skin into one-inch thick garters. Write the same words as above on the garters– the first letter in your own blood, the second with the wolf's blood, and so on, until the end of the phrase.

After you have written the words, and they have dried, line them with white Paduan thread, and attach two violet ribbons to tie them from the top of the knees to the bottom. It is important that no woman or girl see the garters, and to remove them before crossing a river, or else they will lose their strength.

COMPOSITION DE L'EMPLATRE POUR FAIRE DIX LIEUES PAR HEURE

Prenez deux onces de graisse humaine, Une once d'huile de cerf, Une once d'huile de laurier, Une once de graisse de cerf, Une once de momie naturelle, Une demi-chopine d'esprit de vin, Et sept feuilles de verveine. Vous ferez bouillir le tout dans un pot neuf, jusqu'à demi-réduction, puis en formez les emplâtres sur de la peau neuve, et lorsque vous les appliquez sur la rate, vous allez comme le vent ; pour n'être point malade quand vous le quittez, il faut prendre trois gouttes de sang dans un verre de vin blanc.

COMPOSITION OF THE PLASTER TO COVER TEN LEAGUES AN HOUR:

Take two ounces of human fat, an ounce of deer oil, an ounce of laurel oil, an ounce of deer fat, an ounce of natural mummy, a half-pint of wine and seven leaves of verbena. Boil all of this in a new pot, until half-reduced, then make the plaster on a new skin, and when you apply this on the spleen, you will go like the wind. So as not to be sick when you take this off, have three drops of blood in a glass of white wine.

COMPOSITION DE L'ENCRE POUR ECRIRE LES PACTES

Les pactes ne doivent point être écrits avec l'encre ordinaire. Chaque fois qu'on fait une appellation à l'esprit, on doit en changer, Mettez dans un pot de terre vernissé neuf, de l'eau de rivière et la poudre décrite ci-

COMPOSITION OF THE INK FOR WRITING PACTS

The pacts must not be written with ordinary ink. Every time one intends to conjure a spirit, prepare fresh ink. Mix river water and the following powder in a new glazed clay pot. Take fern branches picked on the eve of St. John, vine

après. Alors prenez des branches de fougère cueillies la veille de la S. Jean, du sarment coupé en pleine lune de mars ; allumez ce bois avec du papier vierge, et dès que votre eau bouillera, votre encre sera faite. Observez bien d'en changer à chaque nouvelle écriture que vous aurez à faire. Prenez dix onces de noix de galle, et trois onces de vitriol romain, ou couperose verte ; d'alun de roche ou de gomme arabique, deux onces de chaque ; mettez le tout en poudre impalpable, dont, lorsque vous voudrez faire de l'encre, vous préparerez comme il est dit ci-dessus.

branches cut on the full moon in March. Kindle this wood with virgin parchment, and when the water boils, your ink will be made. Remember to prepare a fresh batch whenever it is needed. For the powder, take ten ounces of gallnuts, three ounces of copper sulfate (Roman Vitriol), two ounces each of rock alum and gum Arabic. Grind all the ingredients into a fine powder, then use this when needed in the preparation of the ink for writing Pacts.

ENCRE POUR NOTER LES SOMMES QU'ON PRENDRA DANS LES TRESORS CACHES, ET POUR EN DEMANDER DE PLUS FORTES A LUCIFUGE, DANS LES NOUVEAUX BESOINS.

INK TO NOTE THE AMOUNTS TAKEN FROM HIDDEN TREASURE, AND TO ASK FOR MORE FROM LUCIFUGE, WHEN THERE IS NEED:

Prenez des noyaux de pèches, sans en ôter les amendes, mette-les dans le feu pour les réduire en

Take peach kernels, without removing the fine hair, and put them into the fire to reduce them to charcoal. Take one part of this charcoal, mixed with soot, and

charbons bien brûlés, alors retirez-les, et lorsqu'ils sont bien noirs, prenez en une partie que vous mêlerez avec autant de noir de fumée, ajoutez-y deux parties de noix de galle concassées ; faites dans l'huile desséchée, de gomme arabique quatre parties ; que le tout soit mis en poudre très fine, et passé par le tamis. Mettez cette poudre dans de l'eau de rivière. Il est inutile de faire remarquer que tous les objets décrits ci-dessus doivent être absolument neufs.

blend with two parts of crushed gallnuts, dried grease and four parts of gum Arabic, to be ground into a fine powder that is sieved and then dissolved in river water. Ensure that all these items are absolutely new and pristine.

Lecteur bénévole, pénètre-toi bien de tout ce que le grand Salomon vient de t'enseigner par mon organe. Sois sage comme lui, si tu veux que toutes les richesses que je viens de mettre en ton pouvoir puissent faire ta félicité. Sois humain envers tes semblables, soulage les malheureux ; vis content.

Dear reader, consider well all that the Great Solomon has written by my hand. Be wise like him, if you wish to have all the wealth that I have the power to grant for your happiness. Be humane to your fellowmen, comfort the unfortunate, live content.

Adieu

Goodbye

APPENDIX – The Red Dragon – A novel

THE RED DRAGON

Or THE ART OF CONJURING SPIRITS
DEMONSTRATED by Facts & Examples
by M. Robville

LE DRAGON ROUGE

THE RED DRAGON

Ceci se passait dans un village de Provence, huit Jours avant la Saint-Jean.

This happened in a village in Provence, eight days before the feast of St. John.

On avait moissonné pendant la journée les blés du Père Michu, et tous les gens de la ferme, rassemblés dans la salle commune, achevaient le repas du soir. Après un dernier coup de piquette, les femmes se mirent à quelque travail de couture, les hommes allumèrent leur pipe et ta conversation s'engagea.

Father Michu's wheat had been harvested during the day. All the people of the farm assembled in the common room for the evening meal. After a final cup of punch, the women began some sewing work, and the men lit their pipes and engaged in conversation.

Parmi les assistants se trouvait un jeune garçon à la mine naïve, à l'air timide, que les filles regardaient parfois en souriant, et qui ne parlait qu'avec une sorte d'hésitation. Il montrait, en un mot, tous les signes d'un caractère faible, d'une intelligence, sinon bornée, du moins peu développée pour son âge, car il avait près de vingt ans.

Among the assistants was a shy young man, with a timid air, whom the girls sometimes regarded with a smile, and who never spoke without a bit of hesitation. He showed, in brief, all the indications of a weak character, of an intelligence, if not limited, at least somewhat underdeveloped for his age, which was nearly twenty years old.

On l'appelait Claude Michu, c'était le fils du fermier.

His name was Claude Michu, the son of the farmer.

Il faut le dire, si Claude n'avait rien de l'assurance virile, c'est que de tout temps il s'était vu l'objet des quolibets et des railleries de ses camarades. Habitué à servir de point de mire aux moqueurs, plein de défiance à l'égard de sa propre force, il s'était résigné longtemps à ce rôle de souffre-douleur qu'on lui avait imposé depuis l'enfance.

It must be said, if Claude had none of the manly assurance, this was because he often faced taunts and quibbles from his comrades. He was used to being the target of ridicule from scoffers and had long resigned himself to the role of scapegoat that had been imposed on him since childhood.

Du reste, laid, grêle et chétif comme il était, il ne pouvait guère triompher de sa destinée et parfois il se prenait à songer qu'un prodige seul serait capable de lui rendre sa valeur morale.

Besides, ugly, spindly and puny as he was, he could hardly triumph over his destiny and sometimes he began to think that a single prodigious event might restore his moral value.

Il avait voulu dire quelques douceurs aux fillettes du voisinage, elles lui avaient ri au nez ; il s'était mis, en tête de faire des expériences agricoles, suivant, les données d'un livre spécial, et aucune de ces expériences n'avait réussi.

He had wanted to say a few sweet words to the neighborhood girls, but they had laughed at him. He had started some agricultural experiments, following the data from a special book, but none of these experiences had succeeded.

Enfin Claude était ce qu'on appelle un homme poursuivi par la mauvaise chance.

Finally, one might say that Claude was a man pursued by bad luck.

En y réfléchissant bien, on aurait vu que cette prétendue mauvaise chance venait tout

Reflecting on it, we would have seen that this alleged bad luck was quite simply due to the

simplement de la fausse direction imprimée à l'esprit du jeune, homme, de sa mollesse intellectuelle et de sa grande hésitation dans toutes les circonstances ; mais on ne s'avise pas de tout.

Quoi qu'il en fût, Claude en était venu à se persuader qu'il serait toujours malheureux, toujours faible, toujours bafoué par les unes, battu par les autres, et finalement qu'on lui avait jeté un sort.

Cette croyance était le résultat naturel de la naïveté de son esprit.

Quand elle lui fut entrée dans la cervelle, il n'eut plus d'autre désir que de combattre ce fameux sort dont il était victime ; mais pour le combattre, il fallait, à son avis, beaucoup découragé, beaucoup d'audace, et Claude sentait bien que ces deux qualités-là n'étaient point de son fait.

On va voir, pourtant, comment il se décida à se révolter contre tous les déboires dont il était incessamment abreuvé.

wrong influences on the young person's mind, his intellectual weakness and his great hesitation in all circumstances, but that was not all.

Whatever might be the reason, Claude had come to convince himself that he would always be unhappy, always weak, always ridiculed by some, beaten by others, and finally that a spell had been cast upon him.

This annoyance was the natural result of the naivety of his spirit.

When his spirit entered his brain, he no longer wished to fight this spell of which he was the victim, but to fight it, he needed, in his opinion, a lot of courage and audacity, and Claude felt that he was severely lacking in these two qualities.

We will see, however, how he decided to revolt against all these setbacks that incessantly swamped him.

La soirée touchait à sa fin lorsque la porte de la ferme s'ouvrit et livra passage à un petit vieillard à l'aspect étrange et à l'accoutrement bizarre.

The evening was coming to an end when the gate of the farm opened and gave passage to a little old man with a strange aspect and bizarre outfit.

Ce vieillard faisait ouvertement profession de berger, mais il était connu dans le pays pour un sorcier qui en savait long, disaient les bonnes femmes en hochant la tête, et qui d'un mot pouvait changer la montagne en plaine et la plaine en montagne, au gré de son caprice,

This old man professed to be a shepherd, but he was known in the region as a wise sorcerer, who at a word could change the mountain to the plain and the plain to the mountain, by his whim, according to the good women, who said this while shaking their heads,

La vérité, c'est que Simounen (ainsi se nommait le sorcier) était une fin matoise vivant sur la crédulité des paysans qui garnissaient sa bourse de beaux écus et lui faisaient des revenus avec leur sottise.

The truth was that Simounen (as the sorcerer called himself) was a wily old man living on the credulity of the peasants who stocked his purse with fine crowns and made his income from their foolishness.

Bon compagnon, gai conteur sachant par cœur tous les noëls et toutes les rondes de Provence. Simounen était reçu partout avec plaisir, peut être avec crainte par certains, car sa réputation d'ensorceleur ne manquait pas de causer quelque inquiétude aux faibles cervelles de l'endroit.

He was a good companion, cheerful storyteller who knew by heart all the songs and tales of Provence. Simounen was received everywhere with pleasure, perhaps with fear because of his reputation as a sorcerer, which did not fail to cause fear in the weak brains of the local people.

Quand il parut dans la maison du père Michu, les filles, qui le

When he appeared at Father Michu's home, the girls, who

connaissaient bien pour lui avoir maintes fois acheté des talismans ou des charmes, le saluèrent joyeusement.

« Bon ! » s'écria Madeloun, une jolie brune, que Claude aimait depuis longtemps et qu'il voulait épouser, sans avoir jamais en le courage de le lui dire, dans la crainte d'une moquerie, « bon, voilà le père Simounen qui va nous raconter une histoire. «

« Je ne dis pas non, petite, » répliqua le berger, qu'est-ce que tu veux que je raconte ? »

« Racontez-nous la légende du Trou-Noir. C'est très-intéressant et ça fait peur »

« Oui ! » Crièrent toutes les voix, « la légende du Trou-Noir ! »

« Bon, écoutez-moi donc, et ne soufflez mot, je n'aime pas qu'on m'interrompe. »

Le cercle des auditeurs se serra autour de Simounen, et le vieillard commença ainsi :

« C'était au temps où la Provence ne s'appelait pas encore la Provence ; il y a de cela plus

knew him well, and often bought talismans and charms from him, greeted him with pleasure.

"Well", cried Madeleine, a pretty brunette whom Claude had loved for a long time and wanted to marry, without having the courage to do it, "Well, that is Father Simounen who will tell us a tale!"

"I won't refuse, little one," replied the shepherd, "What would you have me recount?"

"Tell us the legend of the Black Hole. It is very interesting and scary."

"Yes!" cried all the voices, "the legend of the Black Hole!"

"Fine, listen to me closely, and do not breathe a word, I do not like to be interrupted."

The circle of listeners huddled around Simounen, and the old man began thus:

"This was a time when Provence was not called so, over a thousand years ago. In this

221

mille ans, vivaient alors, dans ce pays-ci, deux frères qui habitaient ensemble avec leur père un vieux château sur la montagne. L'un s'appelai Jehan, l'autre André. André, le cadet, était aussi méchant, que son frère Jehan était bon : cependant il ne laissa rien voir de son mauvais cœur, jusqu'au jour où son vieux père fut sur le point de mourir.

country, two brothers lived together with their father in an old castle on the mountain. The first was called Jehan, the other Andre. Andre, the youngest, was as mean as his brother Jehan was good. Andre left nothing unseen from his evil heart, until the day that his old father was at the point of death.

Alors la jalousie s'empara de lui. Il savait que son frère, suivant les habitudes du temps, allait hériter de toute la fortune et de tous les titres paternels, et que lui. André, ne serait plus dans le château que te premier serviteur de Jehan.

Then jealousy seized him. He knew that his brother, following the habits of the time, was going to inherit all the fortune and all the paternal titles, and that he, Andre, would be no better than the first servant of Jehan in the castle.

Il résolut vite de tuer son aîné et de rester ainsi seul possesseur de tous les biens.

He quickly resolved to kill his elder brother and thus stay the sole possessor of everything.

Une nuit donc, pendant que tout dormait, il s'avança doucement jusqu'à la chambre de son frère, et s'étant jeté comme un loup sur ce dernier, il lui perça la poitrine avec un poignard. Le pauvre Jehan fit : Ah ! et mourut :

One night, while everyone was asleep, he crept slowly to his brother's room, and having thrown himself like a wolf on the latter, stabbed him in the chest with a dagger. The poor Jehan cried 'Ah!' and died.

Puis le meurtrier se sauva dans la tour qu'il habitait et attendit le jour.

Then the murderer hid himself in his tower and awaited the day.

Quand il apprit le lendemain matin ce qui s'était passé, le père des deux jeunes gens expira de chagrin, et André eut ce qu'il avait tant souhaité, la fortune et les honneurs ; car, personne n'ayant osé le soupçonner, on crut que Jehan avait été assassiné par des voleurs qui désolaient alors la contrée. Tel fut, du moins, le bruit que fit répandre le nouveau seigneur.

Et comme il était justement redouté dans son domaine, aucun n'osa le contredire.

Vous croyez qu'il vécut tranquille peut-être, comme cela arrive à bien des coupables ? Non. Si la justice des hommes n'avait pu l'atteindre, celle de Dieu ne lui manque pas.

Juste un an après la mort de son père et de son frère, par une soirée d'hiver où la bise soufflait à déraciner les rochers, le seigneur André était seul dans sa chambre.

Il avait reçu, dans la journée, le montant des dîmes en argent qu'il prélevait sur ses tenanciers, et voulant les mettre en sûreté, il

The next morning, when he learned what had happened, the father of the two young men expired in sorrow, and Andre had what he had wished for so much, the fortune and the honors. Because, no one dared to suspect it, it was believed that Jehan had been assassinated by the thieves who frequented the country. Such was, at least, the rumor that the new lord spread about.

As he was rightly feared in his domain, none dared contradict him.

You believe that he lived a tranquil life, perhaps, as happens to many guilty people? It was not to be so. If the justice of men did not reach him, that of God did not fail.

A year after the death of his father and brother, on a winter evening when the wind blew strong and almost uprooted the rocks, Lord Andre was alone in his room.

In the day, he had received his tenants' rents, and wishing to put them away safely, he had opened the family treasure chest which

avait ouvert le trésor de sa famille où se trouvaient entassés des tonnes gorgées d'or, des corbeilles pleines de diamants et de perles, et de grands coffres emplis jusqu'au couvercle de lingots d'argent.

was piled up with tons of gold, baskets of diamonds and pearls, and large boxes filled to the brim with silver ingots.

Ces richesses merveilleuses, il les contemplait avec orgueil et s'applaudissait du coup qui l'en avait rendu le maître, lorsqu'il entendit au fond de la salle du trésor comme un soupir prolongé.

He contemplated these riches with pride and congratulated himself on the blow that had made him their master, when he heard an extended sigh at the end of the treasure chamber.

Son sang se glaça dans ses veines et il eut à peine la force de regarder devant lui.

His blood froze in his veins and he hardly had the strength to look in front of him.

Tout à coup, une voix l'appela à deux reprises :
— André ! André !

Suddenly, a voice called out to him twice
"Andre! Andre!"

Alors, il se hasarda à jeter les yeux vers le fond de la pièce, et soudain il poussa un cri de terreur.

He ventured his eyes to the end of the room, and suddenly uttered a cry of terror.

Son père était devant lui. Et à côté de son père se tenait Jehan assassiné, portant encore dans la poitrine les deux trous rouges qu'y avait faits le poignard d'André.

His father stood before him, and by his side was the assassinated Jehan, still bearing two red holes in his chest chiseled by Andre's dagger.

— Mon père ! mon frère ! cria le meurtrier ; Grâce ! grâce !

"My father! My father" cried the murderer. "Thanks be to God! Thanks!"

Il tomba à genoux devant les deux spectres immobiles et menaçants.

He fell to his knees before the two motionless and menacing specters.

Et la bise au dehors se mit à souffler plus glaciale et plus violente, et les murs du château tremblèrent jusque dans leurs fondements.

The wind outside began to blow more icy and violent and the walls of the castle trembled in their foundations.

— Grâce, répéta le misérable.

"Thanks be to God," repeated the miserable wretch.

— Dieu t'a jugé, ton heure est venue, prononça lentement le spectre de Jehan. Dieu t'avait donné un an pour te repentir, et tu n'as pas un seul instant maudit ton crime. Meurent donc avec toi et les honneurs dont la source est maudite, et les richesses mal acquises, et ce château que lu as souillé.

"God has judged you, your hour has come," the specter of Jehan pronounced slowly. "God gave you one year to repent, and you have not cursed your crime for one moment. You must die, therefore, with all your cursed honors and the ill-acquired riches, and this castle which you have defiled."

Alors, les deux ombres s'attachèrent aux deux piliers qui soutenaient la salle, et tandis qu'ils les secouaient comme un arbre dont on veut faire tomber les fruits, le vent d'hiver redoublait de rage, et les tours, et les remparts du château vacillaient, sous ses attaques, comme dos échalas mal plantés.

The two shades attached themselves to the two pillars which supported the room. As they shook them as if to bring down their fruits, the wind redoubled its rage and the ramparts of the castle trembled under its attacks, like weakly planted stalks.

Bientôt. André entendit autour de lui des cris surhumains, des hurlements de démons déchaînés : les spectres le regardèrent avec des yeux flamboyants, et soudain les deux piliers de la voûte s'abattirent ; un grand bruit de pierres roulant sur leurs assises retentit ; le sol sur lequel était bâti le château s'effondra, et murailles, tours, or, argent, diamants et richesses de toutes sortes s'engouffrèrent dans la terre avec leur indigne possesseur.

Soon, Andre heard the cries of superhuman demons around him – the spirits looked at him with flaming eyes, and suddenly the two pillars fell down, a great rolling sound was heard and the soil on which the castle stood collapsed and the towers, walls, gold, silver, diamonds and all sorts of riches were engulfed in the earth along with their unworthy possessor.

Là où fut naguère une montagne venait de s'ouvrir un profond abîme ; c'est ce qu'on appelle aujourd'hui le Trou-Noir.

Where once there was a mountain, now opened into a profound abyss. This is what is called the Black Hole today.

Le conteur s'arrêta.

The storyteller stopped.

Claude Michu l'avait écouté avec un intérêt mêlé d'effroi.

Claude Michu had been listening with interest, mixed with terror.

Quant à Madeloun, elle n'avait pas perdu un mot du récit ; pourtant, elle ne déclara pas encore sa curiosité satisfaite.

As for Madeleine, she had not missed a single word of the story, yet she did not declare her curiosity satisfied.

— Père Simounen dit-elle, vous n'avez pas fini. Est-ce qu'il ne court pas dans le pays des bruits terribles sur le Trou-Noir ?

"Father Simounen," she said, "You have not finished. Does one not hear terrible sounds in the region of the Black Hole?"

— Si, ma fille ; on dit qu'à certains jours les démons font leur sabbat au lieu où sont enfouis le corps, le château elles trésors d'André le fratricide.

—On dit aussi, n'est-ce pas, reprit Madeloun, que bien des gens ont voulu conjurer les esprits du Trou Noir et chercher te trésor qui est caché ?

— C'est vrai.

— Mais & ce qu'on affirme, aucun n'a réussi,

—On peut donc, hasarda Claude timidement, conjurer ainsi les dénions et s'approprier les trésors dont ils sont gardiens ?

— Sans doute, fit Madeloun ; mais pour cela il faut être très savant et très courageux. A ce compte, ce n'est pas toi qui pourrais aller au Trou-Noir, mon pauvre Claude.

Claude ne répondit pas à Madeloun, mais interrogeant de nouveau le sorcier :

— À quelle époque entend-on ces bruits de sabbat ?

"Yes, my child. It is said that on some days, the demons make their Sabbath at the place where is buried the body, the castle and the treasures of Andre, the fratricide."

"They also say, don't they," replied Madeleine, "that many people want to conjure the spirits of the Black Hole & search for the hidden treasure?"

"That is true."

"But it is said, none have succeeded."

"One might," ventured Claude timidly, "conjure the demons and appropriate the treasure they guard?"

"No doubt," said Madeleine, "but for that he must be very learned and courageous. As such, it should be anyone but you who should go to the Black Hole, my poor Claude."

Claude did not reply to Madeleine, but questioning once again the sorcerer,

"On which days do we hear these sounds of the Devils' Sabbath?"

— A la Noël, à la Toussaint, et pendant la nuit de la Saint-Jean, répondit Simounen, qui attacha sur le visage de son crédule auditeur un regard plein de malice.

"On Christmas, All Saints Day and during the night of St. John," replied Simounen, who had a malicious look on his face at the sight of his credulous listener.

—La Saint-Jean ! c'est dans huit jours, murmura Claude. Et que fait-on, maître Simounen, pour conjurer les démons et avoir le trésor ?

"The Feast of St. John! That is in eight days," murmured Claude. "What else, Master Simounen, must one do to conjure the demons and possess the treasure?"

—Tu en veux trop savoir, petit. Pour apprendre ces choses-là, ça coule gros, et encore ne les apprend pas qui veut.

"You want to know too much too soon, my little child. This knowledge has a high cost and one may still not fathom what is needed."

Ce disant, le berger cligna de l'œil comme pour dire : « Tout cela, je le sais, moi, et je n'en suis pas plus fier. »

Saying so, the shepherd closed his eye in a wink, as if to say, "I know all this myself, and yet I'm not proud."

Le rusé compère avait flairé dans Claude Michel une dupe facile, et à tout événement, il préparait son terrain. Pendant ce temps-là, Claude, qui était timide surtout par crainte des railleries de ses camarades et se sentait plus fort quand il pensait et agissait isolément.

The wily player had sniffed out in Claude Michele an easy dupe, and at any event he was preparing his ground. Meanwhile, Claude, who was timid by nature, and afraid of being taunted by his comrades, felt braver when he thought and acted alone.

Claude réfléchit que posséder

If he possessed the treasure of

le trésor du Trou-Noir. Ce serait gagner tout d'un coup la considération, le respect des hommes, les sourires des filles, et se débarrasser à tout jamais, grâce à l'aplomb que donne la richesse, de celte faiblesse, ridicule qui l'empêchait d'avouer son amour à Madeloun et de lui demander sa main.

Pour la première fois de sa vie, il se sentit du courage et résolut de tenter la terrible épreuve dont avait parlé Simounen,

Pour cela, il lui fallait gagner la confiance du vieux sorcier et lui arracher même à prix d'argent, le secret de la conjuration qui devait rendre les démons du Trou-Noir dociles à son désir.

Ceci montre à quel point de crédulité te défaut de raisonnement peut pousser un homme et quelle riche mine à escroqueries doivent offrir aux aventuriers de la race de Simounen les bonnes bêtes du genre de Claude Michu.

Quand le berger quitta la ferme, il était dix heures du soir.

the Black Hole, Claude believed he would suddenly win the appreciation and respect of all men, the smiles of the girls, and thanks to the strength of wealth, he would be forever rid of that weakness and ridiculousness that prevented him from confessing his love for Madeleine and be able to ask for her hand.

For the first time in his life, he felt the courage and resoluteness to venture on the terrible ordeal of which Simounen had spoken.

For that, he needed to gain the confidence of the old wizard and induce from him even at a high price the secret of conjuration which would render the demons of the Black Hole submissive to his desires.

This demonstrates the extent of credulity and lack of reasoning that a man can be pushed to and the kind of swindling notions that could be pushed by adventurers such as Simounen on the good beasts of the ilk of Claude Michu.

When the shepherd left the farm, it was ten P.M. in the evening.

Il s'engageait dans un chemin creux conduisant aux premières pentes de la montagne où il avait bâti sa cabane, lorsqu'il entendit derrière lui des pas précipites.

—Bon, dit-il en s'arrêtant, l'histoire da trésor a produit son effet ; voilà mon homme.

Simounen ne se trompait pas : presque aussitôt la voix essoufflée de Claude se fit entendre.

— Père Simounen ! Père Simounen !

— C'est toi Claude que l'arrive-t-il. Mon garçon ? fit le sorcier avec un feint étonnement.

— J'ai à vous parler, père Simounen. Et comme le ne voulais pas le taire devant tout le monde, je vous ai suivi jusqu'ici.

— J'ai à vous parler, père Simounen. Et comme le ne voulais pas le taire devant tout le monde, je vous ai suivi jusqu'ici.

—Bon, explique-toi.

He was at the foot of a sunken road leading to the first slopes of the mountain where he had constructed his hut, when he heard behind him a call to stop.

"Good," he mused while pausing. "The history of the treasure has produced the desired effect – there is my fine man."

Simounen was not mistaken – almost instantly, he heard the breathless voice of Claude behind him.

"Father Simounen! Father Simounen!"

"Is that you, Claude, my boy?" asked the sorcerer with a false note of astonishment.

"I wanted to speak with you, father Simounen. And I did not want to speak in front of everyone, I have followed you here."

"I wanted to speak with you, father Simounen. And I did not want to speak in front of everyone, I have followed you here."

"Well, explain yourself."

— C'est que c'est bien difficile...

"It's very difficult…"

—Allons, tu as peur ? Eh bien ! je vais t'éviter la peine de parler ; je vais te dire ce que Lu me veut.

"Come, are you afraid? Well! I will spare you the difficulty of speaking. I'll tell you what you want from me."

—Vous ? murmura Claude déjà épouvanté de cette pénétration du vieux berger ; pénétration facile à expliquer d'après ce qui s'était passé à la veillée,

"You?" whispered Claude, already terrified of the sharp insight of the old shepherd, although it was easy enough to explain after what had happened at the evening affair.

—Moi ! répéta le vieillard d'un ton solennel.

"Me!" repeated the old man in a solemn tone.

Ecoute : Tu sais que je m'occupe de ces sciences terribles, inconnues aux autres hommes ; l'histoire du trésor du Trou-Noir t'a alléché, et tu viens me demander le secret qui doit t'en assurer la possession

"Listen: You know that I deal with these terrible sciences, unknown to most men. The history of the treasure of the Black Hole tempts you, and you come to me to know the secrets that will assure you its possession."

—Comment savez-vous cela ?

"How do you know that?"

—Je sais tout ce que je veux ; je peux tout ce que je désire, mon garçon, reprit le sorcier affectant une intonation de plus en plus grave.

"I know everything that I choose to discover. I can do anything I desire, my boy," replied the sorcerer, adopting a graver tone.

—Ainsi vous consentiriez...

"So, you would consent…"

231

—A t'apprendre la conjuration des démons.

"To teach you the art of conjuration of demons."

—Oui, si tu as du courage ; non si tu as peur.

"Yes, if you have the courage, but not if you are afraid."

—Je n'aurai pas peur.

"I will not be afraid."

—Tu n'as pourtant pas l'air d'un brave.

"But you do not look like a brave man."

—Ça ne fait rien. Quand on n'est point là pour me regarder et m'intimider, je me sens capable de tout.

"It does not matter. When there is nothing to see to intimidate me, I feel able to do anything."

—Tant mieux alors ; car pour ce que tu veux tenter, il faudra que tu sois seul.

"So much the better – because what you have to do must be done alone."

—Que faut-il faire ?

"What should be done?"

— Doucement, mon garçon as-tu de l'argent, d'abord ?

"Gently, my boy. Do you have any money with you?"

—J'en ai un peu.

"I have a small amount."

— Bon, car sans cela rien n'est possible. Pour les conjurations, vois-tu il faut se procurer divers objets qui ne se donnent pas pour rien. Puis j'ai mon secret et ce secret-là vaut quelque chose comme tu penses.

"Good, because without that nothing is possible. For the conjurations, you see, you must procure various objects that are not free. Then I have my own secrets and they are worth something to you, I believe."

— Je l'entends bien ainsi.

"I hear you loud and clear."

—A la bonne heure. Eh bien ! comme il est tard et que j'en ai long à te dire, va te coucher tranquillement. Demain à la nuit, tu viendras me trouvera la montagne et je t'apprendrai ce que tu dois faire.

"All in good time. Well! As it is late tonight, and I have much to tell you, go to sleep quietly. Tomorrow night come find me on the mountain and I will teach you what is to be done.

Simounen se remit en route et Claude revint à la ferme, le cœur serré et tout ému de l'audacieuse entreprise qu'il allait tenter.

Simounen started on his path again and Claude returned to the farm, his heart beating fast and feeling agitated at the audacious enterprise that he was undertaking.

Le jour suivant, après le souper, pendant que les garçons et les filles de la ferme reprenaient leur veillée, toujours animée par les gais propos ou les chansons rustiques, Claude s'esquiva sans être remarqué et gagna au pas de course la cabane de Simounen.

The next day, after dinner, when the boys and girls of the farm were resuming their evening activities, animated by gay comments or rustic songs, Claude slipped away without being noticed and reached Simounen's hut hurriedly.

Le vieillard l'attendait, assis devant une petite table et lisant, à la lueur d'une chandelle de suif, un livre crasseux à demi déchiré.

The old man was awaiting him, sitting in front of a small table and reading, by the light of a tallow candle, a half-torn dusty book.

L'intérieur de la cabane répondait parfaitement au Caractère que l'opinion publique prêtait au berger.

The interior of the hut corresponded to the public perception of the shepherd.

Sur tes murs crépis à la chaux étaient cloués des oiseaux de proie et des chauves-souris, et se mêlaient, dans un désordre étrange, de vieilles armes, des baguettes de coudrier à bout ferré, des branches de gui sèches, et deux ou trois petits chaudrons de cuivre. Au plafond, pendaient un iguane empaillé — sorte de grand lézard à l'aspect terrible — et un serpent dont la gueule ouverte laissait encore passer une langue fine, desséchée par le temps, et pointue comme un dard.

Birds of prey and bats were nailed to the plastered walls, and mingled in a strange disorder, were old weapons, steel-tipped cedar rods, branches of dry mistletoe, and two or three small copper cauldrons. A stuffed iguana hung on the ceiling – a kind of big lizard with a terrible appearance – and a serpent with an open mouth that still displayed a fine forked tongue, hardened by time and sharpened like a dart.

Sur des bancs de bois

On rough square wooden

grossièrement équarri séchaient des plantes aromatiques. D'autres plantes macéraient dans un cuvier posé près de la table, et des hôtes de diverses formes s'alignaient sur la cheminée, à côté de quelques volumes poudreux.

benches were aromatic plants that were drying out. Other plants macerated in a pot beside the table, and there were holes of various forms by the chimney, with strange powders.

Le sol de la cabane était de terre battue ; deux poules noires y picotaient comme dans une bassecour, et dans un coin sombré étincelaient les yeux ronds d'un de ces crapauds énormes, comme on en trouve dans les carrières.

The floor of the hut was clay — two black hens pecked away as if they were in a farmyard, and in a dark corner glittered the round eyes of one of those enormous toads, often found in quarries.

L'aspect de ce misérable logis n'était pas de nature à rassurer le pauvre Claude Michu. Aussi s'arrêta-t-il sur le seuil avec un mouvement de brusque appréhension.

The sight of this miserable dwelling did not reassure poor Claude Michu. He paused at the threshold with a sudden apprehension.

Il n'osait hasarder son pied dans celle enceinte maudite, et il serait probablement retourné sur ses pas, si Simounen, craignant de voir sa dupe lui échapper, ne lui eût crié d'un ton encourageant :

He dared not step foot in this cursed place, and he would probably have retraced his steps if Simounen, fearing to see his dupe about to make his escape, had not shouted at him in an encouraging tone:

—Bonsoir, Claude. Entre vite, mon ami ; je vois que tu es un garçon exact.

"Good evening, Claude! Come in quickly, my friend. I see that you are a punctual boy."

L'aspirant sorcier comprit qu'il

The aspiring sorcerer saw that

était trop tard pour reculer.

Il secoua un frisson et se risqua dans l'intérieur.

Le berger se leva alors et vint fermer soigneusement la porte.

— Il ne faut pas qu'on nous dérange, fit-il, sommé à lui-même. Les gendarmes ne croient à rien et s'ils nous surprenaient, Ils seraient bien capables, ma foi de jeter du trouble dans nos affaires.

Cette crainte des gendarmés imprudemment exprimée par le sorcier aurait dû inspirer à Claude de judicieuses réflexions ; au lieu de se dire qu'il s'engageait là dans une affaire périlleuse au point de vue de ces intérêts ; au lieu de songer qu'un sorcier qui commande au démon ne doit pas craindre les hommes, le crédule paysan considéra sa tentative comine d'autant plus terrible que Simounen prenait plus de précautions pour en assurer le résultat.
—Allons, lui dit te vieillard au bout d'un instant. Il s'agit ce nous entendre vite. Tu veux aller au Trou-Noir ?

it was too late to retreat.

He shivered and ventured into the interior.

The shepherd got up and quickly closed the door.

"We must not be bothered," he said, speaking to himself. "The police do not believe in anything and if they surprised us, they would be well able, my dear, to cause trouble in our affairs."

This fear of the police recklessly expressed by the wizard should have inspired some judicious reflections in Claude - instead of saying to himself that he was engaged in a perilous affair, instead of thinking that the wizard who could command demons should not be afraid of men, the credulous peasant considered his dangerous efforts even more tentatively, leading Simounen to take precautions to assure his intended result.

"Come," said the old man after a pause. "We must act fast. Do you want to go to the Black Hole?"

—Oui !

"Yes!"

—Et prendre le trésor d'André ?

"And take Andre's treasure?

— Si ça se peut.

"If that is possible."

—Ça se pourra, si tu exécutes bien tout ce que je vais t'indiquer.

"It will be, if you follow my instructions precisely."

—Je ferai tout.

"I will do everything you say."

—Et tu feras bien, car, songes-y, manquer à une seule de mes conditions, c'est perdre la fortune que tu désires et peut-être exposer ta vie.

"And you will do it well, because, think about it, if you miss even one of my conditions, it will mean the loss of the fortune you crave and perhaps even your life."

Claude ne répondit pas. Il commençait à trembler. Pourtant il se remit, fort, de sa première résolution.

Claude did not respond. He began to tremble. Yet he recovered, confidently, his initial resoluteness.

— Dites toujours, père Simounen, reprit-il, après un court silence.

"Tell me everything, Father Simounen," he went on, after a brief silence.

Le sorcier quitta son siège et prit sur la cheminée un petit bouquin imprimé en rouge qu'il ouvrit d'un air solennel.
—Quel est ce livre ? demanda Claude Michu.

The sorcerer left his seat and took a small book printed in red from the mantelpiece.

"What is this book?" asked Claude Michu.

— Ce livre, mon fils, c'est le Dragon rouge ; c'est le trésor de la

"This book, my son, is the Red Dragon. This is the treasure of

237

science ; c'est le code du sorcier. Là, se trouvent les grandes conjurations qui rendent les esprits obéissants.

Claude Michu ouvrit de grands yeux. Simounen continua.

— C'est dans ce livre que nous allons puiser l'invocation qui doit t'ouvrir les abîmes du Trou-Noir.

— Il faut aussi une baguette, n'est-ce pas maitre, Simounen ?

Bien des sorciers se servent d'une baguette, ou verge foudroyante ; mais je n'agis pas ainsi. La baguette est bonne tout au plus pour découvrit les sources; pour les trésors, il faut autre chose.

— Que faut-il donc ?

—Il faut une tête d'âne, mon fils

— Une tête d'âne !

— Oui, répliqua le sorcier, qui venait de trouver là une excellente occasion pour se procurer un âne, bon marché, comme on le verra tout à l'heure.

science; it is the wizard's code. There, one finds the great conjurations which make the spirits obedient to one's will.

Claude Michu opened his eyes wide. Simounen continued.

"It is from this book that we must draw the invocation which will open the abyss of the Black Hole."

"One also needs a wand, doesn't one, Master Simounen?"

"Many wizards use a rod or a Blasting Rod, but I do not work like that. The rod is at best good for discovering the sources – for the treasures, one needs something else."

"What is that?"

"One needs the head of an ass, my son."

"The head of an ass!"

"Yes," replied the sorcerer, who had just discovered an excellent opportunity to procure an ass, cheaply, as we will see.

— Que fait-on avec cette tête d'âne ?

—On l'offre en sacrifice aux esprits, en la faisant griller sur des charbons ; ce sacrifice décide les démons à répondre aux questions qu'on leur adresse.

—Bah ! fit Claude tout hébété, une tête d'âne

— C'est comme je te le dis.

—Alors...

—Alors, il faut qu'avant la Saint-Jean tu t'en Ailles en ville et que lu achètes au marché un âne de deux ans que tu m'amèneras ici, en le conduisant de la main gauche. Tu m'entends bien ?

— De la main gauche, bon ! Mais que ferez-vous de l'animal ? Vous lui couperet ta tête.

—Non pas, je le garderai pour une prochaine occasion et je te remettrai en échange la tête d'un autre baudet que j'aurai préparée en conséquence. Celui que tu m'amèneras sera le prix de la tête magique.

"What do you do with this head of the ass?"

One offers it as a sacrifice to the spirits, burning it on charcoal. The demons choose to respond to your questions if they are satisfied with the sacrifice.

"Bah!" exclaimed Claude, dazed, "the head of an ass!"

"This is what has to be done."

"So…"

"So, you must go to the town before the feast of St. John and buy a two-year-old donkey at the market. Then you must bring him here, leading him by the left hand. Do you hear me well?"

"By the left hand, very well! But what will you do with the animal? Will you chop off its head?"

"Not at all, I will keep it safe for another occasion, and I will give you in exchange the head of another donkey that I have prepared accordingly. The one that you will bring me will be the price of the magical donkey head."

Claude fit la grimace.

Claude grimaced.

— Ça ne te va pas ? fit le sorcier, d'un air fâché. Alors, rien de fait, mon garçon.

"This does not suit you?" exclaimed the sorcerer, angrily. "So, nothing can be achieved, my boy."

— Si, maître Simounen, j'accepte : continuez.

"Yes, Master Simounen, I accept this task. Please continue."

—Quand tu auras la tête d'âne en ton pouvoir, tu l'emporteras chez toi sans la montrer à personne. Puis tu iras cueillir, au clair de la lune, une branche de verveine dont tu décoreras ton talisman.

"When you have the magical donkey's head in your possession, you must take it with you without being seen by anyone. Then you will pick a branch of verbena in the moonlight, that you will use to decorate your talisman."

— La tête ?

"The head?"

—Sans doute. Ensuite tu te rendras au Trou-Noir, |et, après avoir tracé le triangle magique comme je vais te le montrer, lu prononceras la formule indiquée par le Dragon Rouge, et que tu vas apprendre par cœur.

"Yes, of course. Then you will take it to the Black Hole, and after having traced a magical triangle like the one I will show you, you will pronounce the formula mentioned in the Red Dragon, which you will learn by heart."

—Alors, Lucifer t'apparaîtra et tu pourras lui demander ce que tu désires.

"Then, Lucifer will appear to you and grant all your desires."

Le sorcier expliqua alors à son adepte comment se construisait le triangle magique, et voici la figure

The sorcerer then explained to his adept how he was to construct the magical triangle, as shown

qu'il lui en donna

below.

Quand Claude fut suffisamment édifié à ce sujet Simounen passa à la dernière partie de l'initiation

When Claude had been sufficiently informed on this subject, Simounen, continued to the final part of the initiation.

Il ouvrit le terrible Dragon Rouge et son doigt se posa sur une page ainsi conçue :

He opened the terrible book of the Red Dragon and his finger landed on a page:

GRANDE APPELLATION DES ESPRITS AVEC LESQUELS ON VEUT FAIRE PACTE, TIREE DE LA GRANDE CLAVICULE

Empereur Lucifer, mettre de tous les esprits rebelles. Je te prie de m'être favorable dans l'appellation que je fais à ton grand ministre LUCIFUGE ROFOCALE, ayant envie de faire pacte avec lui, je te prie aussi prince Belzébuth, de me protéger dans mon entreprise.

O Comte Astaroth ! Sois-moi propice, et fais que dans cette nuit, le grand Lucifer m'apparaisse sous une forme humaine, sans aucune mauvaise odeur, et qu'il m'accorde, par le moyen du pacte que je vais lui présenter, toutes les richesses dont j'ai besoin.

— O grand Lucifuge ! je te prie de quitter demeure dans quelque partie du monde qu'elle sont pour venir me parler, sinon je t'y contraindrai par la force du grand Dieu vivant, de son cher Fils et du

GREAT INVOCATION OF THE SPIRITS WITH WHOM ONE WISHES TO MAKE A PACT, DRAWN FROM THE GREAT KEY

Emperor Lucifer, master of all the rebel spirits. I pray I find your favor in this invocation that I make to your Prime Minister LUCIFUGE ROFOCALE, wanting to make a pact with him, I also pray to your Prince Beelzebub to protect me in my enterprise.

O Count Astaroth! Be propitious unto me, and grant unto me that this night, the great Lucifer appears to me in a human form without any bad odor and that he grants me, by means of the pact that I will present to him, all the riches I desire.

O Great Lucifuge! I pray you leave your abode in whichever part of the world that you might be to come and speak with me, or else I will have to compel you by the force of the great living God, by

Saint-Esprit ; obéis promptement ou tu vas être éternellement tourmente par la force des puissantes paroles de la Grande Clavicule de Solomon, dont il se servait pour obliger les esprits rebelles à recevoir son pacte : ainsi parais au plus tôt, ou je le vais continuellement tourmenter par la force de ces puissantes paroles de la Clavicule :

his dear Son and by the Holy Spirit; obey me promptly or you will be eternally damned by the force of the powerful words of the Great Key of Solomon, which he employed to force the rebel spirits to accept his pact. Thus, appear at the earliest before me, or I will continually torment you by these powerful words of the Key:

Aglon Tetragram Vaycheon Stimulamaton y ezpares retragrammaton olyoran irion esytion existion eryona onera erasym moym messias soter Emanuel Sabaoth Adonay, te adore et invoco

Aglon, Tetragram, Vaycheon, Stimulamaton y ezpares retragrammaton olyoran irion esytion existion eryona onera erasym moym messias soter Emanuel Sabaoth Adonay, te adore et invoco

Claude Michu eut la patience de passer une partie de la nuit à apprendre par cœur cette baroque formule.

Claude Michu patiently spent a good part of the night memorizing this baroque formula.

Quand il la posséda imperturbablement d'un bout à l'autre, Simounen lui dit :

When he demonstrated this confidently from start to finish, Simounen said to him,

—Maintenant, garçon, te voilà ferré, les diables du Trou-Noir n'ont qu'à se bien tenir. Va sans crainte et dans huit jours tu seras riche.

"Now, boy, here you are! The devils of the Black Hole will not be able to stand against you. Go without fear and in eight days you will be rich."

—Quand reviendrai-je ?

"When should I come back?"

— Tu reviendras l'avant-veille de la Saint-Jean. Tu m'amèneras l'âne que tu auras acheté et tu m'apporteras quatre pièces de vingt francs neuves. En échange, je te donnerai la tête magique qui doit t'ouvrir les portes du trésor

"You must return on the eve of the feast of St. John. You must bring me the donkey that you have bought, and you must bring me four new twenty-franc pieces. In return, I will give you the magical head that will open the treasure gates for you."

Claude Michu trouva le secret un peu cher. « Un âne de deux ans et 80 francs, se disait-il, c'est bien payé. »

Claude Michu found the secret a bit costly — "A two-year-old donkey and 80 francs," he said to himself. "That's a fine price."

Il en fit l'observation au sorcier.

He made this observation to the sorcerer.

— Imbécile, répliqua ce dernier, ce n'est pas 80 francs,

"Imbecile!" replied the latter, "It is not 80 francs, it is 1000

c'est 1000 Fr., c'est 10.000 Fr., que le devrais te demander, Comment ! Je te donne le moyen de gagner des millions et tu marchandes !

francs, or perhaps 10,000 francs, that you should offer me. You ask me, why? This is because I give you the means to win millions and you bargain with me!"

Malgré sa crédulité Claude Michu trouva alors une réplique qui démonta légèrement l'aplomb du faiseur de dupes.

Despite his credulity, Claude Michu suddenly discovered an aplomb that shook the composure of the wily conman.

—Mais père Simounen, dit-il, puisque votre recette est si bonne et vaut tant d'argent, pourquoi donc n'avez-vous pas songé à vous en servir vous-même ?

"But Father Simounen," he said, "Since your recipe is so good and worth so much money, why have you not used it to benefit yourself?"

— Pourquoi ? Pourquoi ?... Balbutia le sorcier étonné de l'objection, parce que…

"Why... Because..." stammered the sorcerer, surprised by this objection, "because…"

Puis, reprenant subitement son sang-froid — Ce mystère-là ne te regarde pas, petit, grommela-t-il — il ne faut pas mettre le nez dans mes affaires, souviens-t 'en à l'avenir ; faute de quoi il pourrait t'en cuire.

Then, suddenly recovering his poise, he said, "This mystery need not trouble you, my child, remember in the future not to poke your nose in my affairs, or you might end up in the cooking pot yourself."

Cette défaite grossière et cette menace qui l'accompagnait eurent tout l'effet qu'en attendait Simounen.

This crude defeat and the threat that accompanied it had all the effect that Simounen intended.

Claude Michu baissa la tête en

Claude Michu lowered his

disant : — Excusez-moi, maître Simounen, je ne voulais pas vous offenser.

head, saying, "Excuse me, Master Simounen, I did not mean to offend you."

Puis il prit congé du rusé compère et revint à la ferme au moment où le jour allait paraître.

Then, he took leave of the wily old man and returned to the farm at the break of dawn.

Le Jeudi suivant, Claude Michu se munit de toutes ses économies, les serra dans une bourse de cuir et partit pour la ville, dans l'intention d'acheter l'âne que l'on avait demandé le berger magicien.

Après s'être promené pendant une heure ou deux dans le marché, il trouva ce qu'il voulait : un bel âne, âgé de deux ans, solide sur les Jarrets et promettant à son acquéreur un utile auxiliaire pour les travaux de la campagne.

C'était bien la brave bête qu'il fallait à Claude Michu, ou plutôt à Simounen, car ce dernier devait profiter seul de la belle acquisition du jeune homme, Claude marchanda le roussin, le paya comptant et ayant passé le licol dans la main gauche, l'emmena au village où il le cacha soigneusement dans une écurie abandonnée.

L'avant-veille de la Saint-Jean, vers le soir, il vint chercher la bête, et par un chemin détourné, la conduisit chez Simounen.

—Ah ! Ah ! s'écria celui-ci, en la voyant, belle bête ! tu réussiras, mon garçon, car tu as bienfait les

The next Thursday, Claude Michu collected all his savings, squeezed them into a leather purse and left for the town, with the intention of buying the donkey the shepherd magician had asked of him.

After walking for an hour or two in the market, he found what he was looking for – a handsome donkey, two years old, strong on the heels and promising to be a useful auxiliary for the purchaser's campaign.

It was the brave beast that Claude Michu needed, or rather Simounen, because it would be he would enjoy himself the beautiful acquisition of the young man. Claude traded the horse, paying in cash, and having held the halter in his left hand, took him to the village where he hid it in an abandoned stable.

On the eve of St. John, by evening, he came to fetch the beast, and by a roundabout route, led it to Simounen's house.

"Ah! Ah!" he cried, on seeing it, "beautiful beast! You will succeed, my boy, because you

choses.

have made a fine purchase."

—Vous trouves, maître Simounen ?

"Do you really think so, Master Simounen?"

—Oui, aussi vais-je m'acquitter à mon tour mais, j'oubliais : où sont les 4 pièces de 20 francs ?

"Yes, also, I will take care of my part, but I forget – where are the four twenty-franc pieces?"

—Les voici.

"Here they are."

Simounen prit l'or, le fit sonner et l'engouffre dans la poche de son gilet, avec une satisfaction évidente.

Simounen took the gold, tapping it to hear the tinkling sound and engulfed it in his vest pocket, with an evident satisfaction.

— Viens, ça, dit-il, ensuite, je vais te remettre la Tête Magique.

"Come," he said then, "I will give you the magical head."

Cette fameuse tête était simplement celle d'une pauvre bourrique qu'on avait abattue peu de jour auparavant, et que Simounen s'était facilement procuré. Il l'avait proprement nettoyée, bourrée de paille et accommodée de façon à satisfaire autant que possible les exigences de la situation.

This famed head was simply that of a poor donkey that had been slaughtered a few days ago, and that Simounen had easily procured. He had cleaned it, stuffed it with straw and modified in a fashion as to suit the needs of the occasion.

Il la prit solennellement sur la table où il l'aval exposée, la plaça avec précaution dans un panier

He brought it solemnly to the table where he presented it, and then placed it carefully in a basket and handed the same to Claude

Michu.

Puis il ajouta en manière d'instruction : Tu feras un feu de bruyère, tu y jetteras la tête après avoir prononcé l'invocation que Je t'ai apprise. Va, ton affaire est dans le sac — mais n'oublie rien ou tu perds ta peine et ton argent.

Then he added in an instructive manner: "You will kindle a fire of briar wood and burn the head after having pronounced the invocation that I have taught you. Go, your case is in the bag – but do not forget anything or you will lose your skin and your money.

—Bon, fit Claude.

"Good," said Claude.

Et il partit plein d'espérance et appelant & lui tout le courage dont il allait avoir besoin la nuit suivante

He left, filled with hope and summoning to himself all the courage he would have need of the following night.

Pendant ce temps, le berger se frottait les mains.

During this time, the shepherd began to rub his hands.

—Allons, pensait-il, il y a encore des imbéciles dans ce monde, et si cela continue, le métier de sorcier ne sera pas le plus mauvais.

"Very well," he thought, "there are still imbeciles in the world, and if this continues, the wizarding profession will not be the worst choice."

Claude rentrait tranquillement au village lorsqu'il rencontra, non loin de la ferme, M. Bernard Morand, le pharmacien.

Claude was returning quietly to the village when he met, not far from the farm, Mr. Bernard Morand, the pharmacist.

—Bonsoir, Claude, lui dit ce dernier, qui était un ami de son père ; d'où viens-tu comme ça ?

"Good evening, Claude," the latter said, who was a friend of his father. "Where are you coming from?"

—Bonsoir, monsieur Morand, je viens de la montagne, sauf votre respect.

"Good evening, Mr. Morand, I am coming from the mountain, thank you."

—Ah ! ah ! Et qu'es-tu allé faire à la montagne, si je ne suis pas trop curieux.

"Ah! Ah! And what were you doing on the mountain, if I'm not too curious?"

Claude rougit.

Claude blushed.

— Je suis allé... me promener..., murmura-t-il

"I went…for a walk…," he murmured.

—Ah ! ah ! Et ta promenade a été fructueuse, a ce que je vois, puisque tu reviens avec ce lourd panier ?

"Ah! Ah! And your walk has been productive, I see, since you return with this heavy basket?"

— Oui... oui..., Monsieur Morand, balbutia Claude, qui perdait la tête.

"Yes…Yes…Mr. Morand," stammered Claude, who had lost his cool.

— Qu'as-tu dans ce panier ?... Des fraises, sans doute c'est la saison...

"What do you have in this basket? Strawberries, without a doubt, it is the season…"

—Non ! ce ne sont pas des fraises...

"No! These are not strawberries…"

—Qu'est-ce donc, alors ? Des cerises ? —Est-ce que tu marauderais par hasard ?

"What is it, then? Cherries? Did you plunder them, by chance?

— Oh ! monsieur Morand, moi un maraudeur Pouvez-vous croire ?

"Oh! Mr. Morand, do you see me as a plunderer? Can you believe that?"

— Je ne crois rien ; — mais tu retires ton panier et lu les caches avec tant de soin, qu'il doit y avoir là-dessous quelque mystère ?...

"I believe nothing – but you hide your basket so carefully that there must be some mystery hidden here?"

La timidité de Claude lui était revenue. — Pressé de questions et trop peu dissimulé pour se tirer d'affaire par un mensonge, il se résolut à tout avouer au pharmacien, en lui demandant le secret.

Claude's natural timidity had returned. Pressed by these questions and unable to dissimulate or lie, he resolved to confess everything to the pharmacist and in return ask him for his confidence and to keep it a secret.

Bernard Morand l'écouta avec stupéfaction ; Il ne pouvait se résigner à comprendre une telle crédulité do la part de Claude, une telle duplicité de la part de Simounen.

Bernard listened with amazement. He could not resign himself to accepting such credulity on the part of Claude and such duplicity on the part of Simounen.

—Ainsi, dit-il, quand le jeune homme eut achevé son récit : ce que tu portes là-dedans, c'est une tête d'âne ?

"So," he asked, when the young man had completed his story, "what are you hiding in there, is that the head of a

donkey?"

—Oui, monsieur Morand.

"Yes, Mr. Morand."

—Eh bien, mon ami, tu es mieux monté que tu ne penses, — au lieu d'une tête d'âne, tu en as deux.

"Well, my friend, you are better off than you think – instead of one donkey's head, you have two."

— Deux ?

"Two?"

— Oui : l'une dans ton panier ; l'autre...

"Yes – the one in your basket, the other…"

— L'autre ?

"The other?"

— L'autre sur tes épaules, imbécile !

"The other on your shoulders, imbecile!"

— Est-ce que tu ne vois pas que Simounen est un vieux filou, qu'il t'a extorqué de l'argent et qu'il s'est moqué de toi ?

"Do you not see that Simounen is an old trickster, that he has extorted you of money and that he has fooled you?"

— Vous croyez ?

"Do you think so?"

— Il faut être simple comme tu l'es pour faire une pareille question? — Comment, tu as reçu une certaine instruction, et tu crois encore aux sorciers, aux évocations, aux sorts, aux talismans et à toute la kyrielle cabalistique ? Mais, tu es malade, mon pauvre garçon, il faut te soigner, Allons, jette-moi vite

"One must be very simple-minded to ask such a question. How do you, since you have received a certain level of education, still believe in sorcerers, evocations, spells, talismans and all the Cabalistic balderdash? You are sick, my poor boy, you need treatment. Go, quickly throw the head of the

dans le fossé ta tête de bourrique, et souviens toi que les vrais prodiges aujourd'hui sont ceux qu'accomplissent la science, l'Intelligence et le travail.

Malgré cette mercuriale, Claude Michel ne bougea pas.

— Que voulez-vous, monsieur Morand, dit-il, je me suis promis de tenter l'expérience, et je le tenterai : —je veux en avoir le cœur net.
—A ton aise, mon garçon ! mais, quand tu seras bien persuadé qu'on t'a pris pour une bête, ta viendras me trouver et je te forai voir, moi, que bien des choses, qu'on pourrait offrir à ton esprit comme des prodiges, ne sont que le résultat d'opérations toutes naturelles. — Va au Trou-Noir ; aies en le cœur net, comme tu dis.
— Avec votre permission, monsieur Morand.

—Oui, va — et bonne chance !
— Vous ne dires rien à mon père.

— Sois tranquille. — Adieu !

—Puis, en s'en allant :

donkey into the ditch and remember that true wonders today are those accomplished by science, intelligence and hard work.

Despite this reprimand, Claude Michel did not move.

"What do you want, Mr. Morand?" he asked. "I promised myself to try this experiment and I will. I want to have a clear heart."

"As you wish, my boy! But when you are convinced that you have been taken for a fool, come see me and I will remind you, that many things which one believes are spiritual miracles, are only the result of natural operations. Go to the Black Hole, with a clear heart, as you would say.

"With your permission, Mr. Morand."

"Yes, go – and good luck!"

"You will not say anything to my father?"

"Don't worry, farewell!"

"Then, I'll take your leave."

— Parbleu, mon garçon, pensa le pharmacien, qui aimait à rire, si tu vas chercher des diables au Trou-Noir, je veux que tu sois servi à souhait.

"Good Lord, my boy," mused the pharmacist, who loved a good laugh, "if you go searching for devils in the Black Hole, I hope that you find them."

L'heure redoutable arrive trop vite au gré de Claude — A mesure qu'elle s'approchait, il sentait faiblir son audace.

The dreadful hour arrived too soon for Claude – as it approached, he faltered in his purpose.

Pourtant il avait pris la chose trop à cœur pour l'abandonner au dernier moment.

Yet, he had taken the task too close to his heart to let it go at the last moment.

Quand les feux de la Saint-Jean s'allumèrent sur la montagne, notre futur sorcier quitta donc la ferme et se dirigea vers le Trou-Noir, situé dans une gorge, à quelque distance du village.

When the fires of the feast of St. John began to light up the mountain, our future sorcerer left the farm and went towards the Black Hole, which was situated in a gorge, some distance from the village.

Il avait plu pendant la journée, et la nuit était sans étoiles ; de gros nuages plombés couraient dans le ciel, chassés par un vent assez vif.

It had rained during the day, and the night was starless and dark. Heavy clouds coursed the sky overhead, driven by a strong wind.

Le silence de la campagne, à peine troublé par les cris du grillon où de la cigale, impressionnait vivement Claude Michu.

The silence of the countryside, barely disturbed by the clicks of the cricket or of the cicada, made a strong impression on Claude Michu.

Il marchait d'un pas rapide, répétant mentalement la formule du Dragon rouge, et regardait d'un œil inquiet autour de lui.

He quickened his pace, mentally repeating the formula of the Red Dragon, and looking around with a worried eye.

Les arbres plantés au bord du chemin prenaient à ses yeux des

The trees planted by the side of the road were, in his eyes, taking

apparences fantastiques, et dans les buissons, il lui semblait entendre des soupirs.

Trébuchant, essoufflé, couvert de sueur, il arriva enfin au Trou-Noir : — c'était une espèce de cratère, tapissé à l'intérieur de chênes et de frênes, et dont l'aspect n'avait rien de bien effrayent, quoiqu'il inspirât à Claude Michu une profonde horreur.

L'élève de Simounen, surexcité par le sentiment de la situation, choisit une place dépouillée d'arbres, pour y faire sa conjuration, et ayant allumé un feu de bruyères, il attendit l'heure de minuit.

Pendant celle veille, qui dura près d'une heure, il sembla à Claude Michu que des plaintes s'élevaient du fond du Trou-Noir ; mais il n'y prit pas trop garde, tout occupé qu'il était d'épier le son de la cloche du village qui devait lui apporter les douze coups de l'heure fatale.

Enfin, minuit sonna !...

Aussitôt, Claude jeta la tête magique dans le brasier qu'il avait

on fantastic appearances, and in the woods, he seemed to hear sighs.

Stumbling, out of breath, covered in sweat, he finally arrived at the Black Hole – it was a kind of crater, covered with oaks and ash trees, and although the appearance was not very scary, it inspired a profound horror in Claude Michu.

Simounen's student, over-excited by the situation, chose a place deprived of trees to perform his conjurations, and lighting a fire of heather, he tended it until midnight.

During the vigil, which lasted almost an hour, it seemed to Claude Michu that complaints would be raised from the bottom of the Black Hole, but he did not pay much heed, occupied as he was with listening to the sound of the village bell that would toll the twelve strokes of the fatal hour.

At last, midnight struck!...

At once, Claude threw the magical head into the fire that he

allumé et prononça d'une voix un peu tremblante la conjuration apprise dans le Livre Rouge.

had stoked and uttered with a loud, albeit tremulous voice, the conjuration taught him from the Red Book.

Puis, il attendit, haletant.

Then he waited, panting.

Then he waited, panting.

Nothing happened.

Alors, il reprit l'invocation d'une voix lente.

Then, he repeated the invocation in a slow voice.

Il avait à peine achevé, lorsqu'un bruit terrible se fit autour de lui : c'étaient des cris, des hurlements, des grincements de chaînes épouvantables.
En même temps, une forme, couverte d'un grand linceul rouge, se montra devant le brasier, tirement éclairée par une nappe de lumière blanche, qui partait du fond de l'abîme.

He had hardly finished, when a terrible noise was heard around him – cries, screams, squeaks of terrible chains.
En même temps, une forme, couverte d'un grand linceul rouge, se montra devant le brasier, tirement éclairée par une nappe de lumière blanche, qui partait du fond de l'abîme.

— Claude Michu, lu m'as appelé, que me veux-tu ? dit l'apparition, d'une voix terrible.

"Claude Michu, you who have summoned me, what do you wish of me?" thundered the apparition, in a terrible voice.

Claude tomba la face contre terre, effrayé de l'effet qu'il avait obtenu.

Claude fell face down, afraid of the effect that he had achieved.

— Le Trésor ! la Trésor ! murmura-t-il, d'une voix étouffée.

"The Treasure! The Treasure!" he mumbled, in a muffled voice.

— Avant de te donner le Trésor que tu demandes, il faut que tu sois vainqueur des esprits de l'abîme, reprit la voix. — A moi, les démons du Trou-Noir

"Before granting you the Treasure that you demand, you must vanquish the spirits of the abyss," replied the Voice. "To me, the demons of the Black Hole!"

Claude qui s'était relevé, plein de terreur, se vit soudainement entouré par une dizaine de spectres, semblables au premier, qui, se prenant par la main, se mirent à décrire autour de lui une ronde infernale.

Claude, who had got up, full of terror, saw dozens of spirits suddenly surrounding him, resembling the first, who took the leader by the hand and began to perform an infernal dance around Claude.

— Grâce ! grâce ! cria Claude, à demi mort de peur, en présence de ces figures horribles, éclairées par la lueur surnaturelle qui venait d'en bas.

"Mercy! Mercy!" cried Claude, afraid and at the point of death in the presence of these horrible figures, who were illuminated by the supernatural glow which came from below.

—Il est à nous ! à nous ! à nous ! hurlèrent des voix sépulcrales.

"He is ours! Ours! Ours!" howled the sepulchral voices.

En même temps, Claude se trouva enlevé de terre par des bras robustes et emporté vers le fond du trou. Il ferma les yeux et se crut perdu.

At the same time, Claude was lifted from the earth by strong arms and carried to the bottom of the hole. He closed his eyes and thought himself lost.

Les démons le laissèrent tomber sur l'herbe ! il pensait qu'on allait le jeter dans quelque chaudière bouillante, quand il se sentit au contraire mouillé de la tête aux pieds.

The demons let him fall on the grass! He thought that he would be thrown into some boiling furnace, when on the contrary, he felt himself wet from head to toe.

Les malins esprits l'avaient jeté dans un ruisseau qui coulait le long des parois du Trou-Noir — ce bain salutaire lui fit du bien, et il allait se familiariser avec son enfer humide, lorsqu'il lueur fantastique qui éclairait la scène s'éteignit tout à coup.

The evil spirits had thrown him into a stream which ran along the walls of the Black Hole – this beneficial bath did him good, and he was relaxing in the warm bath when the fantastic light that lit up the scene went out suddenly.

Surpris et charmé de l'obscurité et du silence qui succédaient subitement à l'éclat des lumières et au bruit des voix Claude Michu se leva et fit quelques se trébucha.

Surprised and bewitched by the darkness and silence that suddenly succeeded the brilliant light and noises, Claude Michu got up and stumbled.

Alors un immense éclat de rire retentit auprès de lui.

Then an immense burst of laughter resounded around him.

Après quoi, une voix railleuse et gaie, fit entendre ces mots : — Eh bien. Claude, es-tu content, et mes démons ont-ils bien fait leur affaire?

After this, a mocking and cheerful voice spoke, "Well, Claude, are you satisfied, and did my demons do their job well?"

Claude reconnaît la voix de Bernard Morand.

Claude recognized the voice of Bernard Morand.

— Eh quoi ! s'écria-t-il, M, Morand, c'était VOUS ?

"Well!" he exclaimed, "Mr. Morand, it is YOU?"

— Moi-même, et les diables qui t'ont si bien arrangé, ce sont tes amis qui ont bien voulu se joindre à moi pour te donner une petite leçon.

"Me and the devils who have put you in such a fine spot, these are your friends who have kindly joined me to teach you a little lesson."

THE COMPLETE ILLUSTRATED GRAND GRIMOIRE, INTERLINEAR EDITION

—Mon Dieu ! mon Dieu ! s'écria Claude, honteux de la mystification dont il venait d'être l'objet, je n'oserai plus retourner au village.

"My God! My God!" cried Claude, ashamed of the mystification that he had been the victim of. "I will not dare return to the village"

— Cela t'apprendra à croire aux contes de grand'mère et aux duperies du vieux Simounen.

"That will teach you to believe in grandmothers' tales and in the deceits of old Simounen."

— Ah ! vous m'avez fait bien peur, monsieur Morand.

"Ah! You gave me a fine fright, Mr. Morand."

— Tant mieux ! ce remède était violent ; la guérison sera sûre.

"Good! This is a violent remedy – the healing will be guaranteed."

— Oh ! je sois guéri, allez.

"Oh! I am healed, let's go."

— A la bonne heure, tu vois qu'il n'y a pas d'autres démons au Trou-Noir que ceux qu'on y amène. Sois, à l'avenir, moins timide, moins crédule et lu réussiras dans ce que tu veux entreprendre, sans avoir besoin de graisser la patte aux sorciers.

"All in good time, you will see that there are no other demons in the Black Hole than those we have brought to it. In the future, be less timid, less gullible and more assured in your efforts, and you will succeed in your enterprises, without needing to grease the palm of sorcerers."

— Mais, monsieur Morand qu'était-ce donc que cette lumière diabolique qui nous éclairait tout à l'heure comme le soleil et qui s'est éteinte tout d'un coup ?

"But, Mr. Morand, how did you produce that diabolical light that was as bright as the sun and then went out suddenly in a flash?"

— Ce n'était pas de la lumière diabolique, mais simplement de la lumière électrique que je produisais au moyen de l'appareil que voici.

— C'est une merveille.

— Une merveille que je t'expliquerai quand tu voudras.

— Demain, et vous voulez, monsieur Morand, j'ai bâté de m'instruira et d'oublier toutes les sottises de Simounen et toutes les jongleries du Dragon Rouge.

—Demain, soit. Pour ce soir, dit le pharmacien, en rassemblant autour de lui les acteurs de la mystification qu'il avait préparée depuis la veille à l'intention de Claude Michu, pour ce soir je vous invite tous à venir prendre chez moi une jatte de vin cuit. Cela nous réchauffera. Gardez à Claude le secret de son aventure, et demain venez avec loi profiter des notions scientifiques que je veux lui donner et des expériences que je veux faire devant lui.

Vous pourrez vous convaincre, grâce à quelques courtes leçons, que toute la force des sorciers réside dans la

"That was not a diabolical light, but simply an electrical light that I produced by means of this device."

"That is marvelous!"

"A marvel that I will explain to you when you wish."

"Tomorrow, Mr. Morand, and if you wish, I would like to be taught to forget all the nonsense of Simounen and all the jugglery of the Red Dragon."

"Tomorrow, then. For tonight," said the pharmacist, gathering around him all the actors who had participated in the mystery play presented to Claude Michu, "for tonight, I invite you all to come to my residence to have a glass of mulled wine. It will warm us up. Keep the secrets of our adventure to ourselves and come tomorrow to benefit from the scientific concepts that I will demonstrate to Claude."

"You will thus convince yourself, thanks to some short lessons, that all the power of the sorcerers resides in the knowledge

connaissance de certaines pratiques qui ne sembleront plus merveilleuses lorsque l'instruction se sera vulgarisée.

Ce qui s'est passé entre Simounen et Claude n'est rien auprès de ce que tentent des aventuriers plus forts que notre vieux berger. Aux yeux du vulgaire ils opèrent des prodiges ; ils font parler les esprits, ils changent do place les objets par la seule forcé de la parole ; ce ne sont après tout que d'habiles prestidigitateurs ou do rusée fripons qui font mauvais usage do leur science en lui prêtant un caractère surnaturel.

Il est peu de phénomènes au monde qui ne puissent s'expliquer suivant les lois naturelles ; c'est ce que je compte vous démontrer, pour vous ôter l'envie de jeter, comme Claude Michu, votre argent par les fenêtres de la sottise.

Tout en courant, Bernard Morand et ses compagnons avaient regagné le village.

Un bol de vin chaud les attendait chez le pharmacien.

of some practices that will not look too marvelous when the techniques are commonplace."

What has transpired between Simounen and Claude is nothing more than some complicated adventures of our old shepherd. To common eyes, they appear to be miracles – being able to speak with spirits, moving objects with the power of words – these are in the end how the clever conjurer or cunning rogues misuse their knowledge of science to given themselves supernatural abilities.

There are few phenomena in the world that cannot be explained by the power of natural laws – this is what I will demonstrate to you, to prevent you from having the urge, like Claude Michu, to throw away your money through the windows of your foolishness.

While having this discussion, Bernard Morand and his companions had returned to the village.

A bowl of mulled wine was awaiting them at the pharmacist's

Tous s'assirent autour de la table ; on but à la santé du héros de la soirée et les paysans se séparèrent, en promettant de se montrer exacts au rendez-vous qui leur avait été donné pour le lendemain.

residence. All of them sat down around the table – they toasted the heroes of the evening and the peasants took their leave, promising to return at the appointed time the next day.

Claude Michu, encore tout penaud de sa mésaventure de la veille, se leva le jour suivant avec la ferme résolution de se corriger de sa crédulité et de ne chercher qu'en lui-même le remède à ses faiblesses d'esprit.

Claude Michu, still a bit sheepish after his misadventure the evening before, rose the next day with a firm resolution to correct his credulity and seek only within himself the remedy for his weaknesses of spirit.

En conséquence, et pour inaugurer immédiatement son nouveau système de conduite, il prit ses plus beaux habits et se dirigea vaillamment vers la maisonnette de Madeloun.

As a result, and to usher in immediately his new mode of conduct, he put on his finest clothes and walked confidently towards Madeleine's cottage.

Son cœur battait plus fort à mesure qu'il approchait do la demeure de celle qu'il aimait ; néanmoins il entra d'un pas ferme après avoir heurté deux fois à la porte.

His heart was beating fast as he approached the home of the person whom he loved more than anyone, however, he entered with a firm step after knocking twice on the door.

Madeloun et sa mère étaient seules au logis. La belle fille peignait ses longs cheveux bruns devant un petit miroir, tandis que la vieille femme préparait le repas du matin.

Madeleine and her mother were alone at home. The beautiful girl combed her long brown hair before a small mirror, while the old woman was preparing breakfast.

A la vue de Claude, Madeloun se retourna.

At the sight of Claude, Madeleine turned around.

— Comme te voilà brave, maître Claude, dit-elle au nouveau venu. Qui t'amène de si bonne heure ?

"How are you, brave Master Claude," she said to the newcomer. "What brings you here so early?"

— J'ai à le parler.

"I would like to speak with you."

— A moi ?

"With me?"

— A toi et à ta mère.

"With you and your mother."

— De quoi s'agit-il ? fit cette dernière, en quittant son ouvrage.

"What is it about," asked the latter, leaving her work.

— Je vous le dirai, quand Madeloun m'aura entendu.

"I will tell you when Madeleine has heard what I have to say."

Puis s'adressant à la jeune fille ; —Viens, fit-il, je veux te conduire à la messe en passant sur la grande place je t'achèterai des bagues de Beaucaire. Le marchand est venu aujourd'hui.

Then addressing the young girl, "Come," he said, "I want to take you to Mass. While passing through the Grand Square, I want to buy you some rings from Beaucaire. The merchant has come today."

Ainsi et sans plus de façon s'entame un roman d'amour dans le bon paya de Provence Les bagues de Beaucaire, anneaux en verre qui s'achètent à la douzaine, jouent un grand rôle dans les préliminaires du sentiment. Les offrir c'est presque dire : je vous aime. Les accepter, c'est à peu près répondre : moi aussi.

So, and without much ado begins a tale of love in the good country of Provence. The rings of Beaucaire, glass rings that are bought by the dozen, which play a big role in the initiation of feeling. To offer them is almost to say – I love you. To accept them, is to implicitly respond – Me too.

Aussi, en entendant la proposition significative de Claude Michu, Madeloun n'eut-

On hearing the significant proposition of Claude Michu, Madeleine was not too surprised.

elle pas médiocrement surprise.

—Qui t'a rendu si hardi ? lui demanda-t-elle.

"What made you so brave?" she asked him.

Hier, tu n'osais pas me regarder, et voilà qu'aujourd'hui tu me parles comme un galant ?

"Yesterday, you dared not look at me, and now you speak to me so gallantly."

—Je t'expliquerai cela Madeloun ; vient toujours.

"I will explain to you, Madeleine, come with me."

D'un regard, la jolie fille consulta sa mère. Celle-ci, flattée de la préférence de Claude Michu, un garçon qui avait du bien au soleil, fit un signe affirmatif, et Madeloun prit sans cérémonie le bras de Claude, qui lui paraissait un assez joli garçon, depuis qu'il avait quitté son air timide et gène.

With a glance, the pretty girl consulted her mother. This lady, flattered by the attentions of Claude Michu, a boy with good prospects, made an approving gesture, and Madeleine without much fuss, took Claude's arm, which he offered her, who appeared to be a handsome boy since he had given up his shy and embarrassed air.

Les deux jeunes gens s'en furent ainsi le long des sentiers et sans doute ils s'entendirent à merveille, car lorsque Claude quitta celle qu'il regardait déjà comme sa fiancée, son visage rayonnait, témoignant hautement de sa satisfaction intérieure.

The two young people went off in this manner on their path and no doubt they got along very well, because when Claude left her, who he already regarded as his fiancée, his face shone, indicating his inner satisfaction.

Le mauvais tort avait cédé, en effet, devant la fermeté du jeune homme. Il avait fait preuve de

The bad luck had, in effect, given way to the young man's firmness. He had shown

volonté et de hardiesse ; il avait trouvé de bonnes et honnêtes paroles pour peindre son amour à Madeloun, et il lui semblait qu'une nouvelle existence allez commencer pour lui.

Cet heureux résultat ; il lé devait à Bernard Morand. Aussi ne manqua-t-il pas de se rendre le soir chez le pharmacien, désireux de profiler de nouveau de ces conseils et de ses enseignements.

Pourtant, ce n'était pas d'amour qu'il devait être question ce soir-là. Le pharmacien s'était promis d'éclairer ses jeunes auditeurs sur divers points qui restent toujours assez obscurs pour les intelligences simples, plus souvent ouvertes aux fables qui se débitent dans les campagnes qu'aux saines données de la science et du raisonnement. Il voulait les mettre en garde contre les croyances naïves les prémunir contre les manœuvres des diseurs de bonne aventure, des jeteurs de sorts, des marchands de charmes et de toute cette engeance qui spécule sur la superstition et sur la crédulité des gens de la campagne.

Quand Bernard Morand vit son auditoire au complet, il alluma

willpower and boldness. He had found good and honest words to demonstrate his love to Madeleine, and it appeared that a new life lay ahead for him.

He owed this happy result to Bernard Morand. Thus, he did not fail to go that evening to the pharmacist's residence, looking forward to benefiting from his teachings and advice.

Yet, it was not love that he had questions about that night. The pharmacist had promised to enlighten his young listeners on various points which seemed too obscure for their simple intelligence, more often open to country tales than to healthy science and reason. He wanted to give them to shy away from naïve beliefs and grant the ability to guard them against the maneuvers of fortune tellers, spellcasters, charm merchants and all people of this ilk that took advantage of the superstition and credulity of the people of the countryside.

When Bernard Morand saw his audience was complete, he lit his

sa pipe, invita les paysans à en faire autant, si bon leur semblait, et commença en ces termes :

« J'ai beaucoup voyagé, mes amis, et comme je suis de ma nature curieux et avide de m'instruire, en voyageant, j'ai beaucoup vu et beaucoup appris. En autre, j'ai étudié une foule de questions dont vous ne soupçonnez même pas l'existence, et que la nature spéciale de mes travaux m'engageait & approfondir.

C'est pourquoi je vais pouvoir vous parler aujourd'hui de beaucoup de choses qui vous intéresseront eu vous instruisant et faire devant vous certaines expériences capables de rendre mes théories plus palpables.

Je ne vous dirai pas comme certains que le diable n'existe pas ; la religion nous apprend qu'il y a dans le monde un esprit du mal que notre vertu doit combattre mais cet esprit-là n'est point celui que vous décrivent les faiseurs de contes : un être noir et cornu se montrant aux hommes qui savent l'évoquer. Personne ne peut se vanter d'avoir va le diable, même ceux qui savent par cœur le

pipe, invited the peasants to make themselves at ease, and started in this manner:

"I have travelled much, my friends, and since I have a curious nature and love learning new things in my travels, I have seen much and learned a lot. Further, I have studied a lot of strange topics that you do not even suspect exist, and that the special nature of my work engaged me deeply.

Therefore, I will be able to speak with you today about many things that will interest you, educate you and perform certain experiments that will prove my theories clearly.

I will not tell you that it is certain that the devil does not exist – religion teaches us that in the world there is a spirit of evil that our virtue must fight but that spirit is not the one described by the storytellers – a horned dark being showing himself to men who know how to evoke him. Nobody can boast of knowing how to bring forth the devil, even those who know by heart the Red

Dragon Rouge (ici, maître Morand cligna malignement de l'œil en regardant Claude qui rougit), et pourtant, depuis un temps immémorial, on croit que le diable se manifeste sous diverses formes parmi nous. De tout temps, les habiles ont tiré parti de cette croyance pour exploiter les bonnes gens, ce qui prouvé que de tout temps aussi, il y a eu des faiseurs de dupes et des imbéciles pour les écouter.

De la foi aux apparitions du démon dérivent tes diverses croyances relatives à l'existence d'êtres fantastiques, doués suivant les uns de pouvoirs surnaturels, suivant les autres, animés de l'esprit infernal.

Leurs noms changent avec les pays où l'on s'en occupe. Tels sont les follets, les dracs, les trêves, les farfadets, les loups garous, les vampires, les lutins, les elfes, et une foule d'autres dont je vais vous dire quelques mots.

Ces renseignements consoleront un peu Claude Michu de sa sotte équipée de l'autre nuit, en lui montrant qu'il n'est malheureusement pas le seul

Dragon (here, Mr. Morand cast a dark look at Claude who blushed), and yet, since time immemorial, it has been believed that the devil manifests in various forms among us. At all times, the cunning folk have taken advantage of this belief to exploit the common people, and this also proves that there are always been con artists and people who would listen to them.

The apparitions of the devil derive from various beliefs regarding the existence of fantastic beings, endowed with supernatural powers, and according to some, animated by the infernal spirit.

Their names change with the countries where they are found. These include the will-o'-the-wisp, water dragons, treves, leprechauns, werewolves, vampires, goblins, elves, and a host of others, which I will describe to you briefly.

These details somewhat consoled Claude after his witless escape the other night, showing him that he was unfortunately not the only person in the world who

homme au monde qui puisse croire aux billevesées des conteurs.

Les follets, dont je vous parlerai tout d'abord parce qu'ils sont les plus populaires, sont, suivant la chronique, des esprits capricieux, bons ou méchants suivant l'occasion, et prenant volontiers la forme humaine. On croit qu'en se montrant la nuit sous l'apparence de lueurs errantes, ils se plaisent à égarer le voyageur et quelquefois à le conduire vers des précipices, où il trouve la mort. On croit aussi que souvent ils se prennent d'amitié pour certaines gens et se mettent bénévolement à leur service. Les follets font alors tout l'ouvrage de la maison ; ils récurent les marmites, étrillent les chevaux, balayent la maison, ni plus ni moins qu'un bon domestique à cent écus de gages par an.

Pour parler le langage de la raison, je vous dirai que les flammes errantes auxquelles on donne le nom de follets, et que l'on croit appartenir à ces esprits singuliers, sont tout bonnement produites par l'Inflammation d'un gaz que nous appelons le

believed in the frivolous tales of the storytellers.

The wisps, of which I will speak with you first, because they are the most popular, are, according to folklore, capricious spirits, good or mischievous according to the occasion, and willingly taking the human form when they choose. It is believed that by showing themselves at night as wandering lights, they like to entertain themselves by misleading travelers and sometimes directing them to precipices, where they fall to their death. It is also believed that they often make friends with some people and put themselves at their disposal. The wisps then do all the housework – they scour the pots, curry the horses, sweep the house, neither more nor less than a good servant at a hundred crowns per year.

To speak the language of reason, I will tell you that the errant flames which one calls the will-o'-the-wisps, and that one believes are produced by these singular spirits, are simply produced by the inflammation of a gas called hydrogen phosphide,

Sesquiphosphure d'hydrogène, gaz qui se forme dans l'intérieur de la terre par la décomposition des matières animales et qui prend feu spontanément, dès qu'il se dégage à la surface du sol. Si donc vous rencontrez des feux follets, n'en soyez pas effrayés et o servez-les comme un des mille phénomènes que la nature offre à chaque instant à votre attention.

Les dracs dont vous entendez beaucoup parler en Provence a la réputation d'être tes propriétaires invisibles des rivières et des ruisseaux. On prétend qu'ils habitent au fond des eaux et que, pour attirer les femmes et les enfants ; dont ils font leurs principales victimes, ils laissent flotter au milieu les joncs des bijoux d'or ou d'argent. On les nomme aussi les trêves. Sous ce nom, ils hantent plus particulièrement les maisons inhabitées d'où ils sortent, pendant la nuit, pour faire leurs mauvais coups.

Les loups garous, dont je vous ai entendu parler souvent, sont éclos dans l'imagination du moyen âge. On voyait en eux des magiciens qui, doués du ou voir de revêtir toutes les formes,

which is formed in the earth's interior by the decomposition of animal matter and which is spontaneously inflammable as soon as it emerges from the surface. So, if you encounter these will-o'-the-wisps, do not be scared and instead observe them as any one of the thousand diverse phenomena that nature offers each instant to your attention.

The mermaids, or water dragons, that one hears about often in Provence have the reputation of being the invisible proprietors of the rivers and streams. It is believed that they live at the bottom of the waters, and that to attract women and children, their principal victims, they float gold or silver jewels amidst the rushes. They are also called treves. Under this name, they particularly haunt uninhabited houses from where they go out at night to perform their dark deeds.

Werewolves, which I heard you talk about earlier, were popular in the imagination of the Middle Ages. One sees in them magicians able to take any form, choosing in this case that of the

choisissaient de référence celle du loup et ainsi métamorphosés, plaisaient à tourmenter leurs voisins Je pourrais vous parler encore des djinns qui jouent en Orient rôle de vos lutins ; des elfes qui habitent les trailles de la terre ou les profondeurs du ciel ; des gobelins qui inondent les travaux des champs et étouffent tes ouvriers au milieu de vapeurs pestilentielles ; du nickar norvégien qui soulève les tempêtes ; des vampires qui s'abreuvent du sang humain, et de toute l'armée des revenants, spectres, larves, démons qui peuplent les légendes populaires, mais je préfère vous montrer, par un exemple écrit, jusqu'à quel point de folie la croyance aux esprits peut pousser un homme.

wolf and thus metamorphosing to torment their victims. I could also tell you about djinns who are the Eastern equivalent of your elves – elves who live in the fires of the earth or the depths of the sky, or tell you about goblins who flood the fields and smother your workers amidst pestilent vapors, or about Norwegian nickar who raise storms, or vampires who drink human blood, and all the armies of revenants, specters, larvae, and demons that are found in popular legends, but I would rather show you, by a written example, to what extent of madness the belief in spirits can push a man.

En 1821, vivait à Paris un homme qui s'était tellement identifié avec le monde surnaturel qu'il en était arrivé à croire que rien ne se faisait ici-bas sans la permission ou sans le secours des esprits, des farfadets auxquels il attribuait une influence souveraine sur les actes les plus simples.

In 1821, a man lived in Paris who had so identified with the supernatural world that he had come to believe that nothing was done here on earth without the permission or the help of the spirits, leprechauns to whom he attributed a sovereign influence over even the simplest acts.

Cet original, ou plutôt, comme je l'ai dit, ce fou et qui se nommait

This unique character, or rather, as I would term him, this

Berbiguier, s'imagina d'écrire un livre dans lequel il dévoilait toutes les ruses, toutes les malices des démons dont il se prétendait obsédé.

fool who was named Berbiguier, imagined he would write a book in which he would reveal all the tricks, all the evil deeds of the demons that were his obsession.

J'ai entre les mains ce livre qui est une curiosité rare, et je veux vous en faire lire un passage.

I have in my hands this book which is a rare curiosity, and I want you to read a certain passage.

Bernard Morand se leva, ouvrit sa bibliothèque et en tira un petit volume qu'il tendit à Claude Michu.

Bernard Morand got up, opened his library and fetched a little book which he handed to Claude Michu.

— Tiens, fit-il, lis à haute voix. Voici l'endroit où le pauvre fou fait la nomenclature des esprits composant la cour infernale.

"Here," he said, reading aloud, "This is the section where the poor fool makes up the nomenclature of spirits constituting the infernal court."

Et Claude lut ce qui suit :

Claude read the following:

COUR INFERNALE PRINCES ET GRAND DIGNITAIRES	INFERNAL COURT PRINCES AND DIGNITARIES
BELZEBUTH. Chef suprême.	BEELZEBUB, Supreme Chief
SATAN, prince détrôné.	SATAN, Dethroned Prince
EURINOME, prince de la mort.	EURYNOME, Prince of Death *(Mermaid daughter of Oceanus & Tethys)*
MOLOCH, prince du pays des larmes.	MOLOCH, Prince of the country of tears
PLUTON, prince du feu.	PLUTO, Prince of Fire
PAN, prince des incubes,	PAN, Prince of the Incubi
LILITH, prince des succubes.	LILITH, Prince of the Succubae
LÉONARD, grand maître des sabbats.	LEONARD, Grand Master of Sabbats *(Three-horned goat, Dict. Inf)*
BAALBEAITH, grand pontife.	BAALBERITH, Grand Pope *(Lord of the Covenant)*
PAOSBERPINE, archi-diablesse	PROSPERINE, Arch-devil *(Roman Goddess of Spring, Wife of Pluto)*

— Voilà une cour bien composée, interrompît le pharmacien, et notre homme fait bien les choses mais, va plus loin, Claude : lis-nous le passage relatif aux loups-garous.

Claude Michu tourna quelques feuilles et reprit :

« Les sorciers et magiciens devaient autrefois être plus nombreux qu'aujourd'hui. Il est certain qu'on comptait parmi eux des rois, des reines, des princes et des potentats qui partageaient leurs travaux ou les protégeaient. Aussi les ménagés étaient presque toujours troublés ou dérangés par l'approche de ces bandits qui voyageaient par troupes ou isolément ! ils cherchaient à s'emparer des esprits les plus faibles, et comme il y en a dans toutes les classes de la société, c'est parmi le peuple qu'il leur était facile de trouver des victimes ; cependant ils en cherchaient parmi les grands, et pour preuve, je vais en donner un exemple :

« Les misérables s'étaient emparés de l'esprit d'une femme de condition, en lui persuadant

"Here is a well-composed court," interrupted the pharmacist, "and our author does this well, but, go on, Claude – read the passage on werewolves to us."

Claude Michu turned a few pages and continued:

"Wizards and magicians were once more numerous than today. It is certain that there were kings, queens, princes and potentates who practiced their arts and who protected them. Also, housewives were often troubled and bothered by the approach of these bandits who traveled either alone or in groups! They sought to seize the weak-willed, and as there are such folk in all classes of society, it was among these people that they found their victims quite easily, however they particularly sought them out among the rich and powerful, and to prove this, I will give you an example:

"The wretched shysters had seized the spirit of a woman of means and persuaded her that she

qu'elle aurait beaucoup de plaisir et d'agrément à corriger son mari de la passion du chassé, qui lui faisait passer des journées entières éloigné d'elle. Ils lui mirent dans l'esprit de prendre la forme d'un loup et de se jeter sur te chasseur quand elle le verrait entrer dans le bois, où il fallait qu'elle se cachât pour l'attendre.

« L'épouse crédule dit à son mari qu'elle avait une visite à faire à une dame des environs, et à l'aide des moyens magiques qu'on lui prêtera, elle prit la forme d'un loup et alla se mettre à la piste.

« Par un hasard assez singulier, son mari ne sortit pas ce jour-là : il vit de sa fenêtre passer un de ses amis qui s'en allait chasser, et qui l'invita & partager ce plaisir. Il s'en excusa et le pria de lui rapporter un peu de sa chasse : ce que l'ami promit.

« Le chasseur, s'approchant du bois, fut attaqué par un gros loup ; il lui tira un coup de fusil qui ne blessa pas cet animal ; mais il s'approcha de lui, le prit par les oreilles, le renversa et lui coupa une patte qu'il mit dans sa gibecière. Lorsqu'il eut fini de

would have a lot of pleasure and agreed to correct her husband's passion for hunting, which made him spend many days apart from her. They put it in her mind to take the form of a wolf and to surprise her husband by leaping on him when she saw him enter the woods, where she would be hiding in wait.

The gullible wife told her husband that she had to visit a lady in the neighborhood, and with the aid of magical means, she took on the form of a wolf and went to the trail.

By a rather singular chance, her husband did not go out that day – he saw one of his friends passing from his window with whom he would go hunting, and who invited him to join in this pleasure. He excused himself and asked for a tale of the chase – his friend promised to do so.

The hunter, approaching the woods, was attacked by a large wolf. He fired a shot at him which did not hurt the animal, and it continued to approach him. He took the wolf by the ears, knocked him down and cut off a paw which he put in his game bag. When he

chasser, il revint chez son ami, et sortit de ta gibecière cette patte de loup qui, à son grand étonnement, se trouva être la main d'une femme, ornée d'un anneau d'or, qui fut reconnu pour appartenir à la femme de celui qui n'avait pas voulu chasser. De violents soupçons s'élevèrent contre elle ; on la chercha dans toute la maison, et on la trouva enfin auprès du feu de la cuisine, se chauffant, et ayant soin de cacher sa main dont elle ne pouvait plus se servir. Son mari la lui présenta ; elle en fut démontée, elle ne put nier ce qu'elle venait de faire ; elle avoua qu'elle s'était effectivement jetée sur le chasseur qu'elle croyait être ton mari. Cette affaire causa beaucoup de rumeur dans le pays, la justice s'empara de la femme loi fit son procès, et l'on reconnut qu'elle avait été ensorcelée par les farfadets, dont elle avait suivi les conseils. Et, pour avoir cédé à de tels moyens qui prouvaient sa férocité et sa condescendance, elle fut condamnée à être brûlée pour crime de sorcellerie et de préméditation d'assassinat.

« Les ressources des farfadets sont bien grandes puisqu'ils ont pour eux le pouvoir de l'invisibilité

had finished the hunt, he returned to his friend's home, and took the wolf's paw out of the bag. To their amazement, they found it had transformed into a woman's hand, adorned with a gold ring which the husband recognized as that of his wife. Violent suspicions arose against her, and they searched for her throughout the house, finding her by the kitchen fireplace, warming herself, and taking care to hide her hand, but she was unable to do so for long. Her husband confronted her, she could not deny what she had done, she confessed that she had attacked the hunter because she believed he was her husband. This case caused a lot of hubbub in the countryside - the woman was arrested and brought before the judge. It was recognized that she had been bewitched by the leprechauns, whose advice she had followed. For having succumbed to such methods which demonstrated her ferocity and premeditation, she was condemned to be burned at the stake for the crime of witchcraft and premeditated murder.

The resources of the leprechauns are rather vast, since they have the power of invisibility,

et qu'ils peuvent nous tourmenter sans qu'on ait voie, et, à plus forte raison, sans qu'on puisse les saisir. C'est désespérant pour les infortunés qui souffrent ; on doit donc considérer le mal farfadets en comme un mal moral, ce qui est bien plus dangereux qu'un mal physique, dont on peut considérer la cause pour la guérir. On dit vulgairement que le diable est partout ; cela veut dire que tous les lieux de la terre lui sont favorables pour exercer les maléfices qu'il nous prépare et qu'il nous envoie. Il se glisse sous telle forme qui lui plaît, contrefait les personnages qu'il veut. »

Sur un mot de Bernard Morand, Claude suspendit sa lecture.

— Voilà une curieuse rêverie, dit le pharmacien, et vous voyez de quelle jolie façon les contes de ma mère l'Oie ont porté fruit dans l'esprit de notre auteur. Ne vous étonnez pas après cela, si, croyant fermement aux farfadets et animé d'un grand feu de charité pour ses semblables, il a cherché le moyen de sauvegarder ces derniers de l'obsession.

and thus they can torment us without being seen, and further, without being able to be caught. It is hopeless for the poor sufferer, we must therefore consider the bad leprechauns as a moral sickness, which is much more dangerous than physical harm – one might almost consider the cause the remedy. We say in common parlance that the devil is everywhere – this means that all the earth is favorable to exercise his maleficent power that he prepares for us and sends our way. He slips into whatever form he chooses, and counterfeits whichever personality he wishes."

At a word from Bernard Morand, Claude paused his reading.

"That's a curious fantasy," said the pharmacist, "and you see how entertaining are the tales of Mother Goose which have influenced our author. Do not be surprised, after that, if firmly believing in leprechauns and animated by a great fire of charity for his fellowmen, he has looked for ways to save them from this obsession."

Le remède qu'il a trouvé est aussi plaisant que le reste de sa théorie. Avant de vous le faire connaître, je vous rappelle que Berbiguier était une pauvre cervelle détraquée, et qu'il ne faut voir dans l'exposition de son système qu'une nouvelle curiosité, bonne à étudier, surtout pour ceux qui, comme Claude Michu, ont besoin d'exercer leur raison un peu faible sur des faits capables de le mettre en pleine révolte. Lis donc, mon cher Claude, l'histoire du *Baquet Révélateur et des Bouteilles prisons* de Berbiguier.

"The remedy he found is as pleasant as the rest of his theory. Before letting you know this remedy, I must remind you that Berbiguier was a poor deranged soul, and that we must not see in the exposition of his system anything more than a novel curiosity, worth studying, especially for those, like Claude Michu, tend to exercise their reason a bit feebly and not apply the facts to logical end. Read on, my dear Claude, the history of the *Revealing Bucket and the Prison Bottles* of Berbiguier.

BAQUET REVELATEUR ET LES BOUTEILLES PRISONS

THE REVEALING BUCKET & THE PRISON BOTTLES

« Qu'entendez-vous par Baquet révélateur et Bouteilles prisons ? me disent la plupart des personnes à qui je parle de ces choses. Je vous, l'apprendrai dans mon ouvrage, leur dis-je d'un air mystérieux ; car j'ai cela de bon, que je sais donner à ma figure l'air qui convient à la situation.

« Voulez-vous savoir ce que j'appelle mon Baquet révélateur et mes Bouteilles prisons ? je vais maintenant vous les faire connaître.

« Mon Baquet révélateur est un vase en bois que le remplis d'eau et que je place ensuite sur ma fenêtre ; il me sert à dévoiler les farfadets quand ils sont dans les nuages. J'ai, je crois, déjà assez appris à mes lecteurs quelle était la puissance du bouc émissaire ; les farfadets sautent dessus pour s'élever dans les airs lorsqu'ils

"What do you mean by revealing buckets and prison bottles?" ask most people when I speak of these things. I tell them, you will understand these as I teach you my methods, in a mysterious air – because I can grant myself an air suitable to the occasion.

"Would you like to know what I call my revealing bucket and my prison bottles? Let me introduce them to you."

"My revealing bucket is a wooden vessel that I fill with water and then place on my window. This serves to unveil the leprechauns who are in the clouds. I think I have already explained to my readers what the power of the scapegoat is – the leprechauns soar and dive on the airstreams when they use their aerial physics.

veulent s'occuper de leur physique aérienne. C'est donc pour les voir travailler en l'air que j'ai inventé mon Baquet révélateur.

« Ce baquet, rempli d'eau, placé sur ma fenêtre, comme je viens de l'annoncer, me répète, dans l'eau, toutes les opérations de mes ennemis ; je les vois se disputer, sauter, danser et voltiger bien mieux que tous les Fortoso et toutes les Saqui de la terre. Je les vois lorsqu'ils conjurent le temps, lorsqu'ils amoncèlent les nuages, lorsqu'ils allument les éclairs et les tonnerres. L'eau qui est dans le baquet suit tous les mouvements de ces misérables. Je les vois tantôt sous la forme d'un serpent ou d'une anguille, tantôt sous celle d'un sansonnet ou d'un oiseau-mouche : je les vois et je ne puis les atteindre ; je me contente de leur dire : Monstres cruels, pourquoi ne puis-je pas vous noyer tous dans ce baquet qui répète vos affreuses iniquités ! Les malheureux que vous persécutez seraient tous en même temps délivrés de vos infamies. Je vous vois dans ce moment, mon baquet est sur ma fenêtre ; Dieu ! quel troupeau de monstres rassemblés !... Dispersez-vous... Ils s'allient. Incrédules, regardez donc dans

I have therefore invented my revealing bucket to see them travel through the air.

This bucket, filled with water and placed on my window, as I mentioned, serves to reflect for me all the operations of my enemies in the water. I see them argue, jump, dance and fly much better than all the acrobats like Fortoso and Saqui in the world. I watch them when they conjure time, when they pile up the clouds, when they cause lightning and thunder. The water which is in the bucket follows all the movements of these wretches. I see them sometimes in the form of a serpent or an eel, sometimes as that of a starling or a hummingbird. I see them and yet I cannot reach them. I must satisfy myself to say to them – Cruel monsters, why can I not drown all of you in this bucket which reflects your ugly iniquities! The unfortunate people whom you persecute would be immediately delivered from your infamy. I see you right now in my bucket on my window. Dear God! What a flock of monsters is assembled here! Begone! They are allied. Incredulous folk look in my

mon baquet, et vous ne me contrarierez plus par vos dé négations.

« Je passe maintenant à mes bouteilles prisons, toutes les opérations dont j'ai déjà rendu compte ne sont rien en les comparant à celles que je fais à l'aide de ces bouteilles. Autrefois, je ne tenais captifs mes ennemis que pendant huit ou quinze jours ; à présent, je les prive de la liberté pour toujours, si on ne parvient pas à casser les bouteilles qui les renferment, et je les y emprisonne par un moyen bien simple ; lorsque je les sens pendant la nuit marcher et sauter sur mes couvertures je les désoriente en leur jetant du tabac dans les yeux ; ils ne savent plus alors où ils sont ; ils tombent comme des mouches sur ma couverture, où je les couvre de tabac ; le lendemain matin, je ramasse bien soigneusement ce tabac avec une carte, et je le vide dans mes bouteilles, dans lesquelles je mets aussi du vinaigre et du poivré. C'est lorsque tout cela est terminé que je cachète la bouteille avec de la cire d'Espagne, et que je leur, enlève, par ce moyen, toute possibilité de se soustraire à l'emprisonnement auquel je les ai

bucket, and you will not annoy me anymore with your denials.

"Let me tell you now about my prison bottles. All the operations I have described are nothing compared to what I am doing with these bottles. Formerly, I did not keep my enemies under captivity for more than eight or fifteen days. Now, I can deprive them of their liberty forever, if their bottles are not opened or broken. I imprison them in a very simple way – when I feel them walking and jumping on my bedcovers at night, I disorient them by throwing tobacco in their eyes – they do not know where they are and fall like flies on my blanket, where I cover them with tobacco. The next morning, I carefully pick up the tobacco grains with a card and I empty them into my bottles, in which I also put vinegar and pepper. I then seal them with Spanish wax and thereby deny them any ability to escape the imprisonment to which I condemn them.

condamnés.

« Le tabac leur sert de nourriture, et le vinaigre les désaltère quand ils ont soif. Ainsi, ils virent dans un état de gêne, et ils sont témoins de mes triomphes journaliers. Je place mes bouteilles de manière à ce qu'ils puissent voir tout ce que je fais journellement contre leurs camarades et une preuve que je n'en impose pas lorsque je dis qu'ils ne peuvent plus sortir du tabac que je leur ai jeté pour les couvrir, c'est qu'en présence de Mme Gorand,

"Tobacco serves to nourish them, and the vinegar quenches them when they are thirsty. So, they are kept in a state of discomfort, and they are witnesses of my daily triumphs. I place my prison bottles in such a way that they can see everything I do and report to their comrades and as a proof that they cannot escape their bottles, I threw the tobacco from one in front of Mrs. Gerand into the fire, at which point we both heard the burning leprechaun sparkle in the brazier as if they were covered in a large quantity of salt grains.

« J'ai eu le plaisir de jeter de ce tabac au feu, et que nous avons entendu les farfadets qui pétillaient dans le brasier comme si on l'avait couvert d'une grande quantité de grains de sel. Je veux faire présent d'une demi-bouteille au conservateur du Cabinet d'histoire naturelle : il là pourra placer dans la ménagerie des animaux d'une nouvelle espèce : il est vrai qu'il ne pourra pas les tenir captifs dans une loge, comme on y tient le tigre et l'ours Martin, mais il les fera voir dans la bouteille, de laquelle il leur est

"I want to present one of the smaller bottles to the conservator of the Museum of Natural History. He would place it among the menagerie of animals as a new species. It is true that he cannot keep them captive in a cage, as one might place a tiger or a bear, but he would show them in a bottle from which they would be unable to escape."

défendu de s'échapper.

« Si parmi les curieux qui vont visiter le jardin des Plantes et le Cabinet d'histoire naturelle, il se trouvait par hasard quelques incrédules ou quelques farfadets, le conservateur n'aurait pour les convaincre de l'existence des malins esprits dans la prison, qu'à remuer cette bouteille, et entendrait, comme je l'entends journellement, les cris de mes prisonniers qui semblent me demander grâce ; les incrédules se tairaient, et les farfadets enrageraient » :

Morand, quand le lecteur se fut arrêté. Il faut en rire et rien de plus, comme il faut rire de tout ce qui est conçu et exécuté en dépit du bon sens. La soirée n'est pas assez avancée pour que nous nous séparions. Je veux employer le temps qui nous resté à vous parler des fées et à vous faire connaître la légende de Mélusine, la femme serpent, une des fées dont se sont le plus particulièrement occupés les chroniqueurs.

Demain, je vous renseignerai

"If among the curious folk who would visit the Botanical Garden and the Natural History Museum, there were perhaps some who did not believe in the existence of leprechauns, the conservator would only have to ask them to stir the bottle to convince them of the existence of evil spirits in their prison, and hear, as I do on a daily basis, the cries of my prisons who seem to ask me for mercy – this would silence the incredulous and the leprechauns would rage on."

"I will not ask you to suspend your disbelief for too long about what you have just heard," said Bernard Morand, when the reader had finished. "We must laugh and do nothing else, at how nonsensical all this, while seeming well-conceived and well-executed. It is too early for us to draw the evening to a close, so let me tell you about the fairies and acquaint you with the legend of Melusine, the serpent woman, one of the fairies who has been well documented by the chroniclers of these tales.

Tomorrow, I will inform you

sur les enchantements, les évocations, les divinations, les métamorphoses, et autres pratiques de sorcellerie ; vous verrez, j'ose le croire, que tout cela n'est pas plus acceptable que l'existence des farfadets.

Le pharmacien replaça le livre de Berbiguier dans la bibliothèque et en prit un autre.

— C'est, reprit-il, en le remettant à Claude Michu qu'il avait, comme on le voit, élevé aux fonctions de lecteur, c'est un mémoire, où se trouve relatée, d'après un récit de Jean d'Arras, imprimé en 1699, la légende de Mélusine. Tu vas nous lire cela tout au long. Laisse-moi te dire d'abord que les fées, appelées *fados*, en idiôme provençal, ont la spécialité de présider aux naissances et d'agir en bien ou en mal sur la destinée de l'enfant auquel elles s'attachent, les mauvaises langues disent aussi qu'elles éprouvent de l'amour pour les hommes, et poursuivent de leur vengeance ceux qui les ont repoussées ou abandonnées. Du reste, vous avec tous lu des contes de Perrault et vous savez, sans plus ample explication, à qui vous avez affaire. Écoutez donc de

about the enchantments, evocations, divinations, metamorphoses and other practices of witchcraft. You will see, I hope, that all these are no more acceptable than the existence of leprechauns.

The pharmacist replaced Berbiguier's book in the library and took another in his hand.

"This," he said, handing it over to Claude Michu, who he had, as we can see, elevated to the function of reader, "is a memoir, where is narrated, according to a story by Jean d'Arras, printed in 1699, the legend of Melusine. You will hear about the legend soon enough. Let me tell you first about the fairies, called *fados*, in the Provencal idiom, who have the specialty of presiding over births and acting as good or bad spirits, over the destiny of the child to whom they are attached. The dark tales say they experience love for men, and never give up, continuing to wreak their vengeance if they are repulsed or abandoned. You have also read the tales of Perrault, and you know, without further explanation, with whom you are dealing. Listen closely – after this,

toutes vos oreilles ; après quoi, je vous dirai bonne nuit.

I will bid you goodnight.

Et Claude, qui ne se sentait pas fatigué, tant il prenait de plaisir à cet entretien, commença aussitôt l'histoire de la fée Mélusine.

Claude, who did not feel tired, as he took much pleasure in this discussion, began immediately to tell the tale of the fairy Melusine.

HISTOIRE DE LA FÉE MÉLUSINE

Notice historique sur les sciences occultes, par M. dé Fontanelle (collection Roret), Précis du roman de Jean d'Arras d'après un mémoire de M. Babinet

« Jean d'Arras, secrétaire du duc de Berri, recueillit en 1387 les traditions populaires sur Mélusine, par l'ordre de Charles V, pour l'amusement de la duchesse de Bar, sœur du roi, Lusignan fut la dernière forteresse que les Anglais possédèrent de r. le Poitou ; après la victoire que Duguesclin remporta sur eux à Chizé, et la prise de Niort qui en fut la suite, les Anglais furent obligés de rendre Lusignan, dont la plus grande partie de la garnison avait péri au combat de Chizé : le Poitou et toutes les provinces cédées à l'Angleterre par le désastreux traité de Brétigny furent délivrées. Ce fut pour célébrer la reddition de la dernière forteresse qui avait, servi de point d'appui aux Anglais, que Jean d'Arras composa le roman de

THE HISTORY OF THE FAIRY MELUSINE

Historical note on the occult sciences, by M. de Fontanelle (Roret Collection), Summary of the novel by Jean d'Arras from a memoir by Mr. Babinet

Jean d'Arras, secretary of the duke of Berri, collected the popular folktales about Melusine in 1387, by the order of Charles V, for the entertainment of the duchess of Bar, sister of the king. Lusignan was the last fortress that the English held in Poitou. After the victory that Dugeusclin won over them at Chize, and the subsequent taking of Niort, the English were forced to return Lusignan. Most of the garrison of Lusignan had perished at the battle of Chize. Poitou and all the provinces ceded to England by the disastrous treaty of Bretigny were delivered to the French. Jean d'Arras composed the novel of Melusine in celebration of the surrender of the last fortress the English held, who was traditionally believed to be the founder of Lusignan.

Mélusine, que la tradition donnait pour fondatrice à Lusignan.

D'après l'histoire ou roman qu'il publia, Mélusine était fille d'Ëlinas roi d'Albanie, et de Perssine. Perssine était fée, et fut rencontrée par Elinas à la chasse. En l'épousant, elle lui fit promettre qu'il ne la verrait pas dans ses couches. Perssine donna le jour à trois filles : Mélusine, Méliar et Palestine.

According to the novel which he published, Melusine was the daughter of Elinas, king of Albania and Perssine. Perssine was a fairy, who met Elinas when he was hunting. As a condition of her marriage, he promised her he would never see her in her bedchamber. She gave birth to three girls – Melusine, Meliar and Palestine.

Nathas, fils d'un premier lit, jaloux de sa belle-mère, engagea son père à manquer à sa promesse ; Elinas entra dans la chambre de sa femme, et au même instant la reine et ses trois filles disparurent.

Nathas, son of the first wife of Elinas, was jealous of his stepmother, and induced his father to break the promise he had made to her. When Elinas entered his wife's bedchamber, the queen and the three girls disappeared instantly.

« Quand Mélusine et ses sœurs furent grandes, leur mère leur raconta leur origine, la manque de foi de leur père, et l'exil dans lequel elles étaient condamnées à vivre, par suite de cette faute. Pour venger les malheurs de leur mère, les trois sœurs saisirent leur père, l'enfermèrent dans une caverne creusée dans une montagne, et l'y condamnèrent à une prison perpétuelle. Perssine irritée du

When Melusine and her sisters grew older, their mother told them of their origins, the betrayal of their father, and the subsequent exile to which they had been condemned to live in, as a result. To avenge the misfortunes of their mother, the three sisters seized their father and imprisoned him in a cavern dug into a mountain, condemning him to a perpetual prison. Perssine,

crime de ses filles, et plaignant un époux qu'elle n'avait cessé d'aimer, chassa, ses trois filles de sa présence en les maudissant. Mélusine fut condamnée à être, tous les samedis, serpent depuis la ceinture. Cependant, si elle trouvait un époux qui consentit à ne pas la voir le samedi, son supplice finissait avec sa vie ; s'il lui manquait de parole, son supplice ne devait finir qu'au jugement dernier, Méliar fut enfermée dans un château d'Arménie, occupée à la garde d'un épervier et Palestine était destinée à veiller, dans le sein d'une haute montagne, à la conservation d'un trésor, jusqu'à ce qu'un chevalier de la maison de Lusignan vînt la chercher pour conquérir la Terre-Sainte.

« Jean d'Arras ne dit point ce que devint Mélusine après la malédiction de sa mère : il transporté ses lecteurs à la cour d'un comte de Poitiers qu'il nomme Aimery. Ce comte, dans une partie de chasse, égaré dans la forât de Colombier avec Raimondin, son neveu, fut surpris par la nuit.

Versé dans l'astrologie, il

irritated by the crime of her daughters, and defending a husband who she had never ceased to love, drove her three daughters from her presence, cursing them. Melusine was condemned to transform, every Saturday, to become a snake from her waist down. However, if she found a husband who agreed not to see her on Saturday, her punishment would end in the present life, if he failed to speak with her, she would be condemned until Judgement Day. Meliar was imprisoned in a castle of Armenia, guarded by a sparrow hawk, and Palestine was destined to watch and protect a treasure in the heart of a tall mountain, until a knight from the house of Lusignan came to fetch her to conquer the Holy Land.

Jean d'Arras does not tell us what happened to Melusine after her mother's curse. He takes his readers to the castle of a Count of Poitiers named Aimery. This count, in a hunting party, was lost in the forest of Colombier with Raimondin, his nephew, during the night.

Skilled in astrology, he

consulta les astres, et vit qu'ils promettaient une fortune brillante à celui qui lui donnerait la mort dans cette nuit. A peine avait-il cessé de faire part à Raimondin de celte triste prophétie, que le sanglier qu'on avait poursuivi tout le jour vint attaquer les deux chasseurs égarés. Raimondin se précipite devant son oncle pour le défendre, le sanglier se détourne et va se jeter sur le comte qui s'était saisi d'un épieu. Raimondin le poursuit, le frappe de son épée, mais la lame glisse sur les soies, et le coup atteignait le comte qui fut percé d'outre en outre, au moment où il enferrait le sanglier de son épieu.

Raimondin, épouvanté de ce forfait involontaire, monta sur son palefroi, et s'éloigna de ce funeste lieu. Laissant guider son cheval au hasard, il erra jusqu'au lendemain matin, tellement troublé du malheur qui lui était arrivé, qu'il ne voyait rien de ce qui l'environnait : enfin il fut tiré de cet état par un mouvement d'épouvante que fit son coursier ;

Il reconnut alors qu'il était dans un lieu très aventureux. Du pied d'un rocher sourcilleux sortait une fontaine merveilleuse appelée la

consulted the stars, and saw that they promised a brilliant future to whoever would kill him that night. Hardly had he ceased to inform Raimondin of this sad prophecy when they were attacked by a wild boar, who had chased them all day. Raimondin rushed in front of his uncle to defend him , but the boar turned away and leapt on the Count who had seized a spear. Raimondin pursued the bear and struck him with his sword, but the blade slipped over its bristles and struck the Count, who was stabbed just as he was spearing the wild boar.

Raimondin, terrified by this involuntary crime, mounted his palfrey and departed from this fatal place. Leaving his horse to wander by chance, he wandered until the next morning, so troubled by the misfortune that had struck him, that he did not pay attention to his environs, until he was at last drawn from this state by a movement of his steed.

He recognized then that he was in a very risky place. He was at the foot of a high rock, from which sprung a marvelous

fontaine do Soif, la fontaine Fée, ou la Font de-Cé, et renommée pour les prodiges qui s'y opéraient.

Là se baignait Mélusine avec deux suivantes : elle fut au-devant de Raimondin, le rassura, lui raconta la prédilection de son oncle et tout ce qui venait de lui arriver. Raimondin, surpris de ce qu'il entendait, crut que la justice divine le poussait dans ce lieu redoutable, pour lui faire subir le châtiment du meurtre de seigneur ; mais rassuré de nouveau parla dame, il s'abandonna à ses conseils, et retourna, à Poitiers, trouva le peuple plongé dans le deuil : la populace imputant au sanglier la mort de son souverain, brûlait devant la porte de l'église où se faisaient les obsèques du comte, le corps du sanglier, comme félon et faux meurtrier.

« Raimondin, suivant les conseils de Mélusine, rendit hommage au nouveau comte, et lui demanda de lui octroyer en fief, autant de terrain qu'une peau de cerf pourrait en enceindre. Le comte, regarda cela comme de peu

fountain called the Fountain of Thirst, the Fairy Fountain or the Bridge of the Seas, and renowned for the wonders which were witnessed thereabouts.

Melusine was bathing there, with two attendants. She met Raimondin and reassured him that the situation of his uncle and all that had transpired was not his fault. Raimondin, surprised by what he had heard, though that divine justice was pushing him to this redoubtable place, to make him undergo the punishment for the murder of his lord, but reassured again by the lady, he gave himself to her counsel and returned to Poitiers to find the people plunged in mourning. The populace, imputing to the boar the death of their sovereign, were burning the body of the wild boar as a felon and false murderer at the door of the church where they were performing the Count's funeral.

Raimondin, following the advice of Melusine, paid tribute to the new count, and asked him to grant him in fief, as much ground as a stag's skin might cover. The count, looking upon this request as having little value, saw no

de valeur, ne fit aucune difficulté, et nomma les commissaires qui devaient délivrer ce don à Raimondin.

En sortant de l'église de Saint-Hilaire, où le comte recevait le serment de ses nouveaux sujets, un homme se présenta à Raimondin, et lui offrit une peau de cerf ; il l'acheta et la donna à un sellier pour la tailler en lanières, ce que l'ouvrier exécuta avec tant d'adresse, que les commissaires furent étonnés quand ils virent combien elles étaient déliées ; mais Raimondin représentant la charte que lui avait fait expédier le comte ils furent obligés de l'exécuter littéralement, ainsi que le demandait Raimondin.

En arrivant à la fontaine dé Soif, ils virent avec surprise que dans ce lieu inhabité, on avait fait une immense tranchée au milieu des forêts séculaires qui le couvraient ; à l'instant deux hommes leur apparurent, prirent le cuir de cerf, et suivant la marche que leur indiquait la tranchée ils parcoururent un circuit de deux lieues (8 kilomètres). Retournés au point d'où ils étaient partis, il leur restait un superflu de lanières, ils le déroulèrent pour agrandir le

difficulty in granting it, and named the commissioners who would deliver this request to Raimondin.

On leaving the church of St. Hiliers, where the count was receiving the vows of his new subjects, a man presented himself to Raimondin and offered him a stag's skin, which he bought and gave to a saddler to cut into strips, which the workman executed with such skill that the commissioners were surprised when they saw how finely it had been sliced, but they were obliged to literally execute the charter the Count had given them, as demanded by Raimondin.

When they arrived at the Fountain of Thirst, they were surprised to see that an immense trench had been dug in this uninhabited place amidst the surrounding forests. At once, two men appeared, took the skin of the stag and following the path indicated by the trench, they covered a circuit of two leagues (eight kilometers). Returning to the starting point, they discovered they had a surfeit of strips. They unrolled these to enlarge the circle

cercle, et au lieu où ils plantèrent le pieu qui devait le fixer il jaillit une fontaine, et les deux hommes disparurent.

Les commissaires, remplis d'étonnement, retournèrent à la cour du comte, et racontèrent les merveilles dont ils avaient été témoins. Quelques jours après, Raimondin revint à Poitiers, invita le comte et toute sa cour à ses noces avec Mélusine, e qui mit le comble à la surprise qu'avait produite le récit des commissaires. Le comte demanda à Raimondin quels étaient la naissance et l'état de sa nouvelle épouse ; il refusa de répondre, et dès lors tout le monde fut persuadé qu'il avait trouvé une aventure près de la Fontaine-Fée.

Les noces se firent avec toute la pompe possible ; le comte et les seigneurs qui l'accompagnaient admiraient l'élégance et le nombre des pavillons préparés en si peu de temps pour recevoir si noble compagnie, et ne pouvaient comprendre d'où venait la multitude des serviteurs qui s'empressaient de pourvoir aux besoins des dames et des chevaliers que la renommée de

and instead of planting a stake to hold it together, a fountain sprung up in the center and the two men disappeared.

The commissioners, filled with astonishment, returned to the Count's castle, and recounted the marvels that they had witnessed. Some days later, Raimondin returned to Poitiers to invite the Count and all his court to his wedding with Melusine, which further increased the surprise that had been caused by the tale of the commissioners. The count asked Raimondin what was the parentage and country of origin of his new wife. He refused to answer and from that moment on, everyone was convinced he had had an adventure near the Fountain of the Fairies.

The wedding was performed with much pomp and circumstance – the Count and the lords who accompanied him admired the elegance and number of pavilions prepared in such a short time to receive the nobles of the country, and could not understand where he had found the multitude of servants who hastened to meet the needs of the ladies and knights who had been

l'événement avait attirés & ces noces merveilleuses. Les grâces de Mélusine captivèrent tous les cœurs, et le comte, qui n'avait d'abord vu qu'avec peine une femme inconnue entrer dans sa famille, laissa les nouveaux époux, persuadé qu'une telle alliance ne pouvait être qu'à l'honneur de son lignage.

attracted to this marvelous marriage by the fame of the event. The gracefulness of Melusine captivated all hearts, and the Count, who had initially felt a challenge at allowing an unknown woman to enter into his family, left the newly married couple, convinced that such an alliance could only increase the honor of his lineage.

« Nous ne devons pas oublier ici que Mélusine, avant de consentir à son mariage avec Raimondin, lui avait fait jurer que jamais il ne la verrait le samedi, ni ne s'inquiéterait de ce qu'elle deviendrait.

"We must not forget that Melusine, before agreeing to marry Raimondin, had made him swear that he would never look at her on Saturday, or ask her what she became.

Mélusine, outre les richesses dont elle combla Raimondin, lui donna comme présent nuptial a deux verges desquelles les pierres avaient grande vertu. L'une, que celui à qui elle sera donnée par amour, ne pourra mourir par nuls coups d'armes ; l'autre, que celui à qui elle sera donnée, aura victoire sur ses malveillants, soit en plaids, soit en mêlée.

Melusine, in addition to the riches that she granted Raimondin, gave him a nuptial present of two wands which had crystals of great value. The first, that he to whom it would be given in love would not die by the stroke of arms, the second, that he to whom it be given would be victorious over his enemies, whether individually or in a group.

Après le départ du comte do Poitiers, Mélusine apprit à Raimondin que son père était originaire de Bretagne, qu'il y

After leaving the Count of Poitiers, Melusine told Raimondin that his father was originally from Brittany, where he had possessed

possédait de grands biens, dont il avait été dépouillé par suite d'un complot ourdi, contre lui par un seigneur breton nommé Josselin, qui possédait toute la confiance du roi de Bretagne, et à qui l'on avait donné les biens confisqués sur son père. Raimondin, par les conseils de Mélusine, alla en Bretagne redemander l'héritage de ses aïeux.

Le roi, pour connaître la vérité des réclamations du chevalier étranger, ordonna le combat judiciaire entre Raimondin et le fils de Josselin. Raimondin fut vainqueur, et demanda la grâce de vaincus ; mais le roi était trop bon justicier, pour ne pas faire pendre sur-le-champ Josselin et son fils déclarés traîtres par le jugement de Dieu.

Le roi breton fit tous ses efforts pour fixer près de lui un si brave chevalier, mais l'amour de Mélusine rappelait Raimondin près le rocher de la Fontaine-Fée : il donna les terres qu'il venait de conquérir à deux de ses cousins qui demeuraient en Bretagne, et laissa le roi aussi plein d'admiration de son courage, que surpris de sa générosité.

Les parents de Josselin,

great property, which he had been deprived of by a conspiracy hatched by a Breton Lord named Josselin, who had the ear of the king of Brittany, and to whom the confiscated property had been granted by his father. Raimondin, on the advice of Melusine, went to Brittany to demand the inheritance of his ancestors.

The king, to know the truth of the claims of the strange knight, ordered a judicial combat between Raimondin and the son of Josselin. Raimondin was victorious and asked for mercy for the vanquished, but the king was too good a judge not to order the hanging of Josselin and his son who were declared traitors in God's judgement.

The Breton king made every effort to keep the brave knight by his side, but his love for Melusine recalled Raimondin to the rock of the Fairy Fountain. He gave the lands he had just conquered to two cousins who lived in Brittany, and left the King as filled with admiration for his courage as for his generosity.

Josselin's parents, wanting to

voulant venger la honte dont Raimondin les avait couverts, lui dressèrent à son retour une embûche qu'il dissipa par sa valeur. Pendant son absence, Mélusine n'était pas restée oisive : à l'aide des ouvriers que sa puissance magique mettait à ses ordres, elle avait bâti en quelques jours un magnifique château sur la montagne et le rocher qui dominaient la Fontaine de Soif.

Raimondin, à son retour crut que ses yeux l'abusaient en voyant une forteresse, et du haut de ses donjons élevés, entendant résonner le cor de la sentinelle, dans un lieu que naguère, il avait laissé désert. Le nouveau château fut nommé Lusignan.

Raimondin y jouit longtemps de la puissance et de la gloire que la sagesse de Mélusine lui procurait, Il en eut neuf enfants : l'aîné Uriana, fut roi de Chypre ; le second, Guyon, roi d'Arménie ; le troisième, Regnault, roi de Bretagne ; le quatrième, Geoffroy & la Grande dent, seigneur de Lusignan ; le cinquième, Fraimon, moine â Maillezais ; le sixième, Antoine, duc de Luxembourg ; le septième, Raimond, comte de Forêts ; le huitième, Thierry,

avenge the shame which Raimondin had given them, set a trap for him on his return, which he dispelled by his valor. During his absence, Melusine had not remained idle – by the aid of her magical powers her workmen had constructed a magnificent castle in a few days on the mountain overlooking the Fountain of Thirst.

Raimondin, on his return thought that his eyes betrayed him when he saw a tall fortress and heard a sentry's horn from the high keep of a place he had left in a deserted condition. The new castle was called Lusignan.

Raimondin ruled over this castle for a long time by the power and glory which he had by the wisdom of Melusine. He had nine children – the eldest, Urania, was king of Cyprus; the second, Guyon, was king of Armenia; the third, Regnault, was king of Brittany; the fourth, Geoffrey of the Great Tooth became Lord of Lusignan; the fifth, Fraimon, a monk at Maillezais, the sixth, Antoine, Duke of Luxembourg, the seventh, Raymond, Count of

seigneur de Parthenay; et le neuvième, qu'on appela l'Horrible, parce qu'il n'avait qu'un œil au milieu du front, fut mis à mort d'après les ordres que donna sa mère au moment où elle s'envola moitié femme et moitié serpent. Sa science magique lui avait appris que, s'il vivait, il détruirait tout ce qu'elle avait fait pour la grandeur de sa maison ; il fut étouffé sous du foin mouillé auquel on avait mis le feu, et enterré dans l'abbaye de Moutierneuf, à Poitiers.

Mélusine et Raimondin vivaient heureux, quand l'envie vint troubler leur félicité. Le comte de Forêts, frère aîné dé Raimondin, jaloux de sa prospérité, ayant su que tous les samedis Mélusine disparaissait, et que personne ne savait ce qu'elle devenait, fit naître dans l'esprit de son frère des soupçons sur la fidélité de sa femme.

Raimondin, enflammé de jalousie, pénètre dans les salles les plus reculées du château, lieux redoutables où il n'avait jamais osé s'avancer ; il est arrêté par d'énormes portes d'airain ; furieux et croyant voir dans ces

Forests, the eighth, Thierry, Lord of Parthenay, and the ninth, named 'The Horrible', because he had but one eye in the middle of his forehead, was put to death according to the orders of his mother when she was half woman and half serpent. Her magical science had taught her that if he lived, he would destroy everything that she had accomplished for the grandeur of her house. He was therefore stifled under wet hay, which had been set on fire, and was interred in the Abbey of Moutierneuf in Poitiers.

Melusine and Raimondin lived happily until envy disturbed their bliss. The Count of Forests, elder brother of Raimondin, jealous of his prosperity, having known that Melusine disappeared every Saturday and no one knew where she went, induced suspicion in his brother about the fidelity of his wife.

Raimondin, inflamed by jealousy, entered the most secret rooms of the castle, formidable places he had never dared advance to. He was stopped by enormous brass doors. Furious and wishing to see inside these barriers - proof

précautions - preuve de l'accusation dirigée contre son épouse, il tire son épée, et appuyant la pointe contre la porte, il tourne sa laine et fait un trou, qui révèle a son œil indiscret le plus déplorable mystère : il voit Mélusine qui faisait sa pénitence moitié femme et moitié serpent. Elle se débattait dans un large bassin, dont elle faisait jaillir l'eau jusqu'aux voûtes de la salle.

Raimondin, saisi de pitié et d'épouvante, de voir une si noble dame dans un misérable état, bouche le trou fatal ; sa fureur se tourna contre son frère qu'il chassa de sa présence, en le menaçant de la mort, s'il ne retourne jamais dans les lieux soumis à son pouvoir ; mais, comme le funeste secret ne lui était pas échappé, le charme n'était pas rompu, et après une nuit pleine d'angoisses, il vit Mélusine revenir le trouver comme à l'ordinaire, il espérait encore le bonheur, quand un malheur domestique vint tout perdre.

« Geoffroy irrité de ce que Fraimon s'était fait moine, va à l'abbaye de Maillezais, et trouvant les religieux réunis pour les offices divins, il fait un énorme bûcher

of the accusations directed against his wife – he drew his sword and pressing the point against the door, he turned the hilt and made a hole, which revealed the most deplorable mystery to his indiscreet eye – he saw Melusine performing her punishment as half woman and half serpent. She was struggling with a large basin, from which she poured water into the vaults of the hall.

Raimondin, seized with pity and terror, to see a noble lady in such a miserable state, shut up the fatal hole. His fury turned against his brother, whom he chased from his presence, threatening him with death, if he ever returned to his domain. But, as the fatal secret had not escaped him, the charm was not broken, and after a night filled with anguish, he saw Melusine return to find him as usual. He still hoped for happiness, but an unfortunate servant caused him to lose everything.

Geoffrey, irritated that Fraimon had become a monk, went to the Abbey of Maillezais, and finding the religious folk gathered for divine offices, made

autour de l'église et la réduit en cendres avec les moines et le couvent ; Raimondin, détestant cet attentat, reproche publiquement à Mélusine, qu'elle et sa postérité ne sont que fantômes, qu'il a été déçu par ses charmes et sortilèges et dévoile le secret de sa pénitence du samedi.

an enormous bonfire around the church and burned the monks and the convent to ashes. Raimondin, angered with this attack, publicly reproached Melusine, that she and her children were only phantoms, and that he was disappointed by her charms and spells and revealed the secret of her Saturday penitence.

Alors la destinée de Mélusine s'accomplit, la malédiction maternelle retombe sur elle ; elle s'élance par une fenêtre sur laquelle reste empreinte la forme de son pied, et s'envole moitié femme et moitié serpent. Raimondin, revenu de la colère, resta dans un long abattement, à l'aspect des désastres qu'il venait d'appeler sur sa tête ; et pour expier autant qu'il le pouvait le malheur dont il avait frappé une femme qui l'avait comblé de bienfaits, il renonce à sa toute-puissance ; va faire un pèlerinage à Rome, et se rend ensuite dans une solitude près de la ville de Montferrat.

Thus, the destiny of Melusine was accomplished – her maternal curse fell on her. She hurled herself out of a window on which remains the mark of her foot and transformed into a half woman, half-serpent form. Raimondin, calming himself from his anger, remained in a long depression, at the sight of disasters that he had called on himself, and to expiate his sins of striking a woman who had showered him with such favor, he renounced all his power and went on a pilgrimage to Rome, before secluding himself in solitude in the town of Montserrat.

Quant à Mélusine, elle n'avait plus d'habitation connue sur la terre: réduite jusqu'au jugement dernier à l'état monstrueux où l'avait jetée la malédiction de sa

As for Melusine, she had no dwelling on earth – she was condemned until Judgement Day to the monstrous state which her mother's curse had placed on her.

mère, sa tendresse pour ses jeunes enfants la rappelait près de leur berceau, et leurs nourrices l'ont rue souvent traîner silencieusement son énorme queue dans leur chambre et leur prodiguer pendant la nuit ses soins maternels.

Her tenderness for her children brought her back to their cradle, and their nurses often dragged her enormous tail into their rooms, and she nourished them during the night with her maternal care.

Dans les siècles suivants, quand une calamité menaçait sa postérité, on l'entendait au milieu d'une nuit orageuse, errer gémissante autour des créneaux du château de Lusignan. Une apparition bien constatée, s'il en existe, est l'aventure suivante.

In the following centuries, whenever a calamity endangered her posterity, she was heard on a stormy night, roaming the battlements of the castle of Lusignan. A well-known apparition, if any exist, is described in the following adventure:

Après que les succès dus à la sagesse de Charles V et à la bravoure de son connétable, eurent abattu la puissance anglaise sur le continent, Jean, duc de Berri et comte de Poitou, se présenta avec une armée sous les murs de Lusignan, seule forteresse que les Anglais tinssent encore dans le Poitou. Serville, qui y commandait, fut obligé de capituler ;

After the successes due to the wisdom of Charles V and the bravery of his constable, who had defeated the English power on the continent, Jean, Duke of Berri and Count of Poitou, brought an army to the walls of Lusignan, the only fortress the English still held in Poitou. Serville, who commanded the castle, was obliged to surrender.

il raconta au duc de Berri que, la nuit précédente, un monstre moitié femme et moitié serpent lui avait apparu ; qu'avec sa queue

He told the Duke of Berri that the preceding night, a monstrous half-woman, half-serpent being had appeared before him, it had

longue de 8 & 9 pieds il frappait sur le lit dans lequel il était couché ; qu'alors il prit son épée pour se défendre ; mais que la serpente ne lui fit aucun mal ; qu'elle alla se chauffer près d'un grand feu qui éclairait toute la chambre, qu'elle y resta toute la nuit ; que même pendant quelque temps, elle reprit la forme humaine ; mais qu'elle n'était vêtue que d'étoffes grossières, comme une pénitente, et paraissait ne pouvoir rester en place.

« Comment, Serville, répondit le duc de Berri, « vous qui avez été en tant de places, avez-vous eu peur de cette serpente ? C'est la dame de cette forteresse qui la fit édifier : sachez qu'elle ne vous fera jamais de mal ; elle vous veut montrer comment il vous fallait dessaisir de cette place. »

« Serville ajouta alors qu'une femme du pays, avec laquelle il charmait les ennuis de la garnison, avait été témoin de l'apparition et n'avait manifesté aucune crainte. Pour ne pas douter de la réalité de ce fait, il faut se rappeler que Jean d'Arras ; étant secrétaire du duc de Berri, écrirait par ordre de Charles V, vainqueur des Anglais, et que, lors de cette apparition, Mélusine,

struck his bed with its long tail, about 8-9 feet long. He took his sword to defend himself, but the snake did not harm him, but went to warm herself by a large fire which illuminated the entire room and stayed there all night. She even assumed her human form for some time, but was dressed in only coarse rags, like a penitent, and seemed unable to defend herself.

"Serville" replied the duke of Berri, "how did you, who have been in so many places, have any fear of this serpent? This was the lady of this fortress, that she had erected – you knew that she would never hurt you. She wanted to show you how you had to withdraw from this place."

"Serville then added that a local woman, with whom he had charmed the boredom of his garrison, had witnessed the apparition and had not displayed any fear. In order to not doubt the reality of this fact, it must be remembered that Jean d'Arras, being secretary of the Duke of Berri had written this down by the order of Charles V, victor over the

loin d'être gémissante, reçut un allégement à ses peines, parce qu'elle put un instant reprendre sa forme naturelle, sans doute parce que le château qu'elle avait construit, allait être délivré du joug de l'étranger. »

English, and that, this apparition, Melusine, far from being troubled, had been able for a brief time to resume her natural human form, no doubt because the castle she had constructed was about to be delivered from the yoke of the foreigner.

Tel est la fidèle analyse du récit de Jean d'Arras.

Such is the faithful analysis of the narrative of Jean d'Arras.

On y retrouve tout le moyen âge avec sa crédulité naïve et son imagination pleine de merveilles.

One finds such tales everywhere in the Middle Ages, with its naïve credulity and its wondrous imagination.

Le jour suivant, Bernard Morand débuta ainsi :

—Toi, Claude Michu, qui as le désir de te faire. bien venir de Madeloun, ta jolie commère, je vais t'apprendre une conjuration magique, dont on se servait, en Allemagne, au temps jadis, pour se faire aimer des filles.

On prenait un cheveu de sa bien-aimée on le plaçait sous ses vêtements, puis on faisait une confession générale ; — puis encore on faisait dire trois messes pendant lesquelles on mettait le cheveu autour de son cou. Au dernier évangile, on allumait un cierge bénit et l'on disait : O cierge, je te conjure par la vertu du Dieu tout-puissant, par les neuf chaînes des anges, par la vertu gardienne, de m'amener celle que j'aime, afin qu'elle m'appartienne.

Que penses-tu de ce procédé, Claude Michu ?

—Je pense, monsieur Morand, que vous vous moquez de moi.

—Je ne me moque pas de toi ; je ne fais que te rapporter une pratique dont beaucoup d'amoureux transis se sont servis.

The following day, Bernard Morand began thus:

"You, Claude Michu, who would like to be attractive to Madeleine, your pretty little busybody, I will teach you a magic conjuration, which was popular in Germany in the old days to ensure one's true love."

One would take a lock of hair of one's beloved and place it in his clothes, then one would make a general confession – and then perform three masses during which the hair was placed around his neck. At the last gospel, one lit a blessed candle and said, "O candle, I beseech you by the virtue of the All-Powerful God, by the nine chained angels, by the guardian spirit, to bring me the one I love, so that she belongs to me."

"What do you think of this process, Claude Michu?"

"I think, Mr. Morand, that you are mocking me."

"I am not making fun of you. I am only describing to you a practice that many lovers had used to their benefit. You will grant me

Tu m'accorderas bien qu'elle n'est pas plus ridicule que celle du Dragon Rouge, et qu'il n'est pas plus sot de faire brûler un cierge que de faire griller une tête d'âne comme lu l'as expérimenté au Trou-Noir ?

Et comme Claude baissait la tête plein do honte :

— Allons, reprit Morand, remets-toi ; je voulais rire un peu avant de nous entretenir des nombreuses formules de divination ou d'enchantement employées par les amateurs de merveilleux à toutes les époques.

La divination a toujours joui d'une grande faveur auprès des esprits faibles.

Connaître l'avenir, voilà pour beaucoup de gens l'affaire importante de la vie. Ils ne songent pas que l'avenir appartient à Dieu et que te devoir de l'homme est de vivre honnêtement dans le présent en laissant à la Providence le soin des choses futures.

Le ciel nous eût fait un présent funeste s'il nous eût donné le pouvoir de lire dans notre

that it is not more ridiculous than that of the Red Dragon, and that it is not as foolish to light a candle as to burn a donkey's head like your experiment at the Black Hole?"

Claude lowered his head in shame.

"Come," said Morand, "compose yourself. I wanted a little laughter before we talk about the many formulas of divination or enchantment used by magical dabblers in all ages."

"Divination has always enjoyed great favor with weak minds."

"To know the future is the most important objective of many people in their lives. They do not think that the future belongs to God and that the duty of man is to live honestly in the present, leaving for Providence the care of future things."

"Heaven would have made us a baneful present if we were given the power to read our own

destinée.

C'eût été nous refuser le bonheur ; car quel homme serait assez hardi pour supporter sans faiblir le poids d'une science qui lui permettrait de sonder les mystères du temps. Il connaîtrait d'avance les épreuves par lesquelles il doit passer, il saurait quel terme est assigné à ses jours, et cette connaissance lui rendrait l'existence insupportable ; il calculerait les heures qui lui restent et vivrait sans cette espérance dans laquelle l'esprit trouve ses plus douces satisfactions.

Les anciens ont beaucoup pratiqué la divination.

— Les météores, la forme des nuages étaient des signes qu'ils interprétaient suivant leurs divers aspects. Ils faisaient aussi des prédictions au moyen de l'alectoromancie ; c'est-à-dire en décrivant sur la terre un cercle qui se divisait en 24 parties, dans chacune desquelles on plaçait une lettre de l'alphabet et un grain de blé.

destiny."

"This would have denied us our present happiness – because which man would be bold enough to support himself without succumbing to the power of a science which allowed him to probe the mysteries of time? He would know in advance the future tests he must pass; he would know what term was assigned to his days, and this knowledge would make life unbearable for him. He would calculate the remaining hours and live without the hope in which the mind finds sweetest satisfaction."

"The ancients had many methods of divination."

"Meteors and the shapes of clouds were signs that they interpreted according to the various forms. They also made predictions by means of alectoromancy – that is, by describing on the earth a circle divided into twenty-four parts, in each of which was placed a letter of the alphabet and a grain of wheat.

Un coq était ensuite introduit dans le cercle et à mesure que le coq mangeait un des grains, on notait la lettre que ce grain recouvrait. Les lettres assemblées formaient l'élément de la prédiction.

"A rooster was then introduced into the circle and as the rooster ate one of the grains, one noted the letter that this grain covered. The letters formed the element of prediction."

Ils connaissaient encore la divination par le sel. C'était un mauvais présage que d'oublier de placer les salières sur la table, ou que de s'endormir avant qu'elles fussent retirées. A notre époque, les gens superstitieux s'effrayent encore d'une salière renversée ; il n'y a d'autre malheur là-dedans que la perte de la salière quand elle se casse, ou celle du sel quand il se répand.

"They also knew divination by salt. It was considered a bad omen to forget to put the saltshakers on the table, or to fall asleep before they were removed. In our day, superstitious people are still frightened by an overturned saltshaker — there is no other misfortune in this than the loss of the saltshaker when it breaks, or that of the salt when it spills.

Mais le goût de la divination ne se bornait pas toujours à ces innocentes remarques ; il a fait commettre des crimes, car bien souvent on a voulu chercher dans les entrailles humaines le secret des destinées futures.

But the taste for divination was not always limited to these innocent examples. They would commit various crimes, such as to search in human entrails for the secret of future events.

Les sacrifices humains offerts par les Druides, nos ancêtres, ont ensanglanté le soi que nous cultivons aujourd'hui, et des milliers d'innocents sont tombés victimes d'un préjugé barbare que le christianisme seul a pu détruire.

The human sacrifices offered by the Druids, our ancestors have bloodied the soil we cultivate today, and thousands of innocent people have fallen victim to barbaric practices that only Christianity could destroy. *(ed. Ironic)*

Les astres, les nombres, les couleurs, le vol des oiseaux, les plantes, ont servi à la divination.

En ce qui concerne les plantes, on peut, sans tourner au sorcier, partager sur un point la confiance qu'on leur accordait. Ainsi, il est positif qu'en examinant certaines plantes, on peut d'une manière à peu près exacte, indiquer l'heure qu'il est. Mais il n'y a rien de merveilleux dans ce fait ; il est purement scientifique et basé sur des notions acquises à l'égard des habitudes des végétaux.

On a reconnu, en effet, que les corolles des fleurs s'ouvrent se ferment à heure fixe. Avec quelques connaissances en botanique, on peut composer une horloge florale et se passer de montre ou de cadran, solaire. Linné s'est donné ce divertissement et adressé un tableau où, en regard des noms des plantes observées, se trouvent inscrites les heures de jour et de nuit auxquelles ces plantes s'ouvrent où se ferment.

Les fleurs m'ont souvent appris à moi-même, pendant mes longues promenades, qu'il était

The stars, the numbers, the colors, the flight of birds, plants were used for divination.

Regarding plants, one can, without turning to sorcery, agree to one aspect about them that the sorcerers claim. It is certain that by examining some plants, one can almost exactly tell what time it is, but there is nothing marvelous about this fact – it is purely scientific and based on acquired notions with respect to plant habits.

It has been recognized, for example, that the corollas of flowers open and close at a fixed time. With some knowledge of botany, one can compose a floral clock and manage without a solar clock. Linnaeus gave this example and constructed a table which shows the hours of day and night that various plants open and close.

Flowers have been my companions on my long walks, until it was time to return home.

temps de revenir du logis.

Ainsi, en voyant le nymphéa blanc replier son calice, je me disais : je suis en retard, il est cinq heures ; car le nymphéa, qui s'épanouit à sept heures du matin, se referme à cinq heures du soir.

So, seeing the white waterlily fold back it's chalice, I tell myself, "I am late, it is five o'clock, because the waterlily, which blooms at 7 A.M. in the morning, closes at five o'clock in the evening.

Toutes les heures sont indiquées de la même façon.

All times are indicated in the same manner.

Il est des plantes qui marquent plus spécialement les heures de nuit. Ce sont, par exemple, le géranium triste, le silène noctiflore et le cactus à grande fleur, qui éclosent à six, à neuf et à dix heures. J'imagine que vous ne pensiez pas avoir autour de vous d'aussi charmantes horloges ; un jour je vous apprendrai à les utiliser d'une manière complète : permettez-moi maintenant de parler de songes dont on prétend encore lute des avertissements concluants.

There are plants that especially mark the night hours. These are, for example, the geranium triste, the Night-flowering catchfly and the large-flowered cactus, which bloom at six, nine and ten o'clock. I imagine that you did not think that you had such charming clocks around you. One day, I will teach you to use them in a more comprehensive manner. Allow me now to speak of dreams in which people still pretend to read hidden warnings.

Ne croyez pas à l'interprétation des songes, mes amis ; n'achetez jamais ces traités absurdes où l'on se flatte de nous dévoiler la signification des images nocturnes ; avec un peu de raisonnement, vous vous convaincrez bientôt de

Do not believe in the interpretation of dreams, my friends – never buy those absurd treatises where one believes one is taught the meaning and significance of dream images. With a bit of reason, you can

l'inanité des observations de ce genre. Ce que l'on voit en songe, songez-y bien, ce n'est pas une représentation des événements futurs, c'est une peinture tantôt vague, tantôt exagérée des événements passés, et je mets en fait qu'il n'est pas de rêves dont on ne puisse reconstitueras éléments. Le rôle de l'âme dans les songes est assez inexplicable. Il est certain cependant, qu'en celle situation, et en dépit de l'inertie physique et de cette insensibilité morale qui ressemble à la mort, l'imagination surexcitée par une cause quelconque continue à agir spontanément. Mais elle agit sans direction ; elle flotte pour ainsi dire dans le vague et reçoit, comme un miroir un peu trouble, l'image confuse des faits accomplis ou des pensées ébauchées pendant la journée. Quelquefois, elle remonte assez loin dans le passé. Un fait lui revient, un fait oublié même pendant la veille, et elle le reproduit en l'accompagnant de détails et de circonstances, créés le plus souvent par une sensation matérielle.

C'est ainsi qu'après s'être endormi sous des couvertures trop lourdes, on éprouve parfois

convince yourself quite easily of the inanity of these observations. What we see in our minds are not representations of future events, but a vague painting, sometimes exaggerated images of past events, and I propose, there are no dreams where one cannot reconstitute the elements. The role of the soul in dreams cannot be explained. It is certain, however, that in this situation, and despite the physical inertia and moral insensibility that resembles death, the imagination is overexcited and continues to act spontaneously, but it is directionless – it floats in the ocean of sleep, so to sleep, and receives, as if in a cloudy mirror, confused images of the day's events or rough thoughts sketched through the day. Sometimes, it goes back quite far into the past. A forgotten fact is remembered, one forgotten even the day before, and it is reproduced, accompanied with circumstantial details, to create the most material sensation possible.

Thus, after falling asleep under heavy blankets, one sometimes feels a sense of discomfort or even

un sentiment de gêne ou même d'angoisse inexprimable. Alors, on se croit serré par une main de fer : l'imagination vous montre un lutin accroupi sur vous et piétinant votre poitrine : c'est le cauchemar ; on se réveille en sursaut, le front en sueur, la respiration haletante ; on rejette loin de soi la couverture trop lourde ; la cause du mal a disparu ; on se rendort tranquillement.

Cependant, dans un cas pareil, allez consulter un sorcier comme le père Simounen ; il trouvera une foule de significations à donner à votre cauchemar ; il ne vous dira pas : Vous étiez trop couvert : il prendre un air solennel et vous affirmera sans rire, que vous avez des ennemis, que ces ennemis vous poursuivent et se préparent à vous faire bien du mal (ce qui est surabondamment prouvé par la sensation anxieuse dont vous avez eu à souffrir) ; il vous demandera trente sous pour la consultation) ; vous les lui donnerez et vous prouverez une fois de plus qu'il y a encore des sots en ce monde.

Tenez, il faut que je vous raconte l'un de mes rêves et les études auxquelles je me suis livré à son sujet.

an inexpressible anxiety. So, we think we are gripped by an iron hand – imagination shows us an elf squatting and stomping on our chest. This is a nightmare – one wakes from it with a start, the forehead sweaty, panting breath. One pushes away the heavy blanket. The cause of evil is thus dispelled, and one goes back to sleep calmly.

However, in such a case, if you were to consult a sorcerer like Father Simounen, he will find a host of meanings to your nightmare. He will not say to you – you were too covered. He will take a solemn tone and assert to you without laughing that you have many enemies, that these enemies are pursuing you and preparing to do you harm (which is superabundantly proved by the anxious sensation you had to suffer). He will ask you for thirty sous for the consultation – you will give him the money and you will prove once more that there are still fools in this world.

Here, I must tell you one of my dreams and the studies I have done myself on this subject.

Vous verrez par quelle induction je suis arrivé à n'expliquer ce qui au premier abord me semblait inexplicable.

Voici ce rêve :

J'étais dans une grande plaine, couverte de fleurs odorantes et peuplée de papillons aux ailes étincelantes : un grand sentiment de bien-être réjouissait mon âme et je marchais lentement, lorsque je m'aperçus que je n'étais pas seul. Un homme venait derrière moi, me suivant pas à pas ; bientôt cet homme appuya sa main sur mon épaule et semait à me pousser en avant. Le mouvement qu'il m'imprima fut d'abord presque insensible ; puis il s'accéléra et acquit une rapidité vertigineuse. J'allais plus rapide que le vent, et tout en courant il me semblait que je perdais terre et que mes pieds s'agitaient dans le vide. Je ne courais plus, je volais. Je volais en tournoyant, et bientôt je ne distinguai plus rien autour de moi : le cœur me manqua et j'allais m'évanouir, quand je me vis soudainement assis devant une table chargée de fruits et de fleurs, en face d'un Turc qui fumait gravement sa pipe et qui m'invita,

You will see by what induction I arrived at an understanding of what initially seemed inexplicable.

Here is my dream:

I was in a great plain, covered with fragrant flowers and populated by butterflies with glittering wings. A great feeling of well-being filled my soul and I walked slowly, when I realized that I was not alone. A man was coming behind me, following me step by step. Soon, this man put his hand on my shoulder, and it seemed he was pushing me forward. The movement was at first insensible, then he accelerated and acquired a dizzying pace. I was going faster than the wind, and while running it seemed to me that I lost contact with the ground and my feet were moving in the air. I did not run anymore, I flew. I flew whirling, and soon I could not distinguish my surroundings. My heart missed a beat and I was going to faint, when I found myself suddenly sitting in front of a table laden with fruits and flowers, facing a Turk who was gravely smoking his pipe, and who invited me to

pour me rafraîchir, à accepter un sorbet. J'obéissais, lorsqu'un nègre entra dans l'endroit où nous étions, apportant une longue aiguille avec laquelle il nettoya la pipe de mon hôte. Ce dernier prit ensuite l'aiguille et me la montrant:

— Tu vois, dit-il, c'est pour compléter ma collection.

Et sans plus de façon, il me passa l'aiguille au travers du corps. Je ne souffris pas ; mais je me mis à agiter lentement les bras et les jambes : puis, je tombai en avant et la peinte de l'aiguille s'appuyant à terre, se mit à tourner, en imprimant à mon corps, dans lequel elle était comme soudée, un rapide mouvement de rotation.

Je perdis pour un instant le sentiment de ma situation et je me trouvai dans une église où une grande foule était rassemblée. Je voulais percer cette foule pour gagner la porte, lorsqu'il me sembla que les murs se resserraient sur moi et allaient m'étouffer.

Je voulais crier à l'aide : ma voix s'arrêta dans ma gorge : je fis un effort pour pousser un cri qui devait me saurer et cet effort me

refresh myself and have a sorbet. I obeyed, when a black man entered the place where we were sitting, bringing with him a long needle with which he cleaned the pipe of my host. The latter then took the needle and showed it to me:

"You see," he said, "this is to complete my collection."

"And without further ado, he passed the needle through my body. I did not suffer, but I began to shake my arms and legs. Then, I fell in front of the table, and the point of the needle began to spin on the ground, imprinting itself on my body, in which it was wedded, in a rapid rotating movement.

I lost for a moment the sentiment in my situation and I found myself in a church where a large crowd had gathered. I wanted to push through the crowd to reach the door, when it seemed to me that the walls were narrowing around me and were going to choke me.

I cried for help – my voice stopped in my throat. I tried to utter a cry and this effort woke me up.

réveilla.

Il était grand jour : je me levai, et tout en me mettant au travail, je songeai à cet amphigouri que je viens de vous raconter.

— Bien sûr, pensais-je, si je consultais un devint au sujet du rêve de cette nuit, il ne manquerait pas de me dire de belles choses. Voir des fleurs est un heureux présage ; entrer dans une église n'en est pas toujours un bon ; ce Turc qui m'a embroché, après m'avoir offert un sorbet, c'est un ennemi qui veut ma perte et qui me cajole pour mieux m'atteindre.

Toute réflexion faite, j'appliquai à mon rêve ma méthode habituelle : je reconstituai la journée de la veille, et, comme vous allez le voir, j'y retrouvai tous les principes de mes visions nocturnes.

La plaine couverte de fleurs, c'était mon jardin où je m'étais promené pendant une heure le matin ; tout en me promenant, je m'étais pris à réfléchir à la locomotion aérienne ; j'avais songé au principe qui fait que les oiseaux, plus lourds que l'air, se soutiennent dans l'espace par le

It was a wonderful day. I got up, and while putting myself to work, I thought of this nonsense verse that I have recounted to you.

"Of course," I thought, "if I consulted a man about this dream, he would not fail to tell me beautiful things. To see flowers is a good omen, entering a church is not always a good one, this Turk who skewered me, after having offered me a sorbet is an enemy who wants my undoing, and who cajoles me to better reach me.

All considered, I applied my usual method to my dream. I reconstructed the previous day, and as you will see, I found all the source elements of my nocturnal visions.

The flower-covered plain was my garden where I had walked for an hour in the morning. While strolling, I had begun to think about aerial locomotion. I had thought of the principle that birds, heavier than air, support themselves in space by the motion of their wings. From these

mouvement de leurs ailes ; passant de ces principes à celui de gravitation des corps, je m'étais amusé à suivre le jet d'une pierre violemment lancée, et à calculer combien de secondes elle met à redescendre au point de départ : ceci me donnait l'explication facile de ma transformation eh homme volant. Mon imagination livrée à elle-même pendant le sommeil, m'avait substitué à l'oiseau, et je m'étais vu à mon tour lancé dans l'espace et m'y soutenant naturellement.

Mais le Turc ? Que venait faire le Turc dans cette affaire ? J'y réfléchis longtemps et je parvins à comprendre d'où tenait le Turc.

En lisant mou journal, j'avais trouvé, aux nouvelles étrangères, le récit d'une fête offerte à Constantinople, par le sultan, au nouvel ambassadeur de France. Cette fête m'avait fait penser aux contes des *Mille et une Nuits* et à toutes les splendeurs de la vie orientale. Cette rêverie m'avait certainement valu l'intervention inattendue de mon Turc.

Mais pourquoi mon Turc me perçait-il d'une aiguille ?

principles I passed to those of gravitation of bodies. I had amused myself by following the thrust of a violently thrown stone, and by calculating how many seconds before it began to descend from the point of departure. This was an easy explanation of my transformation into a flying man. My imagination left to itself during sleep had substituted itself for the bird, and I had seen myself launched into space and supporting myself quite naturally.

But what about the Turk? What was the Turk doing in this affair? I thought about it for a long time and I managed to understand the origin of the Turk.

While reading my journal, I had found, in foreign news, the story of a feast offered at Constantinople, by the Sultan, to the new ambassador of France. This festival had made me think of The Thousand and One Nights & all the splendors of the Oriental life. This reverie had certainly earned me the unexpected intervention of my Turk.

But why did my Turk pierce me with a needle?

Justes représailles ! parce que moi-même j'avais piqué sur un liège, le jour même, un magnifique coléoptère, recueilli dans le champ du père Michu. La pauvre bête, quoique percée de part en part, continuait à agiter ses antennes et ses élytres, comme moi-même j'agitais les bras et les jambes après mon supplice.

Le mouvement rotatoire imprimé au pal qui me transperçait était une réminiscence de la première partie de mon rêve ; je revenais machinalement à mes pensées sur la gravitation

Cependant la situation était critique : à force de tourner comme une toupie, j'avais senti la force m'échapper, et il m'avait semblé que j'allais mourir. L'idée de la mort avait fait naître en moi une pensée religieuse, voilà comment j'explique ma présence spontanée dans une église, vers la fin de mon excursion dans le pays des songes.

L'église expliquée, reste à justifier l'angoisse produite par le resserrement des murailles prêtes à m'étouffer, angoisse tenant du

These were just reprisals! Because I had myself stuck, the same day, a magnificent beetle, collected in the fields by father Michu. The poor beast, though pierced from one end to the other, continued to wave its antennae and forewings, just like I myself had shook my arms and legs after my torment.

The rotary movement imprinted on the needle which pierced me was a memory of the first part of my dream. I mechanically returned to my thoughts on gravitation.

However, the situation was critical – by dint of spinning like a top, I had felt the force escape me and it seemed to me that I was going to die. The idea of death had given birth to a religious thought in me, that is how I could explain my presence in a church towards the end of my journey into the land of dreams.

The church explained, all that remained was to justify the anguish produced by the narrowing walls ready to choke

cauchemar. Ici, ma tâche est facile.

me, an anguish that gripped me in my nightmare. Here, my task was easy.

En me démenant dans mon rôle de toupie, j'avais glissé dans la ruelle et je me trouvais pris entre la muraille et le bois du lit. La pression toujours plus forte à mesure que je m'enfonçais davantage, m'avait procuré la sensation pénible dont j'ai parlé.

When I struggled in my role as a spinning top, I slipped into an alley and was caught between the wall and the wooden bed. The ever-increasing pressure as I plunged deeper gave me the painful feeling that I spoke of.

Ainsi, mes amis, j'avais pu tout enchaîner.

So, my friends, I could have linked all the elements.

Rien ne tenait à l'avenir dans mon rêve : tout, au contraire, se rattachait au passé.

Nothing of the future was represented in my dream – on the contrary, everything related to the past.

Si je me suis étendu aussi longuement sur ce sujet, c'est afin de vous convaincre qu'il ne faut jamais vous effrayer de ces rêves, et en chercher l'explication au-delà d'une succession de faits naturels qui se sont produits en vous ou autour de vous, pendant une période récente.

If I have spent so much time on this subject, it is in order to convince you that you must never be afraid of these dreams, and in seeking explanation for them beyond a succession of natural facts that take place, are produced in you or around you, recently.

Vous écarterez donc comme tous les autres procédés de divination, ceux que les malins de la famille de Simounen voudraient baser sur l'interprétation des

You will therefore give up all the other divinatory procedures which the malignant tribe of Simounen would prefer to base on the interpretation of dreams.

songes.

Je condamne en principe tous les genres de divination ; je n'ai donc besoin de m'étendre ni sur la cartomancie, qui augure de l'avenir, d'après la combinaison des cartes à jouer ; ni sur la chiromancie, qui le lit dans les lignes de la main ; ni sur la nécromancie, qui a pour but d'évoquer les Ames des morts pour les interroger ; ni sur les autres pratiques offertes à la crédulité des adeptes.

Je veux faire devant vous diverses expériences qui n'auraient pu être tentées sans danger pour l'opérateur, il y a deux siècles. A cette époque, il suffisait d'être un peu plus savant que de raison pour mériter la dangereuse qualification de sorcier. Or, les sorciers étaient brûlés vifs sur la place publique, et si le métier était productif, avouez qu'il n'était pas bon au point de vue de la sécurité de celai qui l'exerçait. Il y avait, parmi les sorciers, je le sais, des misérables qui faisaient métier d'empoisonneurs, et dont la perte n'était nullement déplorable ; mais combien de pauvres gens furent condamnés au feu, qui n'avaient contre eux que leur intelligence et

I condemn in principle all the forms of divination. I have no need, therefore, to dwell on cartomancy, which augurs the future, based on the combination of playing cards, nor on chiromancy, which reads it in the lines of the hand, nor on necromancy, which aims to evoke the souls of the dead in order to interrogate them, nor on the other practices offered to the credulity of the adepts.

I want to present various experiments before you that could not have been tried without danger for the operator, two centuries ago. At that time, it was enough to be a little learned to merit the dangerous qualification of sorcerer. However, the sorcerers were burned alive in the public square, and even if the craft was productive, one would admit that it was not safe from the point of view of the security of the practitioner. There were, I know, among the sorcerers who performed the job of poisoners, and whose loss was by no means deplorable, but how many poor people were condemned to the fire, who had nothing against

leur savoir ?

Albert le Grand, qui fut un saint homme et un savant illustre, faillit plusieurs fois encourir une accusation de sorcellerie, parce que, très versé dans les arts mécaniques, il avait inventé des automates et des machines où l'ignorance publique croyait voir l'œuvre des démons.

Del Rio assure, qu'en 1515, à Genève, plus de cinq cents personnes périrent comme convaincues de magie. On brûla jusqu'à des enfants que l'on supposait coupables de pratiques infernales.

Les procès d'Edelin, d'Urbain Grandier, du maréchal d'Ancre et de bien d'autres, sont de tristes exemples de la passion qui aveuglait les esprits.

Bien souvent, il est vrai, comme lorsqu'il s'agit du dernier personnage que je viens de rappeler, l'accusation de magie servait à déguiser une vengeance politique ou privée ; mais il faut détourner les yeux de ces horreurs pour les reporter sur les bienfaits de la civilisation dont nous

them but their intelligence and their knowledge?

Albert the Great, who was a saintly man and an illustrious scholar, nearly failed to incur a charge of witchcraft, because, well-versed in the mechanical arts, he had invented automatons and machines that the ignorant public believed were the work of demons.

Del Rio assures us, that in 1515, in Geneva, more than five hundred people perished under the conviction of magic. They burned children who were supposed guilty of infernal practices.

The trials of Edelin, of Urbain Grandier, of the marshal of Ancre and many others are the unfortunate examples of the passion which blinded the spirits.

Very often, it is true, when one comes to the last person that I have just mentioned, the accusation of magic was used to disguise a political or private vengeance, but we must turn our eyes from these horrors to consider the benefits of the civilization that we enjoy today.

jouissons aujourd'hui.

De nos jours, on ne croit guère au merveilleux ; aussi laisse-t-ou les utopies se produire au grand jour. Les esprits frappeurs, les tables tournantes ont leurs adeptes. On leur permet de proclamer leurs doctrines, qui doivent échouer devant la seule raison. Quant aux devins populaires, aux faiseurs de contes bleus, aux sorciers du rang de Simounen, on tâche de détruire leur influence en généralisant l'instruction. Tant qu'ils se bornent à débiter leurs absurdités aux cervelles bien disposées, on les laisse faire en se moquant d'eux ; mais s'ils s'avisent de faire commerce de leur prétendu savoir, la loi, qui, à juste titre, approuve le commerce de l'escroquerie, la loi les atteint et les punit.

C'est ce qui ne manquera pas d'arriver un de ces jours à Simounen, s'il s'avise encore de jouer à quelqu'un le mauvais tour dont Claude Michu a été la dupe.

Sur ce, mes amis, allez dormir et ne faites pas de mauvais rêves.

Je vous invite à venir demain

In our day, we do not believe in the marvelous, or letting utopias occur in broad daylight. Battling spirits and turning tables have their followers. They can proclaim their doctrines, which must fail before reason. As for the popular diviners, and the printers of the Blue Grimoires, and the sorcerers of Simounen's ilk, one must try to destroy their influence by general education. As long as they confine themselves to telling their absurdities to well-disposed minds, they are allowed to do so by making fun of them, but if they think of making this their profession, the law, which rightly regulates the commerce of fraud, reaches them and punishes them.

This is what will happen one of these days to Simounen, if he still thinks of playing the kind of dirty tricks of which Claude Michu was the dupe.

With that, my friends, go to sleep and do not have bad dreams.

I invite you to come tomorrow

319

assister à mes démonstrations. Vous vous convaincrez que la science, doublée d'un peu d'adresse, n'est pas autre chose que ce que l'on appelait autrefois LA MAGIE.

to attend my demonstrations. You will convince yourself that science, coupled with a little skill, is nothing but what was formerly called MAGIC.

Quand Claude Michu et ses autres amis se trouvèrent réunis pour la troisième fois chez Bernard Morand, le pharmacien ne les reçut pas dans la pièce où avaient eu lieu les réunions précédentes, il les fit entrer dans un vaste laboratoire, ménagé derrière son logement, et dans lequel il avait rassemblé tous les instruments et tous les appareils indispensables à ses études scientifiques.

L'aspect des machines électriques et pneumatiques, des piles, des électro-aimants, des cornues et des ballons, étonna beaucoup les visiteurs qui n'avaient jamais rien vu de pareil.

Avant qu'ils l'eussent interrogé, le pharmacien leur dit : — Tout ce que vous voyez ici, mes amis, est destiné à des travaux fort sérieux, auxquels je vous initierai peut-être plus tard. Pour le moment, je ne veux faire avec vous que de la science amusante ; et, pour commencer, je vais vous montrer un tableau magique.

Bernard Morand prit alors un cadre accroché à la muraille, et le fit passer sous les yeux des auditeurs. Le cadre contenait un

When Claude Michu and his other friends met for the third time at Bernard Morand's home, the pharmacist did not receive them in the room where he had hosted their previous meetings. He took them instead into a large laboratory, setup behind his home, in which he had assembled all the instruments and apparatus necessary for his scientific studies.

The appearance of electrical and pneumatic machines, of batteries, electromagnets, retorts and balloons astonished his visitors who had never seen anything like it.

Before they could question him, the pharmacist told them, "All that you see here, my friends, is for very serious work, which I will probably initiate you into later. For the moment, I do not want to show you any of that amusing science, instead we will begin by viewing a magical painting.

Bernard Morand then took a frame hanging on the wall and passed it under the eyes of his audience. The frame contained a

dessin au trait représentant l'hiver. On y voyait, autour d'une maisonnette, des arbres et des buissons dépouillés de leurs feuilles. Aucun oiseau ne se montrait dans le ciel d'une teinte grise et triste. Devant la cabane, nulle trace de l'homme. Le paysage semblait désert.

drawing representing a winter scene. One could see, around a small cottage, some trees and bushes despoiled of their leaves. No birds were visible in the grey and sad sky. In front of the hut, no one was visible. The landscape seemed deserted.

—Eh bien ! Claude Michu, demanda Morand, que penses-tu de ce tableau ?

"Very well! Claude Michu," asked Morand, "what do you think of this scene?"

—Je dis, Monsieur, que je me sens froid rien qu'à le regarder. Il doit geler joliment dans celle cabane.

"I say, sir, that I get a chill when I view it. It must freeze in that hut."

—En effet : c'est l'hiver.

"Indeed, it is wintertime."

—Et un bon hiver, à ce qu'il me semble. On a dû faire ce tableau là au mois de janvier.

"And a fine winter, it seems. It appears to be the month of January in this scene."

—Sans doute. Eh bien ! que dirais-tu si je me chargeais, sans toucher ce dessin, sans l'enlever de son cadre, de changer cet hiver en printemps et de lui donner la vie qui lui manque ?

"Doubtless. Very well! What would you say if I, without touching or removing this painting from its frame, changed it from winter to springtime and gave it the life it presently lacks?"

—Parbleu ! je dirais que vous êtes un grand sorcier.

"By God! I would say that you are a great wizard."

—Je suis un grand sorcier,

"I am a great wizard, as you call

comme tu dis. Que faudrait-il aux arbres pour reverdir ?

—Du soleil.

—Du soleil, parce que le soleil, c'est la chaleur qui vivifie. Nous n'avons pas de soleil ; mais nous pouvons nous procurer de la chaleur et faire pousser les feuilles.

— Est-ce possible !

—Tu vas voir. Prends dans ce coin cette lampe à réflecteur et allume-la. Elle donnera une chaleur assez forte pour ce que nous voulons faire.

Claude obéit, et Bernard Morand ayant placé le tableau à une courte distance de la lampe, qui le chauffait doucement, dit aux paysans :

— Regardez et attendez. Le printemps s'avance.

Tous les yeux se fixèrent vers l'image ; elle resta un instant telle qu'on l'avait vue précédemment, puis, peu à peu, les feuilles poussèrent, comme par enchantement, sur les arbres et sur les buissons ; de petits bonshommes, à l'allure pleine de

me. How would you say the trees turn green?"

"By the sun."

"By the sun, because of the sun, this is the heat which revives. We do not have the sun, but we can apply some heat and work on the leaves."

"Is that possible!"

"You'll see. Take this lamp reflector in the corner and turn it on. It will provide a warmth strong enough for what we want to do."

Claude obeyed, and Bernard Morand placed the image a short distance from the lamp, which he warmed gently, saying to the peasants:

"Wait and see. Springtime is coming."

All the eyes were fixed on the image. It stayed an instant as they had seen it before, then, little by little, the leaves grow, as if enchanted, on the trees and bushes. Little men, full of cheerfulness seemed to come out of the paper, the sky populated

gaieté, semblèrent sortir du papier, le ciel se peupla d'oiseaux aux ailes étendues, et on vit là lueur rose de l'aurore apparaître & l'horizon. C'était le printemps dans toute sa splendeur. Il ne restait plus rien du dessin primitif.

with birds with wide wings, and one saw the rosy glow of dawn appear on the horizon. It was spring in all its splendor. Nothing remained anymore of the simple primitive drawing.

Les assistants poussèrent un seul cri de surprise.

The assistants uttered a single cry of surprise.

—Comment cela se peut-il ! exclama Claude, en regardant son ami Morand d'un air presque épouvanté.

"How is this possible!" exclaimed Claude, looking at his friend Morand in terror.

—Ne fais pas les yeux ronds, mon garçon, dit le pharmacien, et ne me prends pas pour un damné. L'effet qui vient de se produire est des plus simples, et je vais te l'expliquer.

"Stop looking goggle-eyed, my boy," said the pharmacist, "and do not take me for a damned soul. The effect you have just witnessed is very simple, and I will explain it to you."

Pour faire ce tableau changeant, on dessine d'abord à l'encre noire le paysage d'hiver que tu as vu ; puis, avec d'autres encres qu'on appelle *encres de sympathie*, dont je t'expliquerai la composition, et auxquelles on donne toutes les couleurs désirables, on peint les feuilles, les personnages, les oiseaux et le fond du ciel. Ces encres ont la propriété de devenir invisibles en séchant et de reparaître, dans tout leur éclat,

"To make this changing picture, we first draw this winter scene in black ink, then with other inks that we call *sympathetic inks*, which I will explain the composition of, and to which we give all the desired colors, one paints the leaves, the people, the birds and the horizon. These inks have the property to become invisible by drying and reappearing in all their brilliance when exposed to the sun or

lorsqu'on les expose au soleil ou à l'action d'une chaleur modérée.

C'est ce qui t'explique pourquoi ce paysage, noir tout à l'heure, a subitement revêtu toutes les nuances que tu vois. Il n'y a rien de merveilleux en ceci ; il n'y a que l'application adroite d'un procédé chimique. Veux-tu maintenant que je te montre comment on peut enflammer un morceau de métal en le jetant simplement dans une cuvette d'eau froide ?

— Ceci me semble plus curieux encore.

— C'est pourtant plus élémentaire. Voici l'objet

Et Bernard Morand prit, dans une capsule de porcelaine, un morceau de ce métal connu sous le nom de potassium, et le tendit à Claude Michu.

—Que faut-il que je fasse ? demanda ce dernier.

—Fais l'expérience toi-même ; plonge le métal dans la curette qui est là sur la table, et observe le résultat.

moderate heat."

"This explains why the landscape, which was earlier in black and white suddenly took on all the nuances that you observe. There is nothing wonderful in this, it is only the adept application of a chemical process. Do you want me to show you how one can inflame a piece of metal by simply throwing it in a bowl of cold water?"

"This seems even more curious to me."

"It is perhaps even more elementary. Here is the object."

Bernard Morand took a capsule of porcelain containing a morsel of the metal called potassium and gave it to Claude Michu.

"What must I do?" asked the latter.

"Do the experiment yourself – plunge the metal in that bowl on the table and observe the results."

Claude étendit timidement la main au-dessus de l'eau, s'attendant à quelque diablerie, puis, après une courte hésitation, il y laissa tomber le potassium.

Claude timidly extended his hand over the water, expecting some devilry, then, after a short hesitation, he dropped the potassium in the bowl.

Le liquide se mit à rouler, à l'instant, d'innombrables globules de feu qui donnaient une vive lumière et une chaleur intense.

The liquid began to bubble, and instantly, innumerable globules of fire which had a bright light and intense heat burst forth.

—C'est pourtant vrai, fit Claude ébahi. Dire qu'on pourrait se servir d'un verre d'eau pour mettre le feu à une grange.

"It is true," said Claude, amazed. "One could use a glass of water to set a barn on fire."

—La chose s'explique par ce fait, que l'eau, au contact du métal, est immédiatement décomposée ; la chaleur que ce dernier acquiert alors est telle qu'elle enflamme immédiatement l'hydrogène, un des éléments de l'eau. En même temps, l'oxygène se porte sur le potassium et le dissout après l'avoir changé en potasse.

"This is explained by fact that the water, on contact with the metal, is immediately decomposed. The heat that the latter acquires is enough to immediately ignite hydrogen, one of the elements of water. At the same time, the oxygen contacts the potassium and dissolves it after changing it to potash.

On peut également enflammer deux liquides froids en les mêlant l'un à l'autre. A cet effet, on verse dans de l'essence de térébenthine, de l'acide nitrique et de l'acide sulfurique concentré, et l'on voit jaillir subitement une vive flamme.

One can also ignite two cold liquids by mixing them together. For this purpose, one mixes in turpentine essence and gasoline, nitric acid and concentrated sulphuric acid and one would see a strong flame suddenly burst forth.

—Certes, fit Claude Michu, vous nous montrez là des choses qui étonneraient bien le vieux Simounen ; mais pardon, M. Morand, une question en amène une autre. Vous nous avez parlé de l'hydrogène et de l'oxygène de l'eau, et, pour ma part, je ne sais pas de quoi il s'agit. Que veulent dire ces deux mots ?

— L'eau, mes amis, n'est pas un élément simple comme l'ont cru longtemps les physiciens. Elle se compose de deux parties de gaz hydrogène et d'une partie de gaz oxygène.

Cette vérité, longtemps inconnue, est démontrée par une facile expérience, qui consiste à faire brûler de l'hydrogène et de l'oxygène ; ces deux gaz, en se consumant, se résolvent en eau dont la pesanteur est équivalente à leur propre poids.

Le gaz oxygène qui a porté aussi le nom d'où vital, existe dans la nature à l'état élémentaire, et entre dans la composition de l'air ainsi que dans celle de l'eau. Il est le seul propre à la combustion. Un corps presque éteint, plongé dans une cloche remplie d'oxygène, s'y rallume aussitôt et brûle avec une

"Certainly," said Claude Michu, "you show us that there are things which would even astonish old Simounen, but pardon me, Mr. Morand, a question for you. You have told us about hydrogen and oxygen in the water, but for my part, I do not know what these are. What do these two words mean?

"Water, my friends, is not a simple element as physicists have long believed. It is composed of two parts of hydrogen gas and one part of oxygen gas."

This truth, long unknown, is demonstrated by an easy experiment, which involves burning hydrogen and oxygen. These two gases, in consuming themselves, form water whose specific gravity is equivalent to their weight.

Oxygen gas, which is also the name of our vital element, exists in nature in an elementary state, and is present in air as well as in water. It is the only one suitable for combustion. A burning object almost extinguished, immersed in a bell filled with oxygen, reignites and burns with a bright flame.

THE COMPLETE ILLUSTRATED GRAND GRIMOIRE, INTERLINEAR EDITION

vive lumière.

Le gaz hydrogène brûle avec une flamme bleu âtre ; combiné avec le carbone, il produit le gaz d'éclairage que vous connaissez.

Hydrogen gas burns with a blue flame. Combining with carbon, it produces the lighting gas which you are familiar with.

Mais je m'engage là, réfléchit le pharmacien, sur un terrain trop aride pour vous.

"But I believe I have occupied myself," reflected the pharmacist, "on a terrain too arid for you."

Pour changer, je vais vous faire voir le diable.

"To change the subject, I will make you see the devil."

—Le diable ! s'écria Claude Michu.

"The devil!" exclaimed Claude Michu.

—Oui, un diable que tu ne pourras ni saisir ne toucher, car, tout en restant très-visible, il sera impalpable comme l'air.

"Yes, a devil who you will not be able to seize or touch, because, while remaining very visible, it will be as intangible as air."

Le pharmacien fit rouler au milieu de la pièce un petit piédestal, qu'il disposa à son gré pendant quelques instants ; puis quand il eut terminé ses préparatifs :

The pharmacist rolled a small pedestal in the middle of the room, which he arranged at his own pace in some time, then when he had finished his preparations,

—Le diable que je vais vous montrer, dit-il à Claude Michu, va vous apparaître au milieu de la fumée, comme il contient à tout esprit de ce genre. Éteignez d'abord les lumières.

"The devil that I will show you," he said to Claude Michu, "will appear to you in the middle of the room, as if it contained all the spirits of its ilk. Turn off the lights first."

Le laboratoire une fois plongé dans l'obscurité. Le pharmacien s'approcha du piédestal ; presque aussitôt les assistants en virent sortir une mince nappe de famée,' éclairée par une lumière blanche dont ils ne purent s'expliquer la provenance.

The laboratory was once again plunged into darkness. The pharmacist approached the pedestal. Almost immediately the assistants saw a thin blanket of smoke, lit by a white light which they could not explain.

Puis au milieu de la fumée, sur le piédestal, se montra subitement un petit démon vêtu de rouge.

Then amidst the smoke, on the pedestal, they suddenly saw a little demon dressed in red.

—Prends un bâton, cria Bernard à Claude, et viens chasser l'apparition.

"Take a stick!" cried Bernard to Claude, "and come chase the apparition!"

Claude hésitait.

Claude hesitated.

—Ne crains rien, reprit l'opérateur. Il s'agit seulement de te prouver que mon petit diablotin est impalpable.

"Do not be afraid," replied the operator. "It is only to prove to you that my little devil is intangible."

Le jeune homme s'arma alors d'une canne et en frappa l'apparition qui trembla un instant mais ne fut pas autrement endommagée. Sa canne, comme on le comprend n'avait frappé que le vide.

The young man then armed himself with a cane and struck the apparition who trembled for an instant but was not otherwise damaged. His cane seemed to only strike the void.

Quand l'expérience fut finie, les questions recommencèrent.

When the experience had finished, the questions began once again.

—Ce que vous venez de voir, dit Bernard Morand, est une application de la lanterne magique. Seulement l'image au lieu d'être envoyée directement par la lanterne sur un verre blanc, se projette par la réflexion d'un miroir, sur un cône de fumée qui sort d'une fente pratiquée dans le piédestal.

"What you just saw," said Bernard Morand, "is an application of the magic lantern. Only the image instead of being sent directly by the lantern on a white glass, is projected by the reflection of a mirror, on a cone of smoke coming out of a slot in the pedestal.

C'est un jeu d'enfant qui intéresse les hommes à ce que je vois, puisque vous l'avez suivi avec une si vive attention. Veux-tu, maintenant, Claude

This is a child's toy which interests everyone, from what I can tell, because you have followed it closely and with much attention. Would you like, Claude Michu, for me to show you how one can leave one's money without fear of it being stolen?

— Volontiers, monsieur Morand.

"With pleasure, Mr. Morand."

— Donne-moi une pièce de monnaie. Je veux faire l'expérience au moyen de ta propre bourse. De cette façon tu seras mieux persuadé.

Claude Michu vida son porte-monnaie dans la main de son professeur, qui en jeta tout le contenu sur un carreau de métal.

"Give me a coin. I want you to experience this by your own purse. You will be better persuaded thus.

Claude Michu emptied his wallet into his teacher's hand, who threw all the contents on a metal tile.

Puis poussant Claude vers l'appareil. Essaye, dit-il, de reprendre ce qui t'appartient.

Then pushing Claude towards the device, he said, "Try to take back what belongs to you."

Claude, sans défiance, étendit la main vers son argent ; mais à peine l'eût-il touché du bout des doigts qu'il éprouva une commotion, telle qu'elle faillit le renverser.

— Place-toi ici, reprit maître Morand, et essaye de nouveau.

Cette fois, le résultat fut satisfaisant. Claude Michu toucha impunément le plateau de cuivre et reprit son argent sans difficulté.

—Si tu veux savoir la raison du double effet qui vient de se produire, conclut le pharmacien, regarde cette plaque de fer sur laquelle tu t'es placé d'abord pour opérer. Elle communique par un fil invisible au cuivre sur lequel était posée ta monnaie, et que j'avais fortement chargé d'électricité.

En touchant le cuivre du doigt, tu établissais entre tes deux métaux, cuivre et fer, un courant qui en traversant tout ton corps devait produire la commotion que tu as éprouvée.

Claude guilelessly extended his hand towards the money, but scarcely had he touched it with his fingers that he felt a concussion, which almost knocked him down.

"Put yourself here," said Mr. Morand, "and try again."

This time, the result was satisfactory. Claude Michu touched the copper plate with impunity and retrieved his money without any difficulty.

"If you want to know the reason for the double effect that was demonstrated," concluded the pharmacist, "Look at this iron plate on which you first stood to operate the apparatus. It is connected by an invisible wire with the copper plate on which we placed the money, and which I have heavily charged with electricity."

"Touching the copper plate with your finger, established a circuit between the two metals, copper and iron, a current which in crossing your entire body produced the concussion that you have experienced."

Dans la seconde position, tu as touché simplement le cuivre et l'électricité est restée sans effet.

"In the second position, you simply touched the copper plate and the electricity had no effect."

L'électricité est l'instrument de nombreuses expériences aussi amusantes qu'instructives. C'est grâce à l'électricité que j'ai obtenu cette vive lumière qui t'a si fort effrayé l'autre jour, au Trou-Noir.

"Electricity is the instrument of many experiments which are as amusing as they are instructive. It is thanks to electricity that I produced this bright light which frightened you so much the other day, at the Black Hole."

— D'où venait cette lumière :

"Where did this light come from?"

—Elle se produisait entre deux morceaux de carbone taillés en pointe et tenant chacun à l'un des fils conducteurs d'une pile de Bunsen.

"It was produced between two pieces of carbon cut to a point and holding each to one of the conductors of a Bunsen battery."

Dans un traité de physique dont je veux te faire cadeau, tu trouveras toutes les explications relatives à cet appareil aussi simple qu'intéressant.

"In a physics treatise that I want to gift to you, you will find all the explanations about this device in a simple and interesting manner."

La conversation s'arrêta un instant ; Claude Michu profita de ce répit pour glisser une question qui pressait depuis le commencement de la séance.

The conversation stopped for a moment. Claude Michu took this opportunity to slip in a question that had been pressing him from the beginning of the session.

—Monsieur Morand, fit-il, en nous montrant votre tableau

"Mr. Morand," he said, "while telling us about your changeable

changeant, vous nous ayez parlé des encres de sympathie. Expliquez-nous donc comment se fabriquent ces encres.

— Volontiers, mon garçon. Voici quelques recettes que tu pourras appliquer facilement.

ENCRE POUR FAIRE PARAITRE UN ÉCRITURE BLEUE, ROUGE OU VERTE

Il faut écrire en trempant la plume dans une forte infusion de tournesol, ou dans du suc de fleurs de violettes. En exposant cette écriture à la vapeur du gaz acide chlorhydrique, elle passera au rouge ; soumise à l'action du gaz ammoniaque elle variera du rouge au bleu, si on s'est servi d'encre de tournesol et du rouge au vert, si on a employé le suc de violettes.

ENCRE POUR FAIRE PARAITRE EN VIOLET UNE ÉCRITURE INVISIBLE

painting, you had spoken to us about the sympathetic inks. Could you please explain to us how one makes these inks?"

"Gladly, my boy. Here are some recipes that you can apply quite easily."

INK TO PRODUCE BLUE, RED OR GREEN TEXT

One must write by dipping the feather in a strong infusion of sunflowers, or in the juice of violet flowers. When this writing is exposed to hydrochloric acid vapor, it will turn red; subjected to the action of ammonia gas, it will vary from red to blue, if sunflower ink had been used, and change from red to green, if violet juice had been used.

INK FOR MAKING INVISIBLE WRITING APPEAR PURPLE

Pour cette expérience, on emploie une solution de nitrate de cobalt ; les caractères tracés au moyen de cette solution restent invisibles, mais si l'on passe dessus un pinceau trempé dans l'acide oxalique, ils prennent une teinte violette très prononcée.

For this experiment, a solution of cobalt nitrate is used. The characters traced using this solution remain invisible, but if one passes over them a brush soaked in oxalic acid, a violet hue is produced.

ENCRE POUR COLORER EN POURPRE UNE ÉCRITURE PRESQUE BLANCHE

INK TO TURN WHITE TEXT INTO PURPLE

On écrit avec du nitro-muriate d'or et on mouille l'écriture avec de l'hydrochlorate d'étain étendu d'eau, ce qui suffit à la colorer en pourpre

One writes with gold nitro chloride and then wets the writing with tin hydrochloride diluted with water, which is enough to color the text purple.

ENCRE AU MOYEN DE LAQUELLE L'ÉCRITURE N'APPARAIT QU'EN TREMPANT LE PAPIER DANS L'EAU

INVISIBLE INK WHICH IS REVEALED ONLY BY SOAKING THE PAPER IN WATER

Cette encre se compose d'une solution saturée de sulfate d'alumine et de potasse. Plongés

This ink consists of a saturated solution of aluminum sulfate and potassium hydroxide. Plunged in

dans l'eau les caractères tracés au moyen de cette encre prennent une teinte foncée qui permet de les déchiffrer facilement en les présentant à la lumière.

water, characters traced using this ink take on a dark hue which makes it possible to decipher them easily by placing them in the light.

On peut, en outre, continua Bernard, écrire avec différents liquides incolores et faire paraître ces écritures en les chauffant plus ou moins.

"Further," Bernard continued, "one may write with these different colorless liquids and make the text appear by heating it a bit."

Ainsi, avec le suc de citron, l'écriture parait en brun ; avec l'acide sulfurique faible, en roux ; avec le vinaigre blanc, en rose ; avec le suc d'oignon, en brun noirâtre ; avec le suc de cerise, en vert.

"So, with lemon juice, the writing appears in brown, with weak sulfuric acid, in red, with white vinegar, in pink, with onion juice, in blackish brown, with cherry juice, green."

Quand M. Morand eut donné à Claude Michu les explications qu'il demandait, un des auditeurs lui posa à son tour une question.

When Mr. Morand had given Claude Michu the explanations that he had asked for, one of the listeners posed a question to him.

— J'ai vu, dit-il, à la foire de la ville, où je suis allé dernièrement, une chose qui m'a paru inexplicable. Etant entré dans une loge de saltimbanque, on m'a rendu témoin d'une séance de magnétisme, pendant laquelle un homme, doué de ce qu'il appelait la seconde vue, a deviné tout ce qu'on lui demandait : l'âge, le pays des personnes, ta somme qu'on

"I have seen," he said, "at the city fair, where I had gone lately, an inexplicable thing. Having entered a ring of acrobats, I was sent back for a session of magnetism, during which a man, endowed with what he called second sight, guessed everything that one asked – the age, the country of people, the amount one had in one's pocket, etc., etc."

avait dans la poche, etc., etc.

— C'est curieux, en effet, répliqua M. Morand. Et cet homme opérait-il seul ?

—Non : il y en avait un second qui le magnétisait et qui lui posait les questions.

— C'est cela. Eh bien ces deux hommes étaient deux rusés compères et leur seconde vue une plaisanterie. Ce que lu as vu était tout bonnement un four mieux fait que quelques autres, voilà tout.

—Quoi ! monsieur Morand, vous ne croyez pas au magnétisme ?

—Cela dépend. Je crois au magnétisme, en tant que force physique se produisant entre dans individus, par l'établissement d'un courant électrique ; mais je ne crois pas à ce magnétisme qui prétend sonder l'avenir et lire à travers les murs ; celui-là me paraîtra une jonglerie, jusqu'à preuve sérieuse du contraire.

Le tour dit de la seconde vue n'a d'ailleurs rien à démêler avec le magnétisme, et je vais vous

"That is curious, indeed," replied Mr. Morand. "And did this man operate alone?"

"No, he had a second who was posed questions by the hypnotist."

"That's it! Well then, these two men were two cunning comrades and their second sight a joke. What you saw was simply better than a few others, that's all."

"What! Mr. Morand, do you not believe in magnetism?"

"That depends. I believe in magnetism, as that physical force, which is produced within individuals, by the establishment of an electric current, but I do not believe in the magnetism which claims to probe the future and read through the walls. This seems to me to be a bit of juggling, until serious proof is given for the contrary."

"The second sight has nothing to do with magnetism, and I will explain to you how it is commonly

expliquer comment il se pratique communément.

Pour le réussir, il faut faire preuve de beaucoup de mémoire et aussi beaucoup d'attention.

L'un des compères se bande les yeux et se place à quelque distance des spectateurs ; l'autre se tient au milieu de ces derniers pour recueillir les questions. Tout le mystère de la seconde vue consiste dans la manière dont les questions sont posées.

S'agit-il de chiffres : l'opérateur interroge son partenaire de telle sorte que ce dernier, suivant la lettre qui commence la question, sait tout de suite à quel chiffre il a affaire.

Ainsi le mot Confitures, par exemple, se composant de dix lettres différentes, peut parfaitement correspondre aux dix chiffres de la numération, dans l'ordre suivant :

1. 2. 3. 4. 5. 6. 7. 8. 9. 0.
CONFITURES

Si donc le compère dit au sujet ; —Combien de pièces ai-je dans la main ?

practiced."

"To be successful in this art, one must have a strong memory and also keen attentiveness."

"One of the comrades is blindfolded and placed at some distance from the spectators; the other stands in their middle to collect their questions. All the mystery of the second sight consists of the way in which the questions are asked."

"Are these the numbers?" the operator interrogates his partner so that the latter, following the letter which begins the questions, knows right away which number is used.

So, the word Confitures (Preserves), by example, is composed of ten different letters, which can perfectly correspond to the ten numerals, in the following order:

1. 2. 3. 4. 5. 6. 7. 8. 9. 0.
CONFITURES

If then, the comrade asks the subject: "How many coins do I have in my hand?"

Celui-ci répondra hardiment :
— Une.

Car la lettre C qui commence la phrase employée pour l'interrogation correspond au nombre 1 suivant le principe posé.

Et cela se fait sans que le public ne se doute de rien.

Ainsi, pour les dix chiffres, on prépare une série de question, qui peuvent se présenter ainsi ;

1. Combien?. . . .C
2. Oh ! dites vite. . . .O
3. Ne devinez-vous pas ?. . . .N
4. Faites promptement. . . .F
5. Il faut deviner. . . .I
6. Tâchez de ne pas vous tromper. . . .T
7. Une réponse prompte, allons. . . .U
8. Regardez bien. . . .R
9. Eh bien ? voyez-vous ?. . . .E
9 ou 10. S'il vous plaît, la réponse. . . .S

Cela est bon pour les 10 chiffres simples, fit observer l'interlocuteur de Bernard ; mais si j'ai, je suppose, 22 francs.

Eh bien, on répète le mot

The latter responds boldly: "One!"

Because the letter C which begins the phrase used for the question corresponds with the number 1 in the code word.

And this is done without the public doubting anything.

Thus, for the ten figures, one prepares a series of questions, which can be presented thus:

1. How much? C
2. Oh! say quickly. . . .O
3. Do not you guess? . . . .N
4. Do it promptly. . . .F
5. You must guess. . . .I
6. Try not to go wrong. . . .T
7. Prompt answer, let's go. . . .U
8. Look well. . . .R
9. Well? do you see? . . .E
9 or 10. Please, the answer. . . .S

"This is sufficient for the ten simple digits," observed Bernard's interlocutor, "but if I have, let's suppose, 22 francs."

"Ah well, one repeats the word

indicateur, voilà tout.

"indicator, that's all."

Pour 2 on dirait :

"For 2, it looks like:"

—Oh ! dites vite.

"Oh! I say quickly"

Pour 22, on dira :

"For 22, one will say:"

—Oh ! dites vite. Oh !

"Oh! I say, Oh!"

— Mais, reprit le controversiste, si j'ai encore

"But," replied the controversial inquisitor, "If I have, say, 325. That's difficult"

—Non ! On prononce les trois phrases se rapportant à 3, à 2 et à 5, en ayant soin de s'arrêter un peu entre chacune d'elles, de manière à faire comprendre à l'initié qu'il s'agit d'un nombre composé.

"No! One pronounces the three phrases representing, 3, 2, and 5, taking care to pause a little between each, so as to make the insider understand this is a compound number."

Pour 325, on dirait donc :
Ne devinez-vous pas ? — Oh ! dites vite. — Il faut deviner.

"For 325, one says therefore:"
"Do not you guess? - Oh ! say quickly. - It is necessary to guess."

N, O et J qui forment les initiales des questions s'appliquent très bien, suivant le tableau que je vous ai donné, aux chiffres 3, 2 et 5, et cette méthode peut s'étendre aussi loin qu'on le veut.

"N, O and J which form the initials for the questions easily, following the table that I gave you, for 3,2, and 5, and this method can extend as far as you wish."

Pour les objets que les spectateurs portent habituellement sur eux, tels que : bagues, montres, portefeuilles,

"For the objects that the spectators usually carry on them, such as rings, watches, wallets, purses, etc., the operators have

porte-monnaie, etc., les opérateurs ont des questions indicatives du même genre.

Mais ici les lettres initiales ne jouent aucun rôle. Il s'agit de phrases de convention dont l'énoncé suffit à signaler l'objet sur lequel on appelle la seconde vue. Ainsi :

— Regardez bien peut vouloir dire — Bague
— N'hésitez pas, — Montre.
— Allons ! — Portefeuille.
— Voyez-vous ? — Mouchoir.
— Nous attendons, — Epingle.

Pour les objets imprévus, on se fait un langage à part, et le mot Attention indique qu'on va l'employer.

Alors, on interroge en se servant de mots ou d'exclamations dont chacun commence par une des lettres servant à composer le mot de l'objet.

C'est un art difficile, mais on y devient vite habile en le pratiquant.

D'autres praticiens se donnent moins de peine, mais ils ne peuvent opérer que sur leur

similar indicative questions.

But here the initial letters play no role. These are conventional phrases which serve to announce which object is being signaled to the second sight. So:

Looks good may mean --- Ring
Do not hesitate --- Watch
Come on! --- Wallet
Do you see? --- Handkerchief
We are waiting --- Pin

"For unforeseen objects, one prepares a secret language, and the word Attention indicates that we will use it."

"So, one interrogates using words of exclamation which begins with the letters used to compose the name of the object."

"This is a difficult art, but one gets skilled at it, quite quickly."

"Other practitioners take less pains, but they can only operate on their terrain, and of course on

terrain, et bien entendu sur un terrain préparé.

Ceux-là se servent d'un conduit acoustique qui passe sous le sol et communique avec l'oreille des sujets. Ils affectent d'interroger ce dernier de loin et à l'écart, dans le seul but de pouvoir se placer à l'orifice du conduit, d'où il ne leur reste plus qu'à jeter à leur compère les réponses désirables.

Voilà, mes amis, ce qu'est la plupart du temps la seconde vue. Il faut admirer l'adresse qu'on y déploie, mais ne pas s'émerveiller de la puissance surnaturelle de ceux qui l'exploitent.

Je voudrais bien que Simounen fût ici, lança Claude Michu, en manière de réflexion.

— Si Simounen était ici, c'est qu'il aurait renoncé à son métier compromettant ; mais Simounen est fidèle au Dragon Rouge qui lui rapporte de l'argent, en attendant qu'il lui joue le mauvais tour de le faire mettre en prison.

prepared ground."

"They use an acoustic duct which goes underground and communicate with the subjects. They affect to interrogate the latter in close detail, with the sole objective of placing the information at the ear of the hidden listener, thus giving their comrade the desired answers."

"So, my friends, this is what most of the time is believed to be the second sight. One must admire the method applied, but do not marvel at the supernatural powers of those who exploit it."

"I would like Simounen to have been here," mused Claude Michu, in a reflective manner.

"If Simounen was here, he would have renounced his compromising profession, but Simounen is faithful to the Red Dragon, which pays him his money, waiting for him to take a false step which will put him in prison."

— Si Simounen était ici, c'est qu'il aurait renoncé à son métier compromettant ; mais Simounen est fidèle au Dragon Rouge qui lui rapporte de l'argent, en attendant qu'il lui joue le mauvais tour de le faire mettre en prison.

— Qu'est-ce donc enfin que ce Dragon Rouge ? demanda Claude Michu. Je n'en connais rien que la sotte conjuration que le berger m'a fait apprendre, et je voudrais bien savoir le fond de ce livre auquel Simounen semble donner une si grande importance.

—Je puis te satisfaire, car je le possède, moi aussi, ce livre, comme un échantillon de la sottise humaine. C'est un ramassis d'absurdités, écrites il y a longtemps par un nommé Antonio Venitiana, qui ne manquait pas d'orgueil et de présomption, comme lu pourras t'en convaincre en lisant la préface que voici.

Et Bernard remit le Dragon Rouge à Claude Michu, qui lut les passages suivants au milieu des rires moqueurs de l'assistance :

"If Simounen was here, he would have renounced his compromising profession, but Simounen is faithful to the Red Dragon, which pays him his money, waiting for him to take a false step which will put him in prison."

"So, what is this Red Dragon?" asked Claude Michu. "I do not know anything about it but the stupid conjuration that the shepherd had me learn, and I would like to know the substance of the book which Simounen seems to give so much importance."

"I can satisfy you in this regard, because I possess it, myself, as a sample of human foolishness. It is a bunch of absurdities, written a long time ago, by a man named Antonio Venitiana, who did not lack pride and presumption, as you will be able to convince yourself by reading this preface.

And Bernard gave the Red Dragon to Claude Michu, who read the following passages amidst much laughter from the audience:

PRÉLUDE

PRELUDE

(Note: This is virtually identical to the text of the Red Dragon provided earlier and an interesting comparison)

« L'homme, qui gémit sous le poids accablant des préjugés de la présomption, aura peine à se persuader qu'il m'ait été possible de renfermer dans un si petit recueil l'essence de plus de vingt volumes, qui, parleurs dits, redits, et ambiguïtés, rendaient l'accès des opérations philosophiques presque impraticable; mais que l'incrédulité et le prévenu se donnent la peine de suivre pas à pas lâ route que je leur trace, et ils verront la vérité bannir de leur esprit la crainte que peut avoir occasionnée un tas d'essais sans fruits, tant faits hors de saison ou sur indices imparfaits.

The man who groans under the overwhelming weight of prejudice & presumption will scarcely convince himself that I have been able to contain in this little compendium the essence of more than twenty volumes, which by their expressions and ambiguities, make philosophical operations hardly possible : but the disbeliever and cautious person who takes the pains to follow step by step the route that I guide them on will see for themselves the true banishing from their spirit of the occasional fear one might have from a series of efforts attempted through trial and error, be done out of season, or imperfect circumstances.

« C'est encore en vain qu'on croit qu'il n'est pas possible de faire de semblables opérations sans engager sa conscience ; il ne faut, pour être convaincu du contraire, que jeter un clin-d 'œil (sic) sur la vie de saint Cyprien.

One can perform these operations and still be true to one's conscience, the evidence of which is visible by a glimpse at the life of St. Cyprian.

« J'ose me flatter que les savants

I might dare flatter myself by

attachés aux mystères de la science divine, surnommée occulte, regarderont ce livre comme le plus précieux trésor de l'avenir.

L'auteur du Dragon Rouge ajoute ensuite :

« Ce grand livre est si rare, si recherché dans nos contrées, que pour sa rareté on le peut appeler, d'après les rabbins, le véritable Grand Œuvre, et ce sont eux qui nous ont laissé ce précieux original, que tant de charlatans ont voulu contrefaire inutilement en voulant imiter le véritable, qu'ils n'ont jamais trouvé, pour pouvoir attraper de l'argent des simples qui s'adressent au premier venu, sans rechercher la véritable source.

On a copié celui-ci d'après les véritables écrits du grand roi Salomon, que l'on a trouvés, par un effet du hasard, ce grand roi ayant passé tous les jours de sa vie dans les recherches les plus pénibles et dans les secrets les plus obscurs et les plus inespérés ;mais enfin, il a réussi dans toutes ses entreprises, et il est venu à bout de pénétrer jusqu'à la demeure la plus reculée des esprits, qu'il a tous

noting that the scholars of the mysteries of the Divine Science called Occultism will consider this book one of the most precious treasures of the future.

The author of the Red Dragon then adds:

This great book is so rare and sought after that one might, as the Rabbis say, call this the Great Work. It is they who have left us the precious original of which so many charlatans make useless forgeries, wanting to imitate the truth, which they have never discovered, and which they lack the capacity to grasp, while trying to grab the money of the common people, who approach them without searching for the true source.

This book is based on the true writings of the great King Solomon that were discovered by chance efforts. The great king spent his lifetime searching for the hardest, most obscure and unexpected secrets; but he finally succeeded in all his enterprises, commanding and forcing obedience from even the most secluded spirits by the power of his Talisman or Key. What other

fixés et forcés de lui obéir par la puissance de son talisman ou clavicule; car quel autre homme que ce puissant génie aurait eu la hardiesse de mettre au jour les foudroyantes paroles dont Dieu se servit pour consterner et faire obéir les esprits rebelles à sa première volonté ; ayant pénétré jusqu'aux voûtes célestes pour approfondir tes secrets et les puissantes paroles qui font toute la force d'un Dieu terrible et respectable,

man would have the powerful spirit and audacity to express the devastating words which serve God for commanding obedience and dismay from the rebellious spirits, by the force of his will, penetrating unto the vaulted ceilings of heaven by examining the secrets and powerful words that express the force of a terrible and honorable God?

Il a, ce grand roi, pris l'essence de ces mômes secrets dont s'est servie la grande Divinité, puisqu'il nous a découvert les influences des astres, la constellation des planètes et la manière de faire paraître toutes sortes d'étoiles, en récitant les grandes appellations que vous trouverez ci-après dans ce livre ; de même que la véritable composition de la verge foudroyante et les effets qui font trembler les esprits chassa Adam et Eve du Paradis terrestre, et de laquelle Dieu frappa les anges rebelles, précipitant leur orgueil dans les abîmes les plus épouvantables, par la force de cette verge qui forme les nuées qui disperse et brise les tempêtes, les orages, les ouragans, et les fait

It is this great king, who has captured the most guarded secrets, that serve the grand divinity, since it reveals the influence of the stars, the position of the planets, and the means to manifest all types of spirits, by reciting the great names that you will find later in this book, those which constitute the commanding & powerful Blasting Rod, and the effects that make the spirits tremble, and the effects which make the angels tremble who chased Adam & Eve from the earthly paradise, and from which God struck the rebel angels, thrown by their pride into the dreadful Abyss. The strength of this Rod forms clouds, disperses tempests,   powerful

tomber sur quelle partie de la terre que vous voulez.

thunderstorms, hurricanes, and makes them fall on any part of the earth.

« Voici donc, ci-après, les véritables paroles sorties de sa bouche, que j'ai suivies de point en point et dont j'ai eu tout l'agrément et toute la satisfaction possible, puisque j'ai eu l'honneur de réussir dans toutes mes entreprises.

These are therefore the true words expressed by him that I have followed step by step, and with which I have complete agreement and satisfaction, having had the good fortune to experience success in my endeavors.

« Signé :
ANTONIO VENITIANA
Del Rubina. »

(Signed)
Antonio Venitiana del Rabina.

—On ne peut guère lire, dit le pharmacien, en prenant lui-même le livre, un factum d'aussi mauvais goût et en aussi mauvais français que celui-ci. Et voulez-vous savoir de quelle façon l'ouvrage répond à sa pompeuse préface ? Nous allons en faire quelques extraits, au chapitre intitulé :

"One can hardly read," said the pharmacist, taking the book himself, "a fantasy of such bad taste and in such bad French as this one. And do you want to know how the book responds to his pompous preface? We will take some excerpts from the chapter titled:

SECRETS DE L'ÀRT MAGIQUE DU GRAND GRIMOIRE

SECRETS OF THE MAGICAL ARTS OF THE GRAND GRIMOIRE

Bernard Morand franchit quelques pages, précédées d'une grossière gravure représentant un démon rouge orné de trois cornes et monté sur des pieds de chèvre, et se mit & poursuivre, en les commentant plaisamment, les formules suivantes :

Bernard Morand flipped some pages, preceded by a rough engraving representing a red demon adorned with three horns and mounted on goat's feet, and continued, with pleasant commentary, the following formulae:

POUR PARLER AUX ESPRITS LA VEILLE DE LA SAINT-JEAN-BAPTISTE

TO SPEAK WITH SPIRITS ON THE EVE OF ST. JOHN THE BAPTIST

Il faut se transporter, depuis les onze heures jusqu'à minuit, près d'un pied de fougère et dire
« Prie Dieu que les esprits à qui je souhaite parler apparaissent à

From eleven o'clock until midnight, go near a bed of fern and say:
"I pray to God that the spirits which whom I wish to speak

minuit précis. »
Et aux trois quarts, vous dires neuf fois ces cinq paroles :
« Bac, Kirabace, Alli, Alla, Retragamaton. »

appear to me at midnight."
At three-quarters to the hour, say nine times these five words: " Bac, Kirabace, Alli, Alla, Retragrammaton"

POUR SE FAIRE AIMER

Il faut dire, en ramassant l'herbe des neufs chemins, dite Concordia : Je te ramasse au nom de Seheva, pour que tu me serves à m'attacher l'amitié de N***,

Ensuite, vous mettez ladite herbe sur la personne, sans qu'elle ne le sache ni qu'elle s'en aperçoive et aussitôt elle vous aimera.

Ici Bernard Morand s'interrompit dans sa lecture et fit observer à Claude Michu qu'il était improbable que s'il n'eût employé que ce moyen pour se faire aimer de sa promise Madeloun, il fût arrivé à son but, que l'honnêteté dans les intentions, une conduite régulière et un véritable amour du travail était la meilleure herbe que l'on pût apporter en ménage

TO BE LOVED

It is necessary to say, while gathering the herb of nine shirts, known as Concordia, "I gather you in the name of Sheba, so that you serve me by bringing me the friendship of N____"

Then, you must put the herbs on the person, without her knowing it or noticing it, and she will immediately love you.

Here Bernard Morand interrupted his lecture and remarked to Claude Michu that it was improbable for him to only have used this means to have himself loved by his betrothed Madeline. He had arrived at his goal by the honesty of his intentions, a regular conduct and a true love of work was the best herb that one could bring into the household.

POUR SE RENDRE INVISIBLE

Vous volerez un chat noir, et achèterez un pot neuf, un miroir, un briquet, une pierre d'agate, du charbon et de l'amadou, observant d'aller prendre de l'eau au coup de minuit à une fontaine, après quoi vous allumez votre feu, mettez le chat dans le pot, et tenez le couvert de la main gauche sans bouger ni regarder derrière vous, quelque bruit que vous entendiez; et après l'avoir fait bouillir vingt-quatre heures, vous le mettez dans un plat neuf; prenez la viande et la jetez pardessus l'épaule gauche, en disant ces paroles: *accipe quod tibi do, et nihil ampliùs*;

Puis vous mettrez les os un à un sous les dents du côté gauche, en vous regardant dans le miroir ; et si ce n'est pas le bon, vous le jetterez de même, en disant les mêmes paroles jusqu'à ce que vous l'ayez trouvé ; et sitôt que vous ne vous verrez plus dans le miroir, retirez-vous à reculons en disant:
Pater, in manus tuas commendo spiritum meum

TO MAKE ONESELF INVISIBLE

Steal a black cat, and buy a new pot, a mirror, a briquette, an agate stone, coal and tinder. Take water at the stroke of midnight from a fountain. Then light your fire, place the cat in the pot and hold it covered with your left hand without moving or looking behind you, no matter what sounds you might hear. Then boil it for twenty-four hours and place it on a new plate. Take the meat and throw it over your left shoulder, while saying the following words: *Take what you need and do nothing else.*

Then place the bones under the teeth one by one, while looking at yourself in the mirror. If this does not look right, throw them over your left shoulder, while saying the same words until you find it, and until your reflection disappears. Retreat backwards, saying:
Father, into your hands, I give my spirit

POUR FAIRE LA

TO MAKE THE SEVEN

JARRETIÈRE DE SEPT LIEUES PAR HEURE

Vous achèterez un jeune loup au-dessous d'un an, que vous égorgerez avec un couteau neuf, à l'heure de Mars, en prononçant ces paroles : *Adhumatis cados ambulavit in fortitudine cibi ilius;*

Puis vous couperez sa peau en jarretières larges d'un pouce, et y écrirez dessus les mêmes paroles que vous avez dites en l'égorgeant, savoir, la première lettre de votre sang, la seconde de celui du loup, et immédiatement de même jusqu'à la fin de la phrase.

Bernard Morand ferma le livre en disant à Claude.

— En voilà assez, je pense, et tu es suffisamment édifié à l'égard du Dragon Rouge. Quand Simounen t'en parlera, tu pourras lui répondre, en connaissance de cause, que tu en sais autant que lui, et tu n'auras pas de peine à lui démontrer que son fameux livre est bon à jeter au feu.

Nous avons prolongé, ce soir,

LEAGUE GARTERS

Buy a young wolf, less than a year old, and cut its throat with a new knife, in the hour of Mars, while saying the following words: *Adhumatis cados ambulavit in fortitudine cibi ilius*

Then skin the wolf and slice the skin into one-inch thick garters. Write the same words as above on the garters– the first letter in your own blood, the second with the wolf's blood, and so on, until the end of the sentence.

Bernard Morand, closed the book, saying to Claude:

"That's enough, I think, and you have been sufficiently educated about the Red Dragon. When Simounen speaks to you, you can answer him, knowingly, that you know as much about it as he does, and you will have no trouble in showing him that his famous book is good only to throw into the fire."

"We have extended our

notre séance as delà de la limite ordinaire. Continue à venir me voir ; nous causerons encore de choses qui vous intéressent et je mettrai volontiers à votre service le peu de science que je possède.

session this evening to the limits. Continue to come and see me, we will still have cause to speak of things that interest you and I will gladly put the little science I possess at your service."

Claude Michu et ses amis prirent congé de leur bienveillant professeur, et le fils du fermier, fortif lé dans ses bonnes résolutions par les leçons utiles qu'il avait reçues, se promit bien de ne plus retomber dans les fautes que sa faiblesse lui faisait commettre si souvent autrefois.

Claude Michu and his friends took leave of their benevolent professor, and the farmer's son, strengthened by his good resolutions and by the useful lessons he had received, promised himself not to fall back into the faults his weakness had made him commit so often in the past.

En arrivant deux jours après chez Bernard Morand, Claude et ses amis le trouvèrent de fort bonne humeur.

Arriving two days later at Bernard Morand's place, Claude and his friends found him in a very good mood.

Le pharmacien tenait un journal et riait tout seul en le parcourant.

The pharmacist held a newspaper and laughed as he went through it.

—Accourez, dit-il à ses auditeurs accoutumés ; j'ai du nouveau à vous apprendre.

"Quickly," he said to his usual listeners. "I have something new to teach you."

—Quoi donc ! fit Claude Michu.

"What!" said Claude Michu.

—Je vous ai parlé des sorciers des campagnes ; voici à cette heure, il y a des sorciers à Paris.

"I told you about the country wizards, right now there are sorcerers in Paris."

—À Paris !

"In Paris!"

—Oui, bien. Mais ceux-là n'ont pas été aussi heureux que le père Simounen avec toi. Les Parisiens ont eu bien vite éventé leur malice.

"Yes, indeed. But these were not as pleasant as Father Simounen was with you. The Parisians soon fanned their malice."

— Racontez-nous cela, Monsieur Morand,

"Tell us of this, Mr. Morand."

—Bien volontiers.

"With pleasure."

Le pharmacien posa son journal, s'établit commodément dans un grand fauteuil et le cercle

The pharmacist folded his newspaper, settled comfortably in a large armchair and the circle

se forma autour de lui.

—En vous parlant de la nécromancie, commença- t-il, c'est-à-dire en vous entretenant des pratiques de ces farceurs qui ont la prétention de parler aux morts, j'ai touché de près à une question fort à la mode de notre époque : la question du spiritisme.

Le spiritisme n'est rien autre que la nécromancie. Seulement la chose a changé d'habit en même temps que de race.

Elle ne se présente plus dans le monde, entourée d'un appareil effrayant.

Les *spirites* opèrent dans les salons ; ils se vantent ode communiquer directement avec le monde invisible et de s'entretenir familièrement avec les âmes.

Au besoin, ils évoquent tel ou tel personnage, défunt depuis des siècles, et écrivent sous sa dictée.

D'autres fois, ils mettent en rapport leur auditoire avec les esprits qu'ils fréquentent, et les profanes peuvent sentir alors des

formed around him.

"In speaking with you about necromancy," he began, "that is to say, talking to you about the practices of these jokers who pretend to talk with the dead, I have touched on a very important question pertinent to the fashion of our time – the question of Spiritualism."

Spiritualism is nothing but necromancy. Only the thing has changed clothes at the same time as the race.

It is no longer presented in the world, clothed in a scary appearance.

Spiritualists operate in salons. They vow to communicate directly with the invisible world and converse familiarly with the departed souls.

If necessary, they evoke this or that character, deceased for centuries, and write under his dictation.

Other times, they connect their audience with the spirits they frequent, and the layman can feel their icy hands grab their own, a

mains glacées saisir leurs mains, un souffle sépulcral glisser sur leur visage...

sepulchral breath gliding over their face...

Vous comprenez bien que tout cela n'est qu'une pure jonglerie, et que les prétendus spirites sont tout simplement d'habiles faiseurs de tours.

You understand that this is nothing but pure jugglery, and that the so-called spiritualists are all simply skillful tricksters.

Cependant un grand nombre de personnes ajoutent foi à ces fantasmagories.

However, many people profess belief in this phantasmagoria.

L'intervention des esprits est pour elles évidente. Et mal venu serait l'homme qui se mettrait en tête de les convaincre do naïveté.

The intervention of the spirits is obvious to them, and badly placed would be any man who put it to himself to convince them of their naivete.

Les séances des spirites sont très suivies ; ils gagnent beaucoup d'argent à ces exhibitions de leur propre personne.

The seances of the spiritualists are well attended. They earn a lot of money from these exhibitions of their abilities.

Cette faveur accordée à un spectacle puéril ne tribuera pas peu à grossir le nombre des croyants, et aussi celui des opérateurs.

"This favor granted to a childish show helps increase the number of believers and also those of the operators."

Nous qui foulons tout voir avec les yeux du simple bon sens, nous ne donnerons certainement pas dans le panneau.

We who do everything with simple eyes and clear senses, we will certainly not give in to the presentation.

Et, pour peu que nous fussions disposés à céder à l'entraînement, l'histoire qui me faisait rire tout seul lorsque vous êtes arrivés, nous ramènerait bien vite à la raison,

And, so long as we were willing to surrender to the training, the story that made me laugh out loud when you arrived, we would be quickly restored to reason.

Figurez-vous que, ces temps-ci, il est arrivé d'Amérique deux *blagueurs*, deux frères, cousins germains du diable pour le moins, car ils passaient pour avoir avec lui de fréquents rapports.

Do you know that recently two American jokers have recently arrived in Paris, two brothers, demonic cousins of the devil, who claim to have frequent interaction with him?

A beau mentir qui vient de loin.

"A fine tale which comes from far away."

Paris attendait depuis longtemps les deux sorciers.

Paris has long been awaiting the two wizards.

Les journaux les avaient annoncés depuis longtemps à l'avance, et on disait merveille de leur pouvoir.

The newspapers had announced their coming well in advance, and one has marveled at their powers.

En Amérique, en Angleterre, un peu partout, racontaient les fervents adeptes du spiritisme, ils avaient opéré des prodiges et confondu la voix humaine.

In America, in England, perhaps everywhere, tales have been told by the fervent adepts of Spiritualism that they have performed wonders and confused human voices.

— Que faisaient-ils donc? demanda un vieux dans le groupe des paysans.

"What have they done?" asked an old man in the group of peasants.

— Une chose singulière. Ils se plaçaient dans une armoire, en face l'un de l'autre, assis sur un banc adapté aux panneaux des meubles.

"A singular act. They placed themselves in a cupboard, one facing the other, sitting on a bench with furniture panels.

Une fois assis, on les liait fortement sur leur siège, au moyen de cordes solides.

Once seated, they were tied tightly to their seat by means of strong ropes.

Puis on fermait les portes de l'armoire, dans laquelle se trouvait accrochés, il faut vous le dire, une grande quantité d'instruments bruyants : cloches, tambourins, crécelles, etc., etc.

Then the doors of the cupboard were closed, in which were hooked, I must tell you, a large quantity of noisy instruments – bells, tambourines, rattles, etc., etc.

A peine l'armoire était-elle fermée qu'un vacarme épouvantable se faisait entendre à l'intérieur.

Hardly was the cupboard shut that a dreadful din was heard inside.

La cloche tintait.

The bells rang.

Le tambour roulait.

The drum rolled.

La crécelle grinçait.

The rattles creaked.

Et des mains blanches se montraient par une fenêtre pratiquée dans la porte de l'armoire.

White hands showed through a window cut into the door of the cupboard.

On ouvrait alors le meuble mystérieux.

The mysterious furniture was opened.

Les sorciers étaient toujours

The wizards were still attached

attachés à la même place.

Qui donc avait fait tout ce brait?
Les esprits invoqués par les deux frères, disaient les croyants.

L'armoire était alors refermée et réouverte une seconde fois.

On trouvait les compères plus attachés et plus immobiles que jamais, mais débarrassés de leur habit.

Nouveau prodige.

A la troisième ouverture de la boite à surprise, les Américains étaient debout et libres de leurs liens.

Qui les avait mis en liberté.

Les esprits, toujours les esprits, rien que les esprits !

La plaisanterie a duré jusqu'au jour où un malin s'est aperçu que le siège sur lequel on attachait les spirites s'enlevait à volonté, et leur permettait de quitter et de reprendre eu un clin d'œil les liens dont on les avait chargés.

to the same place.

Who had done all this?
The spirits invoked by the two brothers, said the believers.

The cupboard was closed once again and reopened a second time.

One found the comrades as attached and motionless as before but stripped of their clothes.

A new marvel!

When the box of wonder was opened for the third time, the Americans were standing and free of their bonds.

Who had set them free?

The spirits, always the spirits, none but the spirits!

The joke lasted until the day when a sly fellow realized that the seat on which the spiritualists were seated was movable and allowed them to leave and resume with the wink of an eye the bonds that had been placed on them.

Les faux sorciers en ont été pour leurs frais.

The false sorcerers had been pulling a fast one on the rest.

Ce ridicule les a chassés de Paris, et le spiritisme a reçu un rude coup dont il ne se relèvera pas de longtemps.

This ridicule has driven them from Paris, and spiritualism has received a severe blow, from which it will not recover for a long time.

Si les deux Américains s'étaient présentés comme d'habiles prestidigitateurs, on les aurait volontiers applaudis.

If the two Americans had presented themselves as clever conjurers, we would have gladly applauded them.

Mais point ! Ils ont voulu introduire le merveilleux dans leur commerce, alors on n'a plus songé à admirer la dextérité avec laquelle ils opéraient ; on n'a vu qu'une chose, c'est qu'ils prétendaient prendre pour dupe un public qui passe à bon droit pour être des plus intelligents.

But no! They wanted to introduce the marvelous into their trade, so no one thought of admiring the dexterity with which they had operated. We saw only one thing – that they pretended to take for dupes an audience that rightly passes to be the most intelligent.

Ledit public s'est mis en colère et a envoyé promener les armoires spirites, dont la mésaventure est en train de faire le tour du monde.

The public became angry and exhibited the spirit cabinets, the news of whose misadventure is going around the world.

J'ai connu, dans le temps, un brave homme qui se croyait médium. En spiritisme, on appelle médium tout individu armé du prétendu pouvoir de communiquer avec les esprits.

I knew, in time, a good man who thought himself a medium. In Spiritualism, a medium is an individual armed with the supposed power to communicate with spirits.

Mon homme, dont l'histoire est quelque peu instructive, s'appelait Philippe Larive.

My man, whose story is somewhat instructive, was called Philip Larive.

A tout propos, il se vantait de sa puissance occulte. Suivant lui, rien ne devait lui arriver sans qu'il en fût aussitôt averti par un de ses esprits familiers.

At all events, he boasted of his occult power. According to him, nothing would happen to him without his being immediately warned by his familiar spirits.

Vous allez voir comme ces esprits le recevaient bien !

You will see how well these spirits treated him.

Philippe Larive s'était marié, et sa femme lui avait apporté une dot fort embarrassante, en ce sens qu'elle se composait de droits successifs vivement discutés par un collatéral.

Philip Larive was married, and his wife had brought him a very restricted dowry, in the sense that it was composed of successive rights sharply constrained by a collateral.

Un procès était engagé.

A trial ensued.

Philippe Larive avait des chances de gagner ce procès.

Philip Larive was likely to win this trial.

Mais il fallait pour cela retrouver certaines pièces égarées depuis longtemps et fouiller attentivement dans les archives de la famille de sa femme.

But it was necessary to find certain pieces that had been misplaced for a long time and to search carefully in the archives of his wife's family.

Que fit maître Larive ?

What did Mr. Larive do?

Au lieu de prendre un expert en écriture, comme le lui conseillait son avocat, et de le

Instead of taking on a writing expert, as advised by his lawyer, and charging him with these

charger de ces recherches, il se fia tout bonnement aux esprits et passa ses nuits et ses jours à les appeler à son aide, espérant qu'ils ne tarderaient pas à lui révéler l'existence des papiers et le lieu où ils étaient cachés.

inquiries, he simply trusted the spirits and spent his nights and days calling them to his aid, hoping they would not delay in revealing to him the existence of the papers and the place where they were hidden.

Les esprits ne répondirent point ou répondirent mal, parait-il, car le jour du jugement arriva sans que Philippe pût montrer les preuves de son droit. Il fut condamné, et sa fortune se ressentit tellement de ce coup qu'il dût songer à se créer un état.

The spirits did not respond or rather they responded poorly, it appears, because the day of judgement arrived without Philip being able to show the proofs of his rights. He was sentenced, and his fortune fell so much from this blow that he had to think of setting up his own enterprise.

Le spiritisme dont il faisait profession menaçait de souffrir de cet état de choses.

The Spiritualism he professed threatened to suffer from this sorry state of affairs.

Mais Philippe se faisait fort de mener de front les affaires et le merveilleux.

But Philip made a success of leading his business and the marvelous together.

Avec les débris de son avoir, il acheta un établissement et commença assez favorablement ses opérations commerciales.

With the debris of his assets, he bought an establishment and began his commercial operations quite favorably.

Puis, peu à peu, il négligea ces mêmes opérations pour se consacrer plus exclusivement aux folies pratiques dont il s'était si obstinément coiffé.

Then, little by little, he began to neglect these same operations to devote his time exclusively to the practical follies by which he had so obstinately capped himself.

Dès lors la maison périclita.

From then on, the business house went downhill.

Philippe assistait assez philosophiquement à la ruine de ses espérances.

Philip attended philosophically enough to the run of his hopes.

Il comptait toujours qu'une révélation d'en haut allait lui ouvrir un avenir brillant.

He always counted on a revelation from above that would open a bright future for him.

Sa femme lui fit des reproches.

His wife reproached him.

Il la traita de folle.

He called her crazy.

Il fut sérieusement question alors, de faire enfermer cet insensé qui accusait la raison des autres. Mais, comme sa manie était douce et ne se traduisait par aucun acte en apparence extravagant, force fut de le laisser tranquillement consommer sa perte.

It was seriously considered whether to shut up this fool who challenged the reason of others. But, as his mania was mild and did not translate into any seemingly extravagant appearances, he was forced to tranquilly consume his losses.

Philippe Larive qui fut un rentier, un homme établi, ayant de bonnes terres au soleil, achève aujourd'hui de vivre dans un hospice de vieillards indigents. Comme l'astrologue de La Fontaine, il est tombé dans un puits pour s'être entêté à vivre continuellement le nez en l'air.

Philip Larive who was a landlord, an established man, having good lands in the sun, was now finishing his life in a hospice of indigent old men. Like the astrologer of La Fontaine, he fell into a well for stubbornly having his nose in the air.

Il croyait donc, fit Claude

"He believed then," said

Michu, que ces esprits allaient lui révéler l'avenir ?

— Précisément, il poussait à l'excès la foi en ses croyances : — c'est ce qui l'a perdu.

J'ai oui, reprit Claude Michu, que, malgré tout ce que vous nous avez dit, — je me prends encore à songer que l'avenir peut être dévoilé à certaines gens, — on a va des prédictions s'accomplir de point en point, et cela donne toujours un peu à réfléchir.

— Allons, Claude, tu n'es pas aussi bien guéri que je le présumais.

—Oh ! je ne crois plus aux sorciers.

—Mais tu crois encore un peu aux devins ?

—Sans y croire précisément, je suppose que les choses prédites peuvent arriver quelquefois.

— C'est vrai, souviens-toi pourtant de ce que je t'ai dit touchant la prescience. Dieu nous a fermé l'avenir pour sauvegarder la tranquillité de notre vie. Nul autre que lui ne peut soulever le

Claude Michu, "that these spirits would show him the future?"

"Precisely, he pushed to excess his faith in his beliefs – this is what led to his downfall."

"I believe," continued Claude Michu, "that despite what you have told us, I still think the future may be revealed to certain people. One has seen predictions being fulfilled, point by point, and this view is one that I often consider.

"Come on, Claude, you are not as healed as I presumed."

"Oh! I no longer believe in wizards."

"But you still believe a little in the soothsayers?"

"Without believing in them precisely, I suppose that the things predicted can occur occasionally."

"That is true but remember what I told you about prescience. God has concealed the future to safeguard the tranquility of our life. Only he himself can lift the veil of your destiny."

voile de ta destinée.

Mais comme tu crois à Dieu, tu dois croire que quelquefois il se plaît à punir les crédules par où ils ont péché.

"But like you believe in God, you must believe that sometimes he likes to punish the credulous by which they have sinned."

Ceux à qui on a prédit un malheur font tout ce qui est en leur pouvoir pour y échapper.

Those for who misfortune has been predicted will do their best to try and escape it.

Et souvent, conduits par la main de Dieu, qui veut éprouver leur foi au dernier moment et les châtier de leur défaut de confiance en lui, ils viennent tomber au but funeste qu'ils ont fui avec tant de soin.

Often, led by the hand of God, who wants to test their faith at the last moment and punish them for their lack of self-confidence, they come to the fatal goal they have fled with so much care.

On rencontre sa destinée
Souvent par les chemins qu'on prend pour l'éviter

One meets one's destiny
Often by the paths one takes to avoid it

Puisque ce soir, nous causons au lieu d'expérimenter, je veux vous raconter à ce propos un trait frappant et très véridique,

Since this evening, we are talking rather than experimenting, I wish to tell you about a striking and very truthful trait.

Encouragé par la vive attention de son auditoire, Bernard Morand commença aussitôt le récit suivant.

Encouraged by the keen attention of his audience, Bernard Morand immediately began the following narrative.

BEPPO L'ENSORCELÉ

BEPPO THE BEWITCHED

Beppo Fabrini, était un jeune montagnard des environs de Roquebrune, dans la petite principauté de Monaco.

Il était habitué à sa montagne et descendait rarement en ville, où il se sentait comme étouffé.

Son caractère se ressentait vivement de ces habitudes d'isolement.

Il était fier, rude et naïf à la fois. Son père et sa mère, auprès desquels il habitait, avaient voulu l'envoyer à l'école.

Mais au bout d'un an il avait fallu le retirer.

Beppo dépérissait à vue d'œil dans l'atmosphère lourde de la classe.

Il lui fallait l'air libre des

Beppo Fabrini was a young mountaineer near Roquebrune, in the little principality of Monaco.

He was used to the mountain and descended only rarely to the town, where he felt as if he was being suffocated.

His character was strongly affected by these habits of isolation.

He was proud, rough and naïve, all at the same time. His father and mother, with whom he lived, had wanted to send him to school.

But, after a year, he had to be removed.

Beppo was visibly wasting away in the heavy atmosphere of the classroom.

He needed the fresh air of the

montagnes, les courses en plein soleil, la vie vagabonde des chevriers. Tout en gardant ses troupeaux, il chassait et montrait à cet exercice une grande habileté. Si bien que, des produits de ses chasses, il faisait vivre sa famille pendant une partie de l'année.

mountains, the paths in full sun, the wandering life of the goatherds. While keeping his flocks, he hunted and showed great skill in his exercise. So that, from the products of his hunts, he was able to keep his family fed during part of the year.

Malgré ses instincts légèrement sauvages, il avait pour ses parents une amitié profonde.

Despite his slightly wild instincts, he had a deep amity with his parents.

L'idée qu'il devait les perdre un jour était la seule préoccupation de sa vie.

The thought that he was going to lose them one day was the sole preoccupation of his life.

Vous voyez que Beppo avait du bon.

You see that Beppo was a good sort.

Tout eût été pour le mieux, s'il ne s'était pas montré aussi crédule. Mais, comme tous les gens vivant en dehors de la civilisation, il aimait le merveilleux à la passion.

All would have been well if he had not proven so credulous. But, like all people living outside of civilization, he loved the marvelous with a passion.

La seule lecture dans ses longues stations à la montagne était un vieil ouvrage de magie qu'il avait trouvé par grand hasard dans le grenier de la maison paternelle.

The only reading in his long stations on the mountain was an old volume of magic that he had found by chance in the attic of his father's house.

Les figures symboliques du livre le faisaient longuement rêver, et les formules cabalistiques

The symbolic figures of the book made him dream for a long time, and the cabalistic formulae

exerçaient sur son cerveau une singulière influence.

exerted a singular influence on his brain.

Un jour qu'il était à l'affût dans les taillis, il vit venir à loi une vieille femme dont le costume misérable sollicita tout d'abord sa pitié.

One day, when he was on the lookout in the woods, he saw an old woman come to the house in a miserable attire that evoked pity.

C'était une de ces bohémiennes nomades et qui font profession de dire la bonne aventure à tout venant, moyennant une modique rétribution.

This was one of the nomadic gypsies who make a profession out of telling fortunes to all comers for a modest fee.

La vieille était fière sans doute de son métier, car lorsque Beppo voulut lui glisser une pièce de monnaie dans la main, elle le repoussa en disant :
— Merci, je ne demande pas l'aumône.

The old woman was without doubt proud of her chosen profession, because when Beppo tried to slip a coin in her hand, she pushed him away, saying:
"Thank you, I do not ask alms."

—Qui êtes-vous donc ? interrogea curieusement le chevrier, surpris des allures de la voyageuse.

"Who are you?" the goatherd inquired curiously, surprised by the charms of the traveler.

— J'appartiens à une tribu gitane, et je lis l'avenir dans les lignes de la main des hommes.

"I belong to a gypsy tribe, and I read the future in the lines of a man's hand."

A ce mot, un vif intérêt s'éveilla dans l'esprit de Beppo.

At this moment, a keen interest awoke in the spirit of Beppo.

—Eh bien, dit-il, gardez

"Well," he said, "keep the

l'argent que je vous ai donné, en échange vous m'apprendrez ma destinée.

money I gave you. I return, tell me my destiny."

—Soit.

"So be it."

La vieille s'approcha de Beppo, lui prit la main et en interrogea longuement les lignes.

The old woman approached Beppo, took his hand in hers and studied the lines carefully.

—Eh bien, fit le jeune homme impatient, que voyez-vous ?

"Very well," said the young impatient man, "what do you see?"

—Je ne puis te dire cela,

"I cannot tell you that."

—Pourquoi ?

"Why?"

—Parce que tu te ferais horreur à toi-même.

"Because it would horrify you."

—Dites toujours.

"Tell me everything."

— Tu le veux. Eh bien, retiens ceci : Un jour tu tueras ton père et ta mère.

"As you wish. Well, remember this – one day, you will kill your father and mother."

Beppo se prit à trembler de fous ses membres et une morne stupeur s'empara de lui.

Beppo began to tremble and shake. A dreadful stupor took hold of him.

Quand il reprit ses sens, il chercha vainement autour de loi la prophétesse de malheur. Elle s'était éloignée à travers les bois.

When he regained his senses, he searched in vain for the prophetess of misfortune around his house. She had left through the woods.

Quand Beppo revint le soir à la maison, il jeta sur ses parents un regard sombre et désespéré,

When Beppo returned home at night, he cast a somber and desperate look towards his parents.

Pour son esprit ouvert aux impressions superstitieuses, l'avenir n'était pas douteux.

The future was clear to his impressionable mind, open to superstitious impressions.

Il devait être le meurtrier de ceux qu'il aimait plus que sa vie.

He would be the murderer of those he loved more than himself.

Cette pensée, de plus en plus enracinée dans son cerveau, ne tarda pas à le plonger dans un singulier abattement.

This thought became ever more persistent in his brain, and soon plunged him into a singular depression.

Dès l'aube, il fuyait la maison paternelle et se réfugiait sur les plus hauts sommets de la montagne. Là seulement il trouvait un peu de calme et de soulagement.

At dawn, he fled his father's home and took refuge on the highest peaks of the mountain. There, he found a bit of calm and relief alone.

Ses parents remarquaient avec inquiétude le changement qui s'était fait dans les habitudes de Beppo.

His parents were alarmed by the change in Beppo's habits.

Ils l'interrogèrent avec sollicitude.

They questioned him, with earnest concern.

Mais le chevrier demeura impassible. Sans s'en rendre compte, il comprenait peut-être le

But the goatherd remained impassive. Without realizing it, he understood the ridiculousness of

ridicule de ses préoccupations, et il ne voulait pas les avouer.

Six mois après la prédiction, Beppo disparut

On trouva sur le bord d'un précipice son chapeau et son fusil.

Ses parents le crurent mort. Et ils pleurèrent leur unique enfant, qui emportait en mourant toute leur consolation et une partie de leur bien-être.

Cependant Beppo était vivant.

Pour échapper à sa destinée, il n'avait pas craint d'abandonner ses parents, vieux et déjà infirmer et de les laisser croire à sa perte.

Dieu devait le punir bien cruellement un jour d'avoir cédé à une superstitieuse terreur.

Il avait gagné le port le plus proche et s'était embarqué pour la Corse, où il entra, dès son arrivée, au service d'un riche fermier.

Pendant trois ans, il vécut là, tranquille autant qu'on peut l'être quand on a un remords au cœur.

Aucune nouvelle de ses parents ne lui était parvenue, et il

his preoccupations, and he did not want to admit them.

Six months after the prediction, Beppo disappeared.

His hat and rifle were found on the edge of the precipice.

His parents thought him dead, and wept for their only child, who bore all their solace and a part of their well-being by dying thus.

However, Beppo was still alive.

To escape his destiny, he had not feared to abandon his parents, old and infirm, and preferred to let them believe in his doom.

God would punish him cruelly one day for having yielded to a superstitious terror.

He reached the nearest port and embarked for Corsica, where he entered the service of a rich farmer on his arrival.

He lived there for three years, as quiet as one could be when one has remorse in one's heart.

No news from his parents had reached him, and he had not

n'avait pas cherché à s'en procurer. Après ces trois années de séjour en Corse, Beppo devint amoureux d'une jeune servante de la ferme où il servait, et l'épousa.

Son maître, à cette occasion, lui donna à gérer on petit domaine dans lequel il devait habiter seul avec sa femme et un garçon de labour.

Tout allait bien, Beppo était heureux, et il oubliait peu à peu la cause qui l'avait fait déserter son pays.

Cependant ses parents avaient appris que le jeune homme n'était pas mort. Un habitant de Roquebrune, venu en Corse pour ses affaires, avait rencontré Beppo au marché, et malgré les recommandations pressantes de ce dernier s'était empressé d'aller porter aux deux vieillards l'heureuse nouvelle de l'existence de leur dis.

La première pensée du père et de la mère fut alors d'aller embrasser l'enfant prodigue.

Ils partirent, un beau matin, pour la Corse et, sans se faire précéder d'aucun message, arrivèrent à la maison do Beppo.

sought to procure any. After three years in Corsica, Beppo fell in love with a young servant of the farmer and married her.

His master, on this occasion, gave him a small estate to administer where he lived alone with a wife and a plowman.

All was well, Beppo was happy, and he forgot little by little the cause that had made him desert his country.

However, his parents had learned that the young man was not dead. A resident of Roquebrune, who had come to Corsica on business, had encountered Beppo at the market, and, despite the pressing recommendations of the latter, hastened to convey the happy news of his existence to the two old people.

The first thought of the father and mother was to go and embrace their prodigal son.

They left for Corsica, one fine morning and without being preceded by any message, arrived at Beppo's home.

Une jeune femme était assise sur le seuil.

A young woman was sitting on the threshold.

Le père s'avança tout tremblant vers elle et prononça le nom de Beppo.

The father came forward trembling towards her and pronounced the name of Beppo.

Mon mari ! dit la fermière. Il est à la ville ; mais il rentrera ce soir. Que lui voulez-vous ?

"My husband!" exclaimed the farm woman. "He is in the city but will return this evening. What do you want of him?"

Le vieillard se nomma et ouvrit ses bras à sa belle-fille. Cette dernière voulut faire honneur à ses hôtes. Elle mit toute la maison à leurs ordres, et comme la nuit était tenue et que Beppo n'était point rentré, elle engagea les vieux parents à se coucher et leur céda son propre lit. Puis, comme elle était inquiète de la longue absence de son mari, elle partit à sa rencontre.

The old man introduced himself and opened his arms to his daughter-in-law. The latter wished to do honor to her guests. She put the whole house under their orders, and as night fell and Beppo had not returned, she made the old parents go to bed and gave them her own bed. Then, as she was worried about her husband's long absence, went to meet him.

Cependant Beppo revenait. Pour gagner plus vite son logis, il s'était jeté dans un chemin de traverse ; il no rencontra donc point sa femme. En arrivant chez lui, le jeune homme s'étonna de ne point voir sa femme assise sur le seuil, selon sa coutume.

However, Beppo was coming back. To reach his home quickly, he had taken a side road. He did not meet his wife. Arriving at home, the young man was astonished not to see his wife sitting at the threshold, as was her custom.

Comme il se faisait tard, il

As it was getting late, he

pensa qu'elle s'était couchée et pénétra d'un pas discret dans sa chambre. Puis, sans allumer de lampe, il alla au lit pour embrasser sa femme.

thought that she might have gone to bed and slipped quietly into her room. Then, without lighting a lamp, he went to bed to kiss his wife.

En étendant la main dans l'ombre, il toucha une tête d'homme.

Extending his hand in the darkness, he touched the head of a man.

Beppo recula en étouffant un cri de douleur.

Beppo drew back, stifling a cry of pain.

Le doute n'était pas possible.

He could not doubt himself.

Sa femme profitait de son absence pour le déshonorer, pour se livrer à un autre.

His wife had taken advantage of his absence to dishonor him and indulge with another man.

Une jalousie aveugle le transporta.

A blind jealousy engulfed him.

Il tira son couteau et, se ruant sur le lit, il perçu de mille coups ceux qui, dans sa pensée, venaient de lui faire un aussi sanglant outrage. Comme il sortait à demi fou de rage, une voix l'appela doucement

He drew his knife and jumping onto the bed, he pierced with a thousand blows those, who in his thought, had done him such a bloody outrage. As came out half mad with rage, a voice gently called out to him.

— Beppo ! Et, devant lui, il aperçut sa femme, souriants et tout heureuse do la nouvelle qu'elle avait lui donner.

"Beppo!" And, before him, he saw his wife, smiling and very happy at the news she had for him.

—Qui ai-je donc frappé ? s'écria-t-il, l'esprit saisi d'un

"Who did I strike?" he exclaimed; his mind seized with a

terrible pressentiment.

Il rentra dans sa chambre avec de la lumière et reconnut la sanglante vérité.

La prophétie de la gitane était accomplie. Beppo avait tué son père et sa mère.

—Eh bien, vous voyez ! fit alors Claude Michu comprenant que le récit s'arrêtait là.

—Oui, conclut Bernard Morand, je vols l'esprit faible puni de Dieu, et je regarde l'histoire de Beppo comme un grand enseignement. S'il s'était résigné à vivre auprès de ses parents comme un bon fils, le hasard qui le fit meurtrier à son insu ne se serait pas produit.

Écoutez donc et instruisez-vous.

terrible presentiment.

He returned to the room with a light and recognized the bloody truth.

The prophecy of the gypsy had been accomplished. Beppo had killed his father and mother.

"Well, you see!" said Claude Michu, who realized the story had ended.

"Yes," concluded Bernard Morand, "I note the weak spirit punished by God, and I regard the history of Beppo as a great lesson. If he had resigned himself to living with his parents as a good son, the chance that made him a murderer would not have happened."

Listen and learn well.

TRIBUNAL CORRECTIONNEL DE TOURS (1)

Pauvres d'esprit et sorciers - Escroqueries - Exercice illégal de la médecine.

(1) Le Droit, journal des tribunaux

À la campagne, on croit encore aux sorciers. Peut-être bien y croit-on aussi un peu à la ville, mais alors cela s'appelle d'un autre nom, et les escrocs, pour exploiter les simples avec de prétendues somnambules, n'en sont pas moins des escrocs. La seule différence est que leurs pratiques sont moins grossières.

Les époux Loyau habitent le bourg de Beaumont-la-Ronce, où le mari exerce la profession d'hongreur. Un hongreur, à la campagne, fait un peu de tout : de la médecine, de la chirurgie.,.

Celui-là s'occupait aussi, à l'occasion, de nécromancie.

Ils sont tous les deux prévenus d'escroquerie et d'exercice illégal de la médecine.

CORRECTIONAL TRIBUNAL OF TOURS (1)

Weak minds and sorcerers – sorceries – illegal exercise of medicine

(1) The Law, journal of the Courts

In the countryside, we still believe in sorcerers. Perhaps, people still believe in them a little in the city, but there they are called by another name, and the crooks, to exploit the simple-minded, with so-called somnambulists, who are nothing but crooks. The only difference is that their practices are less coarse.

The Loyau couple live in the village of Beaumont-la-Ronce, where the husband performs his profession of horse-gelding. A gelder, in the countryside, does a little bit of everything – medicine, surgery, etc.

This one, on occasion, undertook necromancy.

They were also warned often of fraud and the illegal practice of medicine.

Leurs victimes, les époux Lihoreau sont des cultivateurs do Rouziers, petite commune peu distante de Beaumont.

Their victims, the Lihoreau couple are farmers of Rouziers, a small community not far from Beaumont.

Sous prétexte de désensorceler leurs bestiaux et un peu eux-mêmes, qui avaient été, selon l'expression pittoresque de Loyau, ensauvâtes par contagion, ce dernier leur a escroqué environ 1,400 fr.

Under the pretext of freeing their cattle and themselves from sorcery, that had enslaved them by contagion, in the picturesque expression of Loyau, the latter swindled them about 1,400 francs.

La femme Lihoreau est morte depuis quelques jours, le récit des pratiques dont elle et son mari ont été l'objet a été fait par elle à M. le juge de paix quelques jours avant sa mort. Nous en extrayons quelques passages qui donneront la mesure de la crédulité do ces pauvres gens :

Mrs. Lihoreau had died recently. She recounted the story of the practices that she and her husband had been the object of to a justice of the peace some days before her death. We will extract some passages which will give a measure of the credulity of these poor people:

En juillet dernier, notre mère vache n'ayant pu vêler, nous envoyâmes chercher M. Loyau, qui réussit à avoir le veau, et qui nous dit ensuite que, si notre mère vache n'avait pu vêler, c'est qu'il y avait du malentendu en elle ; puis, mettant les mains sur les reins d'une jeune taure: il y a aussi du malentendu dans celle-là, et n'en sera comme de la mère vache si vous ne faites pas ce que je vais vous dire.

Last July, our pregnant cow could not calve, we sent for Mr. Loyau, who managed to get the calf, and then told us that if the mother could not calve, this was because there was a misfortune on her. Then, putting the hands on the reins of the young heifer, he said, "there is also a misfortune on this one, and it will not be like the mother if you do not do what I tell you."

Il emmena mon mari à Beaumont, lui remit une fiole avec recommandation de verser le liquide qu'elle contenait sur les quatre ergots de la taure, ainsi que dans les orteils.

... Cette fois, il nous demanda de l'argent et je vis mon mari lui remettre 300 fr. devant moi ! plus une douzaine de volailles, sur lesquelles mon dit Loyau allait passer le mal qui était sur nous.

Une seconde fois avant la moisson, Loyau arrive nuitamment chez nous, entre onze heures et minuit.

Il frappe à la porte ; nous ouvrons, et étant entré, il nous dit qu'un grand mal va tomber sur nous, sur nos bestiaux, sur nos enfants ; que le seul moyen de la conjurer n'est connu que de lui, mais qu'il ne peut rien faire si nous ne lui donnons 375 fr. Puis il nous demande une assiette, qu'il pose au milieu de la place, y verse un certain liquide, y met le feu avec du papier qu'il tire de sa poche. Une flamme bleue s'élève pendant qu'il prononce des paroles que nous ne comprenons pas.

He took my husband to Beaumont and gave him a vial with the recommendation of pouring the liquid it contained on the four spurs of the heifer, as well as in the toes.

…This time, he asked us for money, and I saw my husband give him 300 fr. in front of me! As well as a dozen fowls, on which Loyau told us he would pass the evil which was upon us.

A second time before the harvest, Loyau arrived at our house at night, between eleven o'clock and midnight.

He knocked on the door. We opened and he entered, he told us that that a great evil had fallen on us, on our animals, on our children; that the sole means of conjuring this away is known only to him, but he can do nothing if we do not give him 375 fr. Then, he asked us for a plate, which he placed in the middle and poured some liquid on it and set it on fire with paper from his pocket. A blue flame rose as he uttered words we could not understand.

Quand le tout fut brûlé : « Voyez, dit-il, le fond de votre assiette est sec, celui qui vous en veut doit sécher de même ; mais vous ne pouvez plus vous servir de cette assiette, il faut la jeter dans les broussailles.

When all was burned, he said, "See, the bottom of your plate is dry, whoever harms you must be dry as well, but you cannot use this plate anymore. It must be thrown in the underbrush.

Nous étions morts de frayeur, mon mari et moi. Nous lui donnâmes les 375 fr. qu'il demandait et encore une demi-douzaine de volailles. Il a aussi demandé douze livres de beurre.

We were scared to death, my husband and me. We gave him 375 fr. He asked us for a dozen more fowls. He also demanded twelve pounds of butter.

... Le lendemain matin la femme Loyau me rapporta mon panier.

…The next morning, Mrs. Loyau returned my basket to me.

Elle nous dit alors que le malfaiteur devait nous incendier et, pour nous préserver, elle prit trois cuillerées de cendre froide dans le foyer avec trois charbons éteints, plaça le tout dans un coin de son invention, puis demanda à visiter toutes les pièces de la maison...

She told us that the perpetrator intended to set us on fire, and to preserve us, she took three spoonful of cold ashes from the hearth with three extinguished pieces of charcoal, placing everything it in a corner of her choice, then asked to visit all the rooms of the house…

Enfin elle nous demanda 200 Fr. 75 cents, pour nous préserver de brûler... Nous lui remîmes cette somme.

Finally, she asked for 200 fr. 75 c., to save us from burning… we gave her this sum.

... Une troisième fois, Loyau apporta à la maison deux

…A third time, Loyau brought two rosaries to the house for

chapelets pour lesquels il demanda 200 fr. Mais mon mari, n'ayant plus d'argent, promit de le lui remettre quelque temps après.

Mon mari a fait aussi un voyage à la Chartre, d'après l'ordre de M. Loyau, et y a trouvé celui-ci avec un autre monsieur que nous ne connaissions pas. Cet inconnu a taxé mon mari à donner 4 septiers de blé à M. Loyau pour pouvoir, disait-il récolter du blé.

Les menaces et les pratiques de M. Loyau ont profondément effrayé mon mari et moi, et voilà pourquoi nous lui avons donné jusqu'à notre dernier sou, si bien que nous avons été obligés d'emprunter pour nos besoins.

Après avoir fait retirer les témoins, M. le président interroge les prévenus.

M. le Président au prévenu. — Loyau, vous demeuriez à Beaumont-la-Ronce, quel état y exerciez-vous ?

— R. Celui d'affranchisseur.

D. Peut-être, mais vous exerciez une autre industrie, et si

which he asked 200 fr. But my husband, having no more money, promised to give it to him some time later.

My husband also made a journey to Chartres, following the orders of Mr. Loyau, and there he found himself with another gentleman who we did not know. This unknown person has taxed my husband to give Mr. Loyau four bushels of wheat, to be able to harvest more, he recalled.

Mr. Loyau's threats and practices deeply frightened my husband and me, and that's why we gave him our last penny, and had to borrow for our needs.

After having the witnesses removed, the President of the court questioned the defendants.

The President to the defendant: Loyau, you lived at Beaumont-la-Ronce, what role did you exercise there?

A. That of the postman.

Q. Maybe, but you were practicing another industry, and if

vous donniez des remèdes aux bêtes, vous en donniez aussi aux gens assez crédules pour croire à votre prétendue science ?

you gave cures to the animals, you also gave them to people gullible enough to believe your so-called science.

— R. Une seule fois, j'ai donné de l'eau sédative à une jeune fille qui se plaignait d'avoir mal à la tête.

A. Only once, I gave sedative water to a young girl who complained of a severe headache.

D. Ce que vous avez prescrit n'est pas aussi simple que vous voudriez nous le faire croire. Vous connaissez les époux Lihoreau ?

Q. What you have prescribed is not as simple as you would have us believe. Do you know the Lihoreau couple?

— R. Oui, monsieur.

A. Yes, sir.

D. Vous avez soigné leurs bestiaux... que dites-vous de tout ce qu'ils racontent ? M. le juge d'instruction vous en a donné connaissance. —

Q. You've looked after their cattle… What do you say about everything they have claimed? The examining magistrate has informed you…

R. Que ce n'est pas vrai.

A. That it is not true.

D. Alors ils mentent. Ils racontent que, dans de nombreuses circonstances ils vous ont donné de l'argent, et il faut qu'ils aient été singulièrement émus par vos pratiques pour se dépouiller de tout ce qu'ils avaient, eux si avares !...

Q. So they lie. They say that in many circumstances they have given you money and they must have been singularly moved by your practices to get rid of all they had, being so stingy!...

— R. Comment donc m'auraient-ils donné tout cela ?

A. How then could they have given me all this? Lenoir still has a

Lenoir a encore un billet de moi que je lui ai remis à la suite d'un prêt qu'il m'a fait de 130 fr.

D. Pourquoi ? Parce que vous leur aviez persuadé qu'ils étaient perdus, qu'ils étaient endiablés, ensauvâtes, c'est ce mot dont vous vous service.

— R. Il n'est pas possible qu'un homme soit assez borné pour croire à des choses si bêtes !

D. S'il n'y avait pas de gens assez simples pour ajouter foi à de pareilles absurdités, il n'y aurait pas do fripons, et vous ne seriez pas là.

—R. S'ils m'accusent, c'est qu'ils m'en veulent. Je les mets bien au défi de m'amener des témoins.

D. En effet, il n'y en a pas, parce que vous vous arrangiez toujours de façon à agir dans l'ombre. Mais ces pauvres gens ont parlé, et leur récit a un tel accent de vérité qu'il est difficile de ne pas les croire.

Vous entendrez, du reste, des témoins qui raconteront des choses fort compromettantes

ticket of mine that I gave him following a loan he made me of 130 fr.

Q. Why? Because you had persuaded them that they were lost, that they were frenzied, enslaved, these were the words you used.

A. It is not possible for a man to be so limited as to believe these stupid things!

Q. If there were no people simple enough to believe such absurdities, there would be no rogues, and you would not be here.

A. If they accuse me, it is because they desire me. I challenge them to bring forth witnesses.

Q. Indeed, there are none, because you have always arranged to work in the shadows. But these poor people have spoken, and their story has such an accent of truth that it is difficult not to believe them.

You will hear, moreover, witnesses who will recount very compromising things about you.

pour vous.

Femme Loyau, vous avez assisté à plusieurs entrevues, et vous avez pris une part très-active à toutes ces pratiques?

Mrs. Loyau, you have attended many interviews, and you have taken an active part in all these practices?

— R. Je n'ai jamais aidé mon mari dans ces choses-là.

A. I never helped my husband in these things-

Asseyez-vous tous les deux.

Sit down, both of you.

Huissier, faites entrer Lihoreau.

Usher, show Mr. Lihoreau in.

On entend le bruit de plusieurs voix dans la salle des témoins. C'est celle de l'huissier et de quelques témoins qui ne peuvent faire comprendre à Lihoreau, qui est sourd, que le tribunal l'attend.

One heard several voices in the witness room. These were those of the usher and some witnesses who attempted to make it clear to Lihoreau, who was deaf, that the court was awaiting his attendance.

L'huissier entre enfin, tenant par le bras le Monsieur Lihoreau qui se présente en saluant d'un air hébété.

The usher finally entered, supporting Mr. Lihoreau by his arms, who presented himself with a dazed air.

M le président. Approchez-vous.

The President. Come forward.

Lihoreau regarde à droite et à gauche et se dirige vers l'huissier, auquel il tend son chapeau.

Lihoreau looked to the right and the left, then went towards the usher to whom he held out his hat.

Le témoin. J'entends dur, mon

The Witness: I hear hard, my

bon monsieur, l'entends dur,

good sir, I hear hard.

L'huissier l'amène au bas des marches du tribunal.

The usher brought him to the bottom of the court steps.

D. Votre nom ?

Q. Your name?

— R. J'entends dur, (Il met une main à son oreille en forme de cornet),

A. I hear with difficulty. (He put a hand to his ear in the shape of a horn)

D. (A l'huissier) : Transmettez-lui mes questions.

Q. (To the usher) Repeat to him my questions.

— Vous vous appelés Lihoreau ? Votre âge ?

Q. You are called Lihoreau? Your age?

— J'ai bientôt douze ans…, ah ! dame, oui, soixante et douze.

A. I will soon be twelve years…Ah! Damn! Yes, Seventy-two.

D. Connaissez-vous Loyau ?

Q. Do you know Loyau?

— R. Je le connais sans le connaître ; pour avoir soigné mon cheval et ma bête à corne, dont qu'il a apporté une bouteille pour mon bétail qui était malade, dont qu'après ça il m'a dit que les pauvres bêtes étaient ensavâtees. Là-dessus il s'est mis à jurer des noms de Dieu... Il a dit que nous étions perdus., Je lui ai donné tout ce qu'il a voulu.

A. I know him without knowing him – for having cared for my horse and my ox, when he brought a bottle for my cattle who was sick, after which he told me that the poor beasts were enslaved. There he put the names of God. He said we were lost… I gave him whatever he wanted.

D. Après ?

Q. After?

—Après ça, il m'a dit : Vous ne risquez pas de doubler trois ou quatre fois la somme que vous m'avez remise... J'avais encore deux cents francs en or ; je les y ai donnés... Après ça, comme il disait que nous étions ensorcelés, j'ai emprunté à ma femme. Ma pauvre défunte qui est morte..., lui a aussi donné pas mal d'argent.

A. After that he told me: "You are not likely to double the sum you have given me three or four times…" I still had two hundred gold francs. I gave them to him. After that, as he said, we were bewitched. I borrowed from my wife. My poor deceased wife who has died… also gave me a lot of money.

D. Ne venait-il pas la nuit ? —

Q. Did he not come at night?

R. Mais oui, il venait en pleine nuit Mais oui...

A. Yes, he came in the middle of the night. Yes, yes…

Il se retire en arrière et parait effrayé du regard de Loyau, dont les yeux venaient de rencontrer les siens...

He retreated back and appeared frightened by Loyau, whose eyes had just met his…

D. Que faisait-il ?

Q. What was it?

— R. Un tas d'histoires. — J'avons été pris comme des têtes feubles. —• Il nous a enrôlés sons cette affaire-là. (Rires dans la salle).

A. A lot of stories – I was caught like a feeble headed sort. He has enlisted us in this business. (Laughter in the room)

D. Qu'a-t-il fait encore?

Q. What else has he done?

— R. Il nous a donné à chacun un chapelet et nous a dit qu'il fallait emporter de l'argent au carroir de la route.

A. He gave each of us a rosary and told us that we had to take money to the crossroads.

D. Combien ?

Q. How much?

— R. 200 francs.

A. 200 francs.

D. Quand il vous disait que vous étiez ensorcelé, qu'é prouviez-vous?

Q. When he told you that you were bewitched, what did you say?

— R, J'étais comme malade.

A. I was sick.

D. Si vous étiez malade, que ressentiez-vous ?

Q. If you were sick, how did you feel?

—R. Ma foi, rien, seulement ça m'étouffait... (Hilarité générale).

A. My faith, only that it choked me. (General hilarity)

D. Est-ce qu'il n'a pas fait brûler quelque chose dans une assiette ?

Q. Did he not burn something on a plate?

— R. Oui, et qu'il m'a dit mémé de ne pas me servir de l'assiette,

A. Yes, and he even told me not to use the plate.

D. Qu'en avez-vous fait ?

Q. What did you do with it?

R. (D'une voix sourde), nous l'avons jetée dans les broussailles, mon bon monsieur.

A. (In a muffled voice) we threw it into the bushes, my good sir.

D. Vous aviez donc peur du diable ?

Q. So you were afraid of the devil?

— R. Ah ! dame !

A. Ah! Damn!

D. Et c'est pour cela que vous lui donniez de l'argent?

Q. And that is why you gave him money?

— Oui, puisqu'il disait que j'étions perdus

a. Yes, since he said I was lost.

D. Il parlait donc bien haut que vous entendiez tout ce qu'il disait ? — Est-ce que vous êtes devenu sourd de peur ?

Q. So he spoke so loudly that you heard everything he said? Have you since gone deaf?

—R. Ah ! je l'entendis ben, pour mon malheur !

A. Ah! I heard him well, to my misfortune!

D. Loyau et sa femme prétendent que vous avez organisé un complot contre eux, que vous avez inventé ce que vous avez raconté ?

Q. Loyau and his wife claim that you organized a plot against them, that you have invented what you have recounted?

— R. Non, non, j'ai toujours été fidèle et je le serai jusqu'à la mort. (Hilarité).

A. No, no, I have always been faithful, and I will be faithful unto death. (Hilarity)

D. Vous avez fait des emprunts ?

Q. Did you borrow money?

— R. Mais oui, puisque je lui avais tout donné.

A. Yes, since I gave him everything.

Loyau. Tout cela est faux. Il se venge parce qu'il prétend que je lui ai pris trop cher.

Loyau. All this is false. He takes revenge because he pretends that I took too dear a price from him.

D. Il n'a pas l'air d'un homme qui invente, et je crois qu'il n'a

Q. He does not look like a man who makes things up, and I

jamais rien inventé, le pauvre diable.

believe that he has never invented anything, the poor devil.

Le témoin. J'aurais plus de 1,600 francs de plus dans ma poche sans lui.

The witness. I would have had more than 1,600 francs in my pocket if it were not for him.

D. Et la femme Loyau, l'avez-vous vue?

Q. And Mrs. Loyau, did you see her?

—R. Mais oui, elle est venue, et ma femme lui a donné d l'argent... Ah ! la pauvre défunte !

A. Yes, she came, and my wife gave her money…
Ah! The poor deceased soul!

On entend ensuite plusieurs témoins auxquels le époux Lihoreau ont raconté ce qui s'était passé. D'autres auxquels ils ont emprunté de l'argent.

We then heard several witnesses to whom Mr. Lihoreau had told what had happened. These were others from whom they had borrowed money.

Femme Roussetet. A la Saint-Jean, mes deux tilles, qui étaient malades, m'ont dit qu'elles voulaient se purger.

Mrs. Roussetet: By St. John, my two girls, who were sick, told me that they wanted to purge themselves.

Je leur ai dit : Alors allez chez le médecin. Mais elles ont été trouvées Loyau, qui leur a donné deux bouteilles. — Quand j'ai su ce qui se passait, fait tout reporter.

I said to them: So, go to the doctor. But they were found by Loyau, who gave them two bottles. When I found out what was happening, I did everything to prevent it.

D. Pourquoi allaient-elles chez Loyau ?

Q. Why did they go to Loyau?

—R. Monsieur, c'est que c'est

A. Sir, this is because it was

bien meilleur marché.

much cheaper.

Après l'audition des témoins, la parole est donnée à M. Perrot substitut, qui requiert contre les prévenus une application sévère de la loi et déclare qu'il n'insiste pas sur le chef d'exercice illégal de la médecine, qu'il ne retient au procès que comme renseignement de moralité.

After the testimony of the witnesses, the transcript was given to Mr. Perrot, who required a severe application of the law against the defendants, and declared that he did not insist on the count of illegal practice of medicine, that he retained the trial only as an inquiry of morality.

M. Brisard présente ensuite la défense des deux prévenus.

Mr. Brisard then introduced the defense of the two accused.

Le tribunal rejette le chef d'exercice illégal de la médecine et condamne Loyau à treize mois de prison, sa femme à un mois, et tous deux 100 francs d'amende.

The court dismissed the count of illegal practice of medicine and sentenced Loyau to thirteen months in prison, his wife to one month, and both were fined 100 francs.

— C'est bien fait ! s'écrièrent en chœur les femmes, qui avalent fort goûté cette lecture instructive.

"Well done!" exclaimed the chorus of women, who had strongly found this lecture instructive.

—Tiens, dit Bernard Morand à Claude, en lui tendant le journal, tu feras cadeau de ce compte rendu à Simounen. Cela lui donnera à réfléchir.

"Here," said Bernard Morand to Claude, handing him the paper, "you will give this account to Simounen. This will give him pause."

—Merci, monsieur Morand, je crois que nous prêcherions dans le désert.

"Thank you, Mr. Morand. I believe we would preach to an empty desert."

— C'est bien possible. — Bonne nuit, mes chers enfants, et à bientôt.

"That is quite possible. Good night, my dear children, and see you soon."

Les soirées suivantes furent occupées par de semblables entretiens. Toujours plus attentifs à mesure que leur entendement se pliait davantage aux leçons du pharmacien, les paysans prenaient un véritable plaisir à ces instructions familières et voyaient s'écouler les heures avec une fabuleuse rapidité.

The following evenings were occupied by similar conversations. Always more attentive to the extent that their understanding was bent on the lessons of the pharmacist, the peasants took a real pleasure at these familiar instructions and saw the hours flow with a fabulous pace.

Dans ces réunions, Bernard Morand leur expliqua bien des choses qui jusqu'alors étaient muettes pour eux.

In these reunions, Bernard Morand explained to them many things that had hitherto been unknown to them.

Il leur parla des progrès du siècle, leur donna des explications courtes, mais précises, sur l'électricité, sur la Vapeur, sur toutes les inventions modernes ; il tourna leur esprit vers l'étude des questions agricoles et leur montra que les véritables prodiges étaient ceux que peut accomplir la volonté mise au service d'une idée civilisatrice.

He spoke with them on the century's progress, gave them short but precise explanations of electricity, steam, and all modern inventions. He turned their minds towards the study of agricultural questions and showed them that the true wonders were those which could be accomplished by the will placed in service of a civilizing idea.

En un mot, ceux qu'il avait rassemblés autour de lui étaient des enfants par la simplicité de leur esprit ; il chercha à en faire des hommes.

In a word, those whom he had assembled around him were children by the simplicity of their minds — he sought to make men of them.

Quant à Claude Michu, il dut spécialement à Bernard la

As for Claude Michu, he owed Bernard especially for the

conquête do lui-même. Ce ne fut bientôt plus ce garçon timide et indécis que nous avons connu ? il chassa pour toujours le vieil homme et se montra disposé à entreprendre bien des choses qui jusqu'alors avaient effrayé son courage ou excité sa défiance.

conquest of his own self. He was no longer that shy and indecisive boy we knew. He drove out the old man forever and showed himself well-disposed to undertake many things which had hitherto frightened him or excited his mistrust.

Sous son habile direction, la ferme du père Michu devint un établissement modèle.

Under his able direction, Father Michu's farm became a model establishment.

Au lieu du Dragon Rouge ou autre livre de cette sorte, Claude rechercha les traités d'agriculture, les ouvrages sérieux ; il fut encouragé dans cette voie par le pharmacien, qui mit obligeamment à sa disposition les journaux qu'il recevait de Paris.

In place of the Red Dragon or other books of its sort, Claude sought the agricultural treatises, the serious works — he was encouraged in this by the pharmacist, who obligingly placed at his disposal the journals that he received from Paris.

Notre jeune homme y puisa des théories excellentes et les appliqua avec une intelligence et un soin qui furent couronnés d'un plein succès.

Our young man drew excellent theories from them and applied them with an intelligence and care which were completely successful.

Parfois il se prenait à songer à ses essais d'autrefois, essais souvent malheureux, et il se disait avec raison qu'on ne réussit en ce monde qu'à la condition de déployer, en toute occasion, beaucoup de fermeté et beaucoup de persévérance, qualités

Sometimes he would think of his past efforts, often unhappy trials, and he rightly said to himself that one succeeds in the world only on the condition of deploying, on every occasion, a great deal of firmness and perseverance, precious qualities

précieuses dont il avait été privé longtemps.

which he had been deprived of for a long time.

De temps en temps, Claude allait rendre visite à Madeloun.

From time to time, Claude would visit Madeline.

En voyant entrer chez elle ce brave garçon, au teint hâlé, à l'air résolu, la jolie fille ne riait plus comme autrefois.

Seeing this good looking, tanned, resolute young man entering her house, the pretty girl did not laugh as much as before.

Elle lui tendait la main et on devinait bien vite qu'elle serait heureuse le jour où il lui serait donné de s'appeler Mme Michu.

She held out her hand and it was clear that she would be happy on the day when she would be called Mrs. Michu.

Au milieu de ses préoccupations et de ses idées nouvelles, Claude avait gardé une pensée de rancune contre le vieux Simounen et il s'était promis de dire son fait au berger.

Amid his preoccupations and new ideas, Claude had kept a spiteful thought against old Simounen, and he promised himself to tell the shepherd what he had done.

Malheureusement celui-ci avait quitté momentanément le pays ; il était allé conduire des troupeaux dans la Crau et ce devait revenir qu'au printemps.

Unfortunately, he had left the country momentarily. He had gone to drive herds in the Crau, at the confluence of the Durance and the Rhine, and would return in the spring.

Claude Michu oubliait peu à peu sa rancune, lorsque le retour inopiné de Simounen vint la lui rappeler.

Claude Michu gradually forgot his rancor, when the unexpected return of Simounen came to remind him.

Le vaillent fermier surveillait

The valiant farmer was

un jour les travaux du domaine, quand il entendit non loin de lui sur le chemin, la voix railleuse du vieillard, qui lui crait :—Eh, bonjour Claude, comment vas-tu ?

overseeing the work of the estate one day, when he heard not far from him on the road, the mocking voice of the old man, who cried to him: "Hello Claude, how are you?"

Simounen aurait été sans doute à l'abri des reproches de son ancienne dupe, s'il se fut présenté eu malheureusement, il était monté sur ce bel an qu'il devait à la naïveté de Claude.

Simounen would doubtless have been safe from the reproaches of his former dupe, if he had presented himself poorly. Unfortunately, he had risen in the fine year that he owed to Claude's naivete.

Cette circonstance ralluma toute la colère en dormie dans l'esprit de ce dernier, en lui rappelant sa sottise d'autrefois.

This circumstance rekindled all the sleepless anger in his mind and reminded him of his old foolishness.

— Bonjour, répondit-il sèchement.

"Good morning," he answered curtly.

— Et ! comme te voilà, mon garçon, quelle mouche t'a piqué ?

"How are you, my boy, what fly has stung you?"

— Je suis comme je dois l'être avec un blagueur de votre espèce, père Simounen.

"I know I'm talking with a cunning rogue. The affronts! I will confront you before the judge."

—Bah ! pourquoi ne pas me lâcher aux trousses deux ou trois des démons à qui vous commande !

"Bah! Why don't you release two or three of the demons you command!"

—Et si je le faisais ?

"And if I did so?"

—Vous êtes libre, ça nous amusera un peu !

"You are free to do so; it would be amusing!"

—Ah ça ! petit, dit le berger que le ton ironique de Claude embarrassait et qui voulait porter la conversation sur un autre terrain, ah ça ! lu n'as donc pas réussi au Trou-Noir ?

"Oh well! Little one," said the shepherd, who was embarrassed by Claude's ironic tone and wanted to take the conversation to another level, "Oh well Have you not been successful at the Black Hole?"

—Si, j'ai réussi à me faire extorquer 80 francs et la belle bête que voilà ! c'est tout ce que j'ai gagné sans compter tes plaisanteries de mes amis.

"Yes, I have succeeded in being extorted of 80 fr. and the fine beast I see before me! That is all I have won, not counting the jokes from my friends."

—Ce n'est pas ma faute. Tu auras oublié quelque détail.

"That is not my fault. You have perhaps overlooked some detail."

— Dites donc, père Simounen, assez plaisanté! je vais vous donner un conseil. Gardez mon argent et mon âne puisque vous les avez, mais ne vous vantez pas de ce que vous avez fait ; je ne veux pas vous dénoncer à la justice, toutefois, il faut vous tenir tranquille à l'avenir, entendez-vous ?

"What do you say, father Simounen, what a joke! I will give you some advice. Keep my money and my donkey since you have them, but do not boast of what you have done. I do not want to denounce you to the law; however, you must keep quiet in the future, do you understand?

A ce compte-là, nous serons encore bons amis, et, je ne vous fermerai pas la porte, quand vous

On this account, we will still be good friends, and I will not close the door on you, when you come to ask me for a glass of wine and a

viendrez me demander un verre de vin et un morceau de fromage.

slice of cheese."

—C'est bien parlé, ça garçon, fit le berger rassuré, mais tu ne crois donc plus à rien ?

"Well said, my boy," said the shepherd, reassured, "but do you not believe in anything?"

—Si, je crois à beaucoup de choses.

"Yes, I believe in many things."

— A la bonne heure.

"That is good to hear."

— Je crois, par exemple, que j'ai été un imbécile et que vous en avez profité ; je crois que si vous pouviez vendre le moyen de se procurer des trésors vous seriez plat riche que vous ne l'êtes ; je crois enfin, comme dit M. Morand, qu'il n'y a pas d'autres moyens de succès au monde que la probité, l'intelligence et le travail.

"I believe, for example, that I have been an imbecile and that you took advantage of me. I also believe that if you could sell the means to procure treasures, you would be very rich indeed. I also believe, finally, as Mr. Morand says, that there are no other means of success in the world than probity, intelligence and hard work."

— Il y a du bon dans ce que tu dis ; mais, bah ! un petit peu de mystère ça fait de mal à personne et ça fait plaisir à tant de gens !

"There is truth in what you say, but, bah! A little bit of mystery hurts no one and is good for many people."

—Ce qui veut dire, père Simounen, que vous n'êtes pas corrigé et que vous ne vous générez pas pour vendre encore vos recettes aux bonnet âmes !

"Which means, Father Simounen, that you have not improved and that you would be willing to sell yourself to exploit more good souls."

—Pourquoi pas, si ça se trouve

"Why not, if it be so!"

!

—Bon? et s'il se trouve aussi qu'on vous arrête et qu'on vous mette en prison.

"Good? And if it so happens that they arrest you and put you in prison?"

—On est malin, mon garçon.

"One is smart, my boy."

— Allons, tant mieux. Dieu veuille que vos prévisions ne se réalisent pas.

Adieu, père Simounen !

"Very well, all the better. God grant that your predictions are not realized.

Goodbye, father Simounen!"

—Au revoir, mon garçon.

"Goodbye, my boy."

Malgré sa forfanterie, Simounen profita un peu du conseil désintéressé de Claude Michu. Il cessa de se poser en familier du monde surnaturel, mais en même temps qu'il se débarrassait de sa peau de nécromancien, il s'adonna à une autre branche d'opérations non moins dangereuses que celles de la magie, au point de vue de sa tranquillité personnelle.

Despite his boasting, Simounen did profit a little from the selfless advice of Claude Michu. He stopped pretending to be familiar with the supernatural world, but at the same time that he was getting rid of his necromantic robes, he devoted himself to another branch of operations no less dangerous than magic, from the point of view of his personal tranquility.

En un mot, il se mit à débiter des remèdes où l'élément merveilleux jouait aussi son rôle. C'étaient des drogues d'une énergie peu commune qu'il fallait administrer ou absorber en prononçant certaines formules et que le vieux berger livrait aux

In brief, he began to sell remedies in which the marvelous element also played a part. They were drugs of unusual energy that had to be administered or absorbed by pronouncing certain formulae and that the old shepherd delivered to the

consommateurs avec toutes sortes de recommandations touchant leur emploi et toutes sortes de louanges, au sujet de leur incontestable efficacité.

Claude Michu ne tarda pas à apprendre ce qui se passait, et il en parla à son ami Bernard Morand

— Oui, dit ce dernier, Je sais que le vieux Simounen me fait concurrence, mais, outre que sa concurrence m'est assez indifférente, je ne suis pas d'humeur à le mettre aux prises avec la justice. Un Jour viendra, où il se livrera de lui-même, en commettant quelqu'une de ces bévues qui sont la fin de l'histoire de tous les marchands de remèdes de bonne femme.

Dans les campagnes où les médecins sont rares, il serait à désirer que les paysans possédassent parfaitement certaines règles d'hygiène dont l'application les préserverait de beaucoup de maladies et leur éviterait l'occasion de se mettre entre les mains des marchands d'onguents contre tous les maux.

Un de nos grands praticiens l'a

consumers with all sorts of recommendations concerning their use and all kinds of praise about their indisputable efficacy.

Claude Michu was quick to learn what was going on and he spoke with his friend Bernard Morand.

"Yes," said the latter, "I know that old Simounen is competing with me, but besides being indifferent to his competition, I am in no mood to put him to the test with the law. A day will come, where he will deliver himself, by committing some of those blunders which are the end of the story of all the merchants of old wives' remedies.

In the countryside, where doctors are scarce, it would be desirable for peasants to have certain rules of hygiene, the application of which would prevent many diseases and avoid the risk of placing them in the hands of snake oil salesmen and their various evil deeds.

One of our great practitioners

dit: « La richesse du pauvre, c'est la propreté. »

Je voudrais que nos campagnards songeassent à méditer cette maxime. La propreté est la sœur de la santé : elle doit régner partout, chez l'homme et autour de l'homme.

Il faut que le corps soit propre, mais il faut que les vêtements ; le linge et la main son le soient aussi.

Je vois, avec regret, beaucoup de nos voisins amonceler auprès de leurs maisons des tas d'ordures.

C'est une mauvaise chose, il s'exhale de ces immondices des gaz délétères qui peuvent faire naître et propager des maladies contagieuses.

Tous les rebuts de la ferme qui ne peuvent être employés comme engrais doivent être soigneusement brûlés, les animaux morts doivent être profondément enfouis et non pas abandonnés à la voirie comme on le fait communément.

La question de la nourriture doit aussi être l'objet d'une vive attention. Il faut manger peu et à heures fixes ; manger quand on a

said, "The wealth of the poor is cleanliness."

I would like our countrymen to consider this maxim. Cleanliness is the sister of good health. It must reign everywhere, in man and around him.

The body must be kept clean, but also the clothes, the linen and the hands should be clean.

I see, with regret, many of our neighbors have piles of garbage near their homes.

This is a bad habit - filthy deleterious gases emerge from these piles which can cause and spread contagious diseases.

Any farm scraps that cannot be used as fertilizer must be carefully burned, dead animals must be buried deeply and not abandoned on the roadside, as is commonly done in the countryside.

The question of food must also be the subject of great attention. It is necessary to eat little and at fixed times. To eat

le temps et prendre beaucoup de nourriture, sous prétexte qu'on en prend pour plus longtemps, est une habitude qui, peut devenir nuisible.

when you have time and to consumer too much, under the pretext that it takes longer, is a habit that can become harmful.

L'estomac est une machine bien organisée, sans doute, mais elle se détraque facilement ; il lui faut un régime sévère ; lui donner trop ou trop peu de nourriture la lui donner irrégulièrement, c'est compromettre l'ordre de ses fonctions.

The stomach is a well-organized machine, without doubt, but it breaks easily; it needs a strict diet. To have too much or too little food induces irregularity in digestion, which compromises the order of its functions.

On gagne à ce système une terrible affection qui s'appelle la gastrite.

We can gain from this approach a terrible affliction called gastritis.

Il faut manger peu de viande, mais il faut en manger. La viande donne au sang et aux muscles la force nécessaire aux travaux des champs. Les aliments végétaux doivent être intelligemment combinés avec la viande dans l'ordinaire de la journée. On peut les prendre par quantités assez grandes, en évitant autant que possible de faire abus de ceux que leur acidité peut rendre dangereux.

One must eat a little meat, but it must be digested. Meat gives blood and muscles the strength needed for field work. Plant foods must be intelligently combined with meat in the ordinary course of daily meals. They can be taken in fairly large quantities, avoiding as much as possible the acidic foods which can be dangerous.

Les fruits sont bons, à la condition d'être mangés en pleine maturité ; ils rafraîchissent pris modérément, quand on en mangé

Fruits are good, provided they are eaten when ripe. They refresh moderately, when eaten too often, they overload the stomach and

trop ; ils chargent l'estomac et affaiblissent l'économie.

weaken the bodily economy.

Tous ces principes, je te sais, ne peuvent être régulièrement appliqués par les pauvres gens qui prennent ce que Dieu leur donne ; mais il est bon de les connaître et de s'y conformer autant que possible.

All these principles, I would grant, cannot be regularly applied by the poor people who take what God gives them; but it is good to know them and conform to them as far as possible.

Les vêtements des campagnards doivent être larges, afin de faciliter les mouvements du corps. Il faut éviter de se serrer trop le cou, à cause des congestions fréquentes, surtout pendant la chaleur.

Country clothes should be loose to facilitate body movements. It is necessary to avoid choking the neck, because this causes frequent congestion, especially during the heat.

Les habits d'été sont bons en toile, et meilleurs en laine légère. Au soleil, la laine laisse passer moins de chaleur que la toile, et quoique plus lourde, elle tient moins chaud.

Canvas is good for summer war, and light wool even better. In the sun, wool lets in less heat than canvas, and although it is heaver, it is less warm.

Le coton doit être préféré au fil pour le linge de corps, parce qu'il absorbe mieux la sueur et conserve à la peau une chaleur plus normale.

Cotton should be preferred closer to the skin, because it absorbs sweat better and keeps the skin warmer than usual.

Dans l'hiver, il faut craindre de rester dans un appartement trop chauffé ; il faut craindre surtout d'en sortir sans augmenter le

In winter, it is necessary to avoid staying in an apartment that is too hot. Do not go outside without increased layers of

nombre de ses vêtements.

C'est plutôt à l'exercice qu'au feu qu'on doit demander un remède contre le froid. La chaleur naturelle est la meilleure ; celle du feu, surtout celle des poêles en fonte, dessèche la peau, irrite le système nerveux et cause parfois de violents maux de tête.

Pendant les jours caniculaires, lorsque le travail des champs couvre les membres d'une sueur abondante, on doit s'abstenir avec soin de l'ombre des noyers et de certains autres arbres dont le feuillage garde une fraîcheur malsaine et parfois mortelle.

Il vaut mieux laisser la sueur se vaporiser lentement.

Boire frais quand on a très chaud est également nuisible ; quand la soif est trop ardente, il est bon de tremper ses mains dans l'eau, et si on le peut, de prendre un bain.

L'eau entre alors dans le corps par tous les pores, qui sont autant de petites bouches, et la soif disparaît sans qu'il soit nécessaire de se charger l'estomac d'une quantité de liquide qu'il a de la

clothing.

It is better to prefer exercise over fire as a remedy against the cold. Natural warmth is the best; that of fire, especially that from cast iron stoves, dries the skin, irritates the nervous system and sometimes causes violent headaches.

During the hot days, when one is covered in sweat from field work, one must carefully refrain from the shade of walnut trees and certain other trees whose foliage keeps an unhealthy and sometimes mortal freshness.

It is better to let sweat slowly vaporize.

Drinking fresh water when one is very hot is also harmful; when one is very thirsty, it is better to dip one's hands in water, and if one can, take a bath.

The water then enters the body through the pores, which are like many small moths, and the thirst disappears without having to load the stomach with a quantity of liquid which cannot be digested

peine à contenir sans fatigue.

without fatigue.

Tels sont à peu près les principes que je voudrais voir graver dans l'esprit de tous nos paysans.

Such are the principles which I would like to see engraved on the minds of our peasants.

Mais ce ne sont là que des moyens préventifs.

But these are just preventive approaches.

Quand une maladie se déclare, il ne faut pas attendre une aggravation possible pour réclamer les soins du médecin. Ceux qui, par économie, atermoient, ou que par ignorance appliquent des remèdes de bonne femme dont nous parlions tout à l'heure, ceux-là perdent plus d'argent qu'ils n'en épargnent, car plus la maladie empire, plus elle coûte cher à soigner.

When an illness occurs, do not wait for possible aggravation before claiming the care of a doctor. Those who, by economy, procrastinate, or ignorantly apply old wives' remedies, which we spoke of a moment ago, lose more money than they save, because the worse the disease becomes, the more expensive it is to treat.

A ces soins purement matériels, j'en voudrais joindre d'autres, si j'étais libre d'arranger à mon gré les affaires de ce monde. Je voudrais m'occuper de l'esprit aussi bien que du corps, de l'intelligence aussi bien que de la santé.

To this purely material care, I would like to add others, if I were free to arrange the affairs of this world at my pleasure. I would like to take care of the mind as well as the body, of the intelligence as well as that of the health.

De nos jours, il est peu de communes qui n'aient un instituteur. Grâce aux lois actuelles, l'instruction tend à se

Nowadays, there are few communities who do have a schoolmaster. Thanks to the current laws, the instruction tends

généraliser ; eh bien, à mon sens, on trouve encore trop de paysans qui refusent les bienfaits de cette instruction qui leur cst si libéralement offerte.

to be generalized. Well, in my opinion, we still find too many peasants who refuse the benefits of this instruction which is so freely offered to them.

L'enfant est envoyé à l'école assez volontiers tant que ses petits bras sont encore trop faibles pour manier la brouette ou le râteau ; mais, dès qu'il atteint 10 ou 12 ans, on coupe court à son éducation pour l'envoyer au champ avec les hommes ; qu'il sache lire ou non peu importe. Ce qu'on voit en lui, avant tout, c'est un auxiliaire de plus.

The child is sent quite willingly to the school as long as his little arms are too feeble to handle the wheelbarrow or the rake, but as soon as he reaches the age of ten or twelves, his education is cut short and he is sent to the fields with the men, whether he can read or not. What we see in him, above all else, is another menial helper.

Je n'aime pas ces tendances : outre qu'elles accusent un égoïsme peu excusable ; elles sont contraires aux intérêts du cultivateur. S'il considère l'instruction primaire comme inutile, ou du moins comme indifférente à ses intérêts, il a tort et grandement tort.

I do not like these tendencies – besides the fact that they lead to a selfishness that cannot be excused, they are contrary to the interests of the farmer. If he considers primary instruction as useless, or at least as indifferent to his interests, he is wrong, and greatly misled.

Il faut qu'un homme, dût-il pousser la charrue toute sa vie, sache au moins lire, écrire et compter.

A man, even if he must push the plow all his life, should be able to at least read, write and count.

Ces trois notions lui inspireront le désir d'en acquérir de nouvelles.

These three notions will inspire in him the desire to acquire new ones.

Pendant les loisirs que lui laisse son labeur, un esprit trouvera un aliment sérieux : il ira moins au cabaret et sa bourse s'en trouvera mieux ; il lira de temps en temps quelques livres simples appropriés à sa nature, qui lui donneront d'utiles enseignements sur les choses qu'il doit savoir ; il saura calculer plus exactement le rendement de ses terres, et sur ces calculs, il basera des entreprises plus productives.

Enfin, il se moralisera, car je ne crois pas à cette honnêteté que certaines gens font résider dans l'ignorance absolue de toutes choses.

— Il y a peut-être une bonne raison qui empêche le cultivateur de faire donner à ses enfants une éducation élevée, objecta Claude Michu, c'est qu'il craint d'être dédaigné par eux, lorsqu'ils se trouvent plus savants que lui.

— C'est vrai, il est de mauvais esprits et de mauvais cœurs qui rougissent de l'ignorance de leurs parents : mais contre ceux-là le remède est facile.

En voici un exemple : J'ai un

During the leisure his labors grant him, his spirit will find a serious repast – he will go less to the cabaret and his purse will be heavier. He will read from time to time some simple books appropriate to his nature. Which will give him useful lessons on the things he ought to know. He will be able to calculate more exactly the yield of his lands, and on these calculations, he will base more productive enterprises.

Finally, it builds morale, because I do not believe in this honesty that some people claim resides in the absolute ignorance of everything.

"There may be a good reason which prevents the farmers from giving his children a higher education," objected Claude Michu, "because he fears he will be disdained by them when they are more learned than him."

"True, there are evil spirits and bad hearts who blush at the ignorance of their parents, but the remedy is easy against them."

To take one example – I have

ami du nom de Guillaume Hervieux, son père était un riche propriétaire des environs de Marseille. N'ayant reçu qu'une instruction insuffisante, ce brave homme s'était dit que son fils, envoyé régulièrement à l'école pourrait plus tard devenir pour lui un utile auxiliaire.

Dans ce but, il s'imposa des sacrifices et le plaça dans une des bonnes pensions de la ville. Au bout de trois ans l'enfant était un élève fort distingué.

Ses maîtres engagèrent Hervieux à pousser plus loin son instruction. Le fermier n'hésita pas, malgré le blâme de ses amis.

Quand Guillaume revint pour la seconde fois, il se mit de bon cœur à l'ouvrage de la maison ; mais un jour, Hervieux ayant voulu l'envoyer au marché, vendre deux bœufs, il se révolta contre cette exigence.

Tu refuses, dit sévèrement le fermier ?

Oui, mon père, vous ne m'avez pas fait si bien instruire, pour faire de moi un meneur de bœufs.

a friend named William Hervieux. His father was a rich proprietor near Marseilles. Having received only a limited education, this good man said to himself that his son, who went to school regularly would be an able assistant to him in the future.

For this purpose, he imposed sacrifices on himself and placed him in one of the good hostels of the city. In three years, the child was a very distinguished student.

His masters urged Hervieux to push his education further. The farmer did not hesitate, despite the ridicule of his friends.

When William returned for the second time, he set himself heartily to the work of the house, but one day, Hervieux wanted to send him to the market to sell two oxen, he revolted against this demand.

"You refuse?" asked the farmer sternly.

"Yes, my father, you have not educated me so well, to make me a leader of oxen."

Le père ne répondit pas, mais quand Guillaume voulut se lever le lendemain, il trouva, au lieu de ses habits de la veille, une méchante blouse, un pantalon de toile et des sabots.

The father did not respond, but when William wanted to get up the next day, he found, in place of his clothes from the night before, a nasty shirt, canvas trousers and clogs.

A partir de ce jour, prononça Hervieux, je ne veux pas nourrir une bouche inutile : si tu veux manger, tu gagneras ton pain. Mon garçon de labour m'a quitté hier, je te donne sa place.

"From today," announced Hervieux, "I do not want to feed a useless mouth. If you want to eat, earn your bread. My workman left me yesterday, I give you his place."

Guillaume se jeta tout repentant dans les bras de son père. Il avait compris cette rude leçon.

William threw himself repentantly in the arms of his father. He had understood this hard lesson.

Dès ce moment, il s'occupa de tous les travaux de la ferme, et, grâce à ses connaissances, il en fit le domaine le plus riche et le mieux tenu du département.

From that moment on, he took care of all the hard work of the farm, and thanks to his knowledge, he made the estate the richest and best kept domain in the department.

— Je profiterai de tout ce que vous venez de me dire, maître Morand, fit Claude Michu, et j'en ferai profiter mes enfants, je vous en réponds.

"I will take advantage of everything you have taught me, Mr. Morand," said Claude Michu, "and I will make my children profit by it, I promise you."

—Tes enfants ? Il faudrait te marier d'abord.

"Your children? You should get married first."

— C'est ce que je vais faire.

"This is what I'm going to do.

405

Dans un mois, je mènerai Madeleine à l'église, et si vous voulez être mon témoin, ce sera un grand honneur pour moi.

Bernard Morand promit.

Un mois après, Claude et Madeleine étaient les plus heureux époux de toute la Provence.

Que devint le vieux Simounen ? Hélas ! la prédiction de Claude et de Bernard se réalisa.

Simounen vendit un jour à un cultivateur trop crédule un de ses fameux remèdes qu'il lui fit, par parenthèse, payer fort cher, en égard sans doute à la vertu magique qu'il lui prêtait.

La drogue était si rude et elle opéra si bien qu'en deux jours le malade mourut.

Simounen s'en consola, mais la justice se montra moins philosophe : elle voulut savoir la raison de l'événement, et notre vieux berger reçut la visite des gendarmes qu'il redoutait tant.

On découvrit alors toutes les

In a month, I will lead Madeleine to the church, and if you will be my witness, it will be a great honor to me."

Bernard Morand promised this to him.

One month later, Claude and Madeleine were the happiest couple in all Provence.

What became of old Simounen? Alas! The prediction of Claude and Bernard was realized.

Simounen sold one of his unbelievable remedies to a grubby farmer one day, which he was paid dearly for, doubtless in consideration of the magical virtue it granted him.

The drugs were so harsh and worked so well that in two days, the patient died.

Simounen consoled himself, but justice was less philosophical. It wanted to know the reason for the event, and our old shepherd received a visit from the police whom he dreaded so much.

We then discovered all the

manœuvres auxquelles il se livrait depuis longues années ; on sut qu'il abusait de la crédulité des gens pour les rançonner, et que ses pratiques soi-disant bienfaisantes laissaient fort à désirer sous le rapport de la probité.

maneuvers which he had been engaged in for a long time. It was known that he abused the credulity of the people to exploit them, and that his so-called beneficent practices left much to be desired in terms of probity.

Bref ! le père Simounen fut condamné à plusieurs mois de détention.

In short! Father Simounen was sentenced to several months in prison.

Les loisirs de la prison ont dû lui inspirer des réflexions salutaires et le guérir pour toujours de la malencontreuse idée d'appliquer au pauvre monde les recettes surnaturelles du Dragon Rouge.

The prison activities must have inspired him with salutary reflections and healed him forever from the unfortunate idea of applying to the poor world the supernatural recipes of the Red Dragon.

INDEX

About the Authors

Aaman Lamba is a researcher, occultist and student of magic, astrology and philosophy, as well as a computer science professional. His articles have been published in leading newspapers. He was the editor and publisher of an online magazine. He lives in Virginia and has had a passion for French ever since high school. He is currently working on additional translations of texts that deserve greater attention as well as a book on ways of engaging with the world for solitary magicians.

Arundell Overman is a 20-year practicing magician, who went through all the grades of the Golden Dawn order and built a vault of the Adepti. He has experience in Yoga, Toltec, Taoist, Ninja, and Witchcraft arts, and his specialty is the Grimoires known as the Lesser Key of Solomon, The Grand Grimoire, and the Grimorium Verum. He worked the Lesser Key in the traditional manner for 20 years before founding the Ordo Al Ghoul system of magic

Printed in Poland
by Amazon Fulfillment
Poland Sp. z o.o., Wrocław

62079283R00249